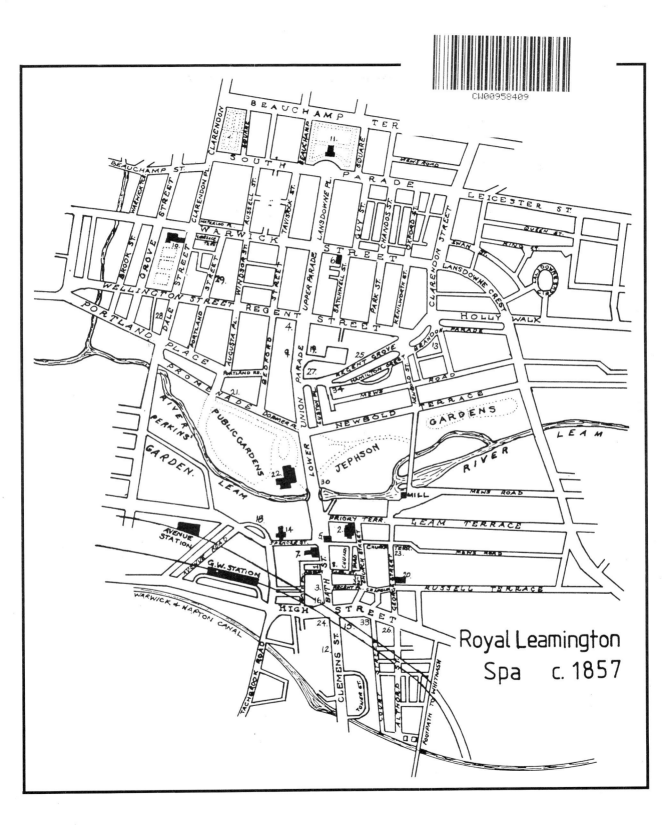

Royal Leamington Spa   c. 1857

ROYAL LEAMINGTON SPA

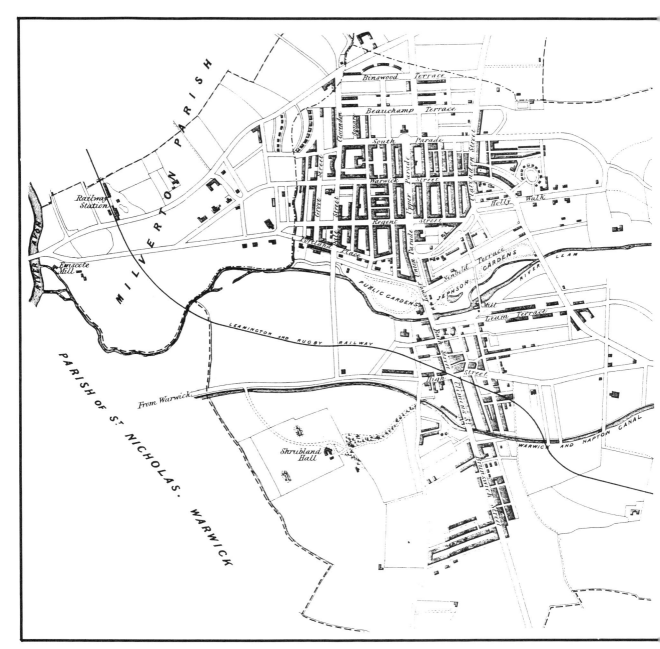

Leamington in 1850, from the report of the General Board of Health's inspector.

ROYAL LEAMINGTON SPA

Its History and Development

Lyndon F. Cave

Phillimore

1988

Published by
PHILLIMORE & CO. LTD.
Shopwyke Hall, Chichester, Sussex

ISBN 0 85033 520 5

Printed and bound by Richard Clay Ltd.,
Chichester, Sussex

Contents

List of Illustrations

Frontispiece: Leamington in 1850

Endpapers: Street map, central Leamington

Acknowledgements
Numbers 1, 2, 5, 7-12, 15, 17, 19, 25, 28, 29, 31, 32, 34, 35, 42-5, 47, 48, 50-5, 58 and the endpapers are reproduced by permission of the Warwickshire County Library Service, Leamington Divisional Library. Numbers 18, 20, 22, 23, 26, 27 and 59, the originals of which are in the Leamington Divisional Library, are reproduced by permission of Mr. W. G. Gibbons. Number 21 is reproduced by permission of Mr. George Hall and number 39 by permission of The Warwickshire County Record Office.

Preface

Leamington Spa or, more correctly, Leamington Priors, one of England's rapidly expanding towns during the early 19th century, was for a long time almost ignored by historians. When the author first began to investigate the town's development, about twenty years ago, little had been written on its history since T. B. Dudley's *Complete History of Royal Leamington Spa* was published at the end of the 19th century. A revival of interest in Leamington and other spa towns has brought forth numerous books and pamphlets, but almost without exception these have dealt with specific aspects of the town's past rather than its overall development. There has been no comprehensive account of the spa since Dudley's.

This book attempts to provide a full up-to-date history and is based partly on sources not available to earlier writers. The most important of these documents, the personal journal of Bertie Bertie Greatheed, gave a contemporary account of the early development of the 'New Town', written by one closely involved in it. Another important source of information has been the views expressed by the editors of the local newspapers, particularly *The Warwick Advertiser* and *The Leamington Spa Courier*, as they recorded and commented on current events. Their biases must have influenced the views of the present writer, just as today's editorials will influence future writers. Nevertheless, consulting a town's newspapers is a good introduction to understanding the reasons for its growth or decay. There is also an overwhelming amount of material, needing much time to sift out the significant details, in the hundreds of property deeds now deposited in the County Record Office; the historian must select from such a mass and trust that no important evidence will inadvertently be ignored. It is not possible to list all the sources of information used by the author over many years, so the Bibliography lists only the most important manuscript and printed sources consulted for the book; the town itself offers to the observant many clues to its history.

New facts will be unearthed at intervals to fill in the blanks in present knowledge, so no history can ever be complete, but it is hoped that this book will answer many questions about Leamington's development, its buildings and streets, and the people who came to try the waters. The author hopes that readers will be encouraged to consider Leamington's past and so help to ensure the future of one of England's few 'Regency' towns. Such an architectural heritage demands protection from further erosion of its unique character.

The author, as always, accepts responsibility for the finished book and the interpretations it contains. He wishes to acknowledge, however, the help and information provided by a great number of people, including: Christopher Arnison; John Drew; Neil Einarson; W. G. Gibbons; George Hall; Miss Kathleen Hanks and the members of the Leamington Literary Society; H. M. Jenkins; the members of the Leamington Society, past and present; T. H. Lloyd; Mrs. Margaret Slater, formerly Curator of Warwick District Council Art Gallery and Museum, and other members of the staff of Warwick District Council; and John M. Winterburn. He wishes also to acknowledge the help of Robin Chaplin, Daniel Roth and Mrs. Frances O'Shaughnessy, particularly with Chapter 17, who, sadly, died before this book was completed.

The patient staff of the Leamington branch of the Warwickshire County Library provided invaluable assistance, especially J. W. Paxton, the Librarian, and Barry Hickman, until recently the assistant librarian in charge of the Local History Collection. Mr. Hickman has been particularly helpful with the illustrations for the book. Michael Farr, the County Archivist, and his staff provided essential advice and guidance to the documents relating to Leamington Spa in their care. Dr. Richard Morris of the History of Art Dept., University of Warwick, provided much needed aid with the photographing of documents and plans in the County Record Office.

Finally the assistance and patience of Noel Osborne and John Stedman of Messrs. Phillimore should be acknowledged, as without their encouragement this book would never have been published. Their forebearance in waiting much longer than expected for the manuscript's completion was appreciated, and their skill in editing and book production were essential to the attractiveness of the final publication.

Introduction

At the end of the 18th century Leamington was an obscure, small village with one muddy mineral spring – its transformation into a large and fashionable spa town amazed all who came to 'take the waters'. During the early years of the 19th century gushing descriptions advertised the curative properties of the waters, the rustic charms of the surrounding countryside and the fine streets and houses of the new town. Favourable reports came from visitors, including Charles Dickens, John Ruskin and Nathaniel Hawthorne, as well as from many doctors interested in promoting the properties of its copious supplies of mineral water. A hundred years on, Royal Leamington Spa gave the impression of genteel dilapidation, as John Betjeman depicted in *Death in Leamington*, one of his earliest poems. It also stirred memories of Regency stylishness, contrasted with modern impecunious elegance in a popular, tinkling, little ditty taking a sly dig at the *Ladies of Leamington*. The town may have changed drastically since its heyday as a fashionable spa, but it owes its very being to its mineral waters.

Among those attracted to the new spa were many members of the court. Besides the Prince Regent, who visited the town briefly in 1819, they included his sisters, Princess Augusta, who in August 1822 stayed at 9 Upper Union Parade, later renamed Augusta House, and the Duchess of Gloucester, who shortly afterwards stayed a month, with her husband the Duke, in a house near the corner of Regent Street and the Parade later called Gloucester House. There were also influential aristocrats such as the Duke of Wellington, who came in 1827 to visit his sister-in-law then taking a course of the waters, the Duke and Duchess of Bedford, the Duke and Duchess of Argyll, the Duchess of Gordon, the Duke and Duchess of St Albans, the Earl and Countess of Bradford and the Duke and Duchess of Grafton. Some of them visited the spa several times.

On Monday 2 August 1830 the Duchess of Kent and her daughter Princess Victoria, with ladies in waiting and attendants, set out from Kensington Palace in four carriages to go to Malvern. On reaching Stratford-upon-Avon the following day they made a detour to visit Leamington Spa, to sample the waters already tasted and talked about by members of the court. The travellers arrived in Leamington at six o'clock in the evening and proceeded to *The Regent Hotel* where they stayed the night. Three triumphal arches, decorated with evergreens and surmounted by the crown, had been hurriedly erected near the hotel, which was illuminated during the evening. The Princess, then between 11 and 12 years old, appeared several times at a window of the hotel to acknowledge the loyal greetings of the townsfolk and visitors. The next day the party resumed its journey to Malvern. Their stay was brief, but it was a symbol of the town's respectability and growing success as a spa.

The sequel to this visit took place in 1838, a year after Victoria became Queen. A formal application for a new 'title' for the town was made in a letter to Lord Melbourne, the Prime Minister, on 3 July. On 18 July a deputation consisting of Lord Eastnor, Major Hawkes and Mr. John Hampden attended a royal levee and presented a loyal address on behalf of the inhabitants of Leamington Priors. It was 'most graciously received'. On the following day the Queen granted the request of the townspeople that they might be permitted in future to call the town Royal Leamington Spa. The deputation bearing the news returned to the town at ten p.m. on 24 July. A crowd waiting to greet them outside the Town Hall cheered their speeches announcing that the privilege of styling the town 'Royal' belonged to no other place in the kingdom. Their carriage was then pulled by the crowd to *The Regent Hotel* for more speeches. Since then the town has proudly borne the name as a sign of royal approval. Doubtless it contributed to Leamington's success as a spa.

Queen Victoria came to the town once more, on 17 June 1858. She was on her way from Stoneleigh Abbey to board a train at Kenilworth Station while travelling to Birmingham to open Aston Hall Museum. She did, however, pass through the Great Western Railway station a number of times on her journeys to and from Balmoral, when local people turned out in large numbers to see the train pass.

This year is the 150th since the grant of Leamington's 'title'. To mark the anniversary a number of events have been held or are planned. Perhaps the most appropriate of these, certainly the most popular, was the official visit of Her Majesty the Queen, on 24 March, her first to the town. There she opened the new Royal Priors shopping centre, unveiled a plaque at the Town Hall commemorating the 150th anniversary of the granting of the royal warrant to the spa by Queen Victoria, and visited *The Regent Hotel* where her ancestor had stayed.

Chapter One

Leamington Priors before 1800

> If a man were seeking the bustle of Society, he might find it more readily in Leamington than in most other Engish towns. It is a permanent watering-place, a sort of institution to which I do not know any close parallel in American life . . . Leamington seems to be always in flower and serves as a home for the homeless all the year round. Its original nucleus, the plausible excuse for the town's coming into prosperous existence, lies in the fiction of a chalybeate well, which, indeed, is so far a reality that out of its magical depth have gushed streets, groves, gardens, mansions, shops and churches, and spread themselves along the banks of the little river Leam. This miracle accomplished the beneficent fountain has retired beneath a pump-room and appears to have given up all pretensions to the remedial virtues formerly attributed to it.

Nathaniel Hawthorne, the American writer, produced *Our Old Home. A Series of English Sketches* in 1863. He had stayed at 10 Lansdowne Circus, Leamington, for several months about ten years previously when the town was at the height of its popularity as a spa. This book will attempt to portray the growth of Royal Leamington Spa, as it became known in 1838, from a small village to a large, prosperous town in less than a century.

There were two villages in Warwickshire bearing the name Leamington. Leamington Hastings belonged to the Hastings family, Leamington Priors, a few miles away, took its name from the Priory of Kenilworth, by which it was once owned. The first is still a comparatively small village, the second has become Royal Leamington Spa. In Domesday Book this village was called Lamintone. Although scholars have held differing views, the generally accepted meaning of the name is 'a farm on the River Leam', the word 'leam' meaning a pool or lake. Whatever the precise meaning, there was a settlement near the river before the Saxon period, as during the last century traces of prehistoric man were found when boreholes were sunk in search of further mineral springs.

The first landowner about whom there is evidence was Turchill, the last Saxon Earl of Warwick, who possessed 'a farm on the bank of the river Leam'. In the Domesday survey Leamington appeared as a manor of about 240 acres, valued at £4, with two mills. Their sites are uncertain: one was perhaps near the present church, possibly on the site occupied in the 19th century by Oldham's Mill, and the other at Newbold Comyn, just to the east of the original village.

After the Conquest William I presented the manor to Henry de Newburgh, the first Norman earl of Warwick, who was soon succeeded by Roger de Montgomery. Roger's family supported William Rufus; after Rufus' death the new monarch, Henry I, therefore seized the estate and in 1100 gave it to the bishop of Coventry and Lichfield. After about sixty years the bishop of the time disposed of the property to Geoffrey de Clinton, who was the son-in-law of the earl of Warwick and founder of Kenilworth castle and priory. Geoffrey's son presented the manor of Leamington to the Prior of Kenilworth who held it for nearly 300 years until the Dissolution of the Monasteries.

One of the results of the acquisition of the manor by the priors of Kenilworth was the change of its name. Previously known simply as Leminton, it became Lemynton Prioris and in 1533 was first recorded as Lemyngton Priors. In 1539 when Henry VIII dissolved the priory the value of the manor had increased from the £4 a year at Domesday to £533 15s. 4d. It remained crown property for a number of years. The village continued to be called Leamington Priors until the middle of last century when, by special permission of Queen

Victoria, it was renamed Royal Leamington Spa. The old name has been retained by the ecclesiastical parish which is in the modern Diocese of Coventry, the parish church being known as All Saints, Leamington Priors.

A church was perhaps established at Leamington before the Conquest since there was a priest recorded there in Domesday Book, but not until 1315 is the name of the vicar, Henry de Keton, first known. Before the 14th century the church at Leamington was a chapel belonging to Leek Wootton, formerly an extensive parish a few miles away between Warwick and Kenilworth. Henry de Keton held the living until 1338 when he was succeeded by Thomas de Lemyngton, a vicar whose name suggests he was a local man. He was followed briefly in 1348 by William de Leycester – there were three vicars in 1349, the year of the Black Death. In 1429 Richard Bennett, vicar of the adjacent parish of Whitnash, was appointed vicar of Leamington and held the two livings jointly until 1436; Whitnash is now part of the built-up area of Leamington Spa.

A mineral spring at Leamington was first recorded about 1480 by John Rous, a chantry priest at Guy's Cliffe near Warwick, in his *Roll of the Earls of Warwick* which records the history of the earls and their estates. Rous tells us that 'in little more than a mile from Warwick is a salt well and many springs about where might be made many wells and have salt water running the whole year and the river Leam that runs by oft time flows over them'. From this account we learn that in the 15th century there were a number of springs besides the principal one, later known as the 'Old Well', and that the supply was considered sufficient to provide for several other wells.

In 1539, at the time of the Dissolution of the Monasteries, Richard Willes of Ufton and William Morcote of Leamington jointly purchased the farm of Newbold Comyn on the north bank of the river, just to the east of the village. Willes died in 1564 possessed of the whole of Newbold Comyn having married Morcote's heiress. It remained Willes family property until the middle of the 20th century, a significant fact in the later development of the spa town.

The manor of Leamington Priors by 1564 included land on both sides of the river. It was granted by Elizabeth I to 'the noble and good Ambrose Dudley, Earl of Warwick', the heir and third son of John Dudley, Duke of Northumberland, but Ambrose died in 1589 without issue and the manor reverted to the crown.

On 22 April 1596 the queen granted the advowson of the parish church of All Saints to William Borne and Jacob Orange, of the Middle Temple, London, 'with all its rights, lands, tenements, glebe lands and hereditaments belonging to the same Rectory, which had previously belonged to the Monastery of Kenilworth, together with the rights of patronage of the parish church, that they, their heirs and assigns for ever should have, hold and enjoy'. Borne and Orange were required to pay yearly to the crown £16 16s. after the death of Anne, Countess of Warwick. Their heirs held the patronage of the church, as well as the land adjacent to the Newbold Comyn estate, until about 1693 when all their property passed into the hands of Edward Willes of Newbold Comyn, who thus acquired the lands belonging to the church as well as the right to appoint the vicar. The combined estates remained as agricultural land until the beginning of the 19th century when some was sold and built on as the 'New Town' developed on the north bank of the river.

At the end of the 16th century the spring was becoming better known. It was mentioned by William Camden in his *Britannia*, published in 1586. He briefly described the situation of Leamington and its mineral spring, and later generations named the original spring the Camden Well in his honour. John Speed, in his *Theatre of the Empire of Great Britain* published ten years later, remarked that 'at Leamington so far from the sea a spring of salt water boileth up', but gave no details of the location of the spring.

William Dugdale observed in *The Antiquities of Warwickshire* that 'nigh to the east end of

Called Lord Aylesford's Well

1. The original well-house and the parish church as they appeared between 1804 and 1813.

2. A cottage formerly on the corner of Mill Street and New Street, drawn before 1842.

the church there is a spring of salt water not a stone's throw from the river Leame whereof the inhabitants make much use for seasoning of meat'. This was an error by the author as the spring was at the west end of the church and Dr. Thomas in his revised edition of the book, dated 1730, corrects this and adds 'that the villagers used the water for making their bread and strangers drink it as a purging water with much success'. In 1662, a few years after Dugdale's book appeared, the spring was described as follows by Dr. Fuller in his *History of the Worthies of England*:

> At Leamington, two miles from Warwick, there issues out, within a stride of the womb of the earth, two twin springs, as different in taste and operation as Jacob and Esau in disposition; the one salt and the other fresh. This the meanest countryman does plainly see by their effects while it would puzzle a consultation of physicians to assign the cause thereof.

This was a period when there was a growing interest in the medical use of mineral springs and among the first of many books on the subject was that published in 1691 by Dr. Guidott, a medical practitioner at Bath who had devoted his life to the study of the therapeutic effects of the waters at different places. There is no doubt that he visited Leamington to examine the water, which he declared to be from a nitrous spring. This opinion was generally accepted until the mid-18th century when later writers claimed that the spring provided brine. At the time that Dr. Guidott wrote the spring was obviously not very well known to people outside the district, since Celia Fiennes, who visited any mineral spring she heard of, did not visit Leamington Priors when travelling from Warwick to Daventry in 1697.

In the years which followed, debate about the nature of the spring continued. In 1740 Dr. Short wrote a *Treatise on Mineral Waters* in which he announced it to be 'a brine spring, possessed of a considerable quantity of calcareous nitre'. This was disputed by Dr. Rutty, who was, according to Dudley in his *Complete History of Royal Leamington Spa* (1896), the 'most profound and correct inquirer of all the early writers into the nature and properties of mineral waters'. In his *Methodical Synopsis of Mineral Waters*, published in 1757, Rutty declared the water to be from a 'saline nitrous spring', the evidence being an analysis which found each gallon of water to contain 960 grains of sediment, 30 of which were calcareous earth and the rest marine salt. His view has been accepted by almost all of the later writers.

In 1767 Parliament passed an act entitled 'An Act for Dividing and Inclosing the Open and Common Fields, Common Meadows and Commonable Lands on the South and West Parts of the River Leam in the Manor and Parish of Leamington Priors in the County of Warwick'. This enclosure affected the ownership of all land adjacent to the village, especially the land on which the expanding spa town was built in the following century. A copy of the enclosure award can be seen in the County Record Office in Warwick, while it is also summarised in Dudley's *History*. It will be discussed in a later chapter so only brief details need mentioning here. Before the act the land was farmed under the common-field system, each landowner's property being divided into scattered strips.

The manorial rights were confirmed as belonging to the Earl of Aylesford, who then lived at Packington Hall, near Coventry. He was one of the largest landowners in the county although he only owned just over 21 acres in Leamington, including the site of the first saline spring. Mr. Matthew Wise was the chief landowner south of the Leam although small plots of land were owned by other local people, many on important sites in the centre of Leamington. North of the river the principal owners of the land destined to become the site of the New Town were the Greatheed family of Guy's Cliffe near Warwick, whose land was immediately opposite the church and near the only bridge over the river, and Mr. Edward Willes of Newbold Comyn whose large estate lay on either side of the 64 acres belonging to the Greatheeds. This pattern of land ownership remained intact until the middle of the 19th century, influencing the layout of the spa town from its inception.

The Hearth Tax returns of 1662 and 1663, although often unreliable, offer some idea of the size of the village in those years. The Hearth Tax was a levy of 2s. a year on each hearth or stove in a house. People who occupied dwellings or land whose rent was less than 20s. a year and whose property was worth less than £10 did not have to pay it. There were 46 cottages or houses, the number being the same in each year; tax was paid on 49 hearths and 17 were exempt. The large houses included that occupied by Edward Willes, gent., who had four hearths in 1662, making the house at Newbold Comyn the largest in the parish. John Boddington had three hearths, Thomas Lees four, Nathaniel Olney, gent., four, all in 1662, while Richard Olney, gent., occupied the same property in 1663, probably on the death of his father. Francis Raborne had three hearths in 1663, succeeding Edward Raborne who had had two the previous year, and Francis Horne and Tarry Lees had three each. The remaining dwellings had one hearth each, including the 17 cottages whose occupiers were too poor to pay the tax. These were let at very low rents and were evidently small, poorly-built dwellings in a bad state of repair. The village green would have been the nucleus of a village consisting of several farms and the cottages of the farm workers, housing some 200 people, while the large houses such as Newbold Comyn stood a little apart.

This community was large enough by 1625 to support at least two alehouses. The names of the alehousekeepers are given in an order of the Warwickshire Court of Quarter Sessions suppressing them.

> For as much as the Court was this day informed by a certificate of dyvers of the inhabitants of Leamington Priors in this Countie, that William Mills and Margett Walsgrave, two victuallers who in the saide towne keepe very ill order and rule in their houses, so that their neighbours are offended and wronged thereby, besydes, as this Court be informed the said Margett selleth without a Lycense, in contempt of this Court. It is therefore ordered that the said William Mills and Margett Walsgrave shall be from henceforth absolutely suppressed from offering or selling ale, beer or victualls, any more, which if they continue then the Constable there is required to apprehend . . . bring them before some Justice of the Peace of this County, there to find sufficient sureties to forebeare selling ale, beer and victuals which if they refuse to do so then to comitte them to this Majesties gaole . . .

Part of Leamington was described in 1693; that year the bishop of Lichfield and Coventry held a visitation at the parish church and a 'terrier' was laid before him describing the property belonging to the vicar and churchwardens. This property consisted of the vicarage, a dwelling-house of two bays which suggests it was a timber-framed building, a barn of one bay, several meadows, a churchyard and a small church.

As the first census did not take place until 1801 it is only the first ground plan of the village, dated 1783, that gives some idea of the population and layout of Leamington Priors between the Hearth Tax and its rapid growth in the late 18th century. Only six persons were eligible to vote in the 1774 election, all having property and houses in the parish; in contrast Warwick had 316 and Kenilworth 135 voters at this election. The 1783 plan suggests that there were few more dwellings in Leamington in that year than in 1663, perhaps 50 cottages housing a population of under three hundred. The buildings shown include the parish church, the vicarage, the mill and mill house, two public houses – *The Old Bowling Green* and *The Dog* – the post office, well-house, parish poorhouse, the smithy, stocks and cattle pound, as well as ten groups of cottages ranging in number from two to five dwellings.

Most of the buildings shown on the 1783 map have disappeared, although some are recalled by place or street names. The mill on the south bank of the Leam near the spot where the suspension bridge is today, which became Oldham's Mill in the early 19th century, is remembered by Mill Street. Not far away was Richard Court's farmhouse, the family being remembered by Court Street. The footpath from Lillington to Whitnash survives as a right of way passing near the site of the Old Post Office, the house of Benjamin Satchwell, which is now occupied by a warehouse. In Priory Terrace some of the cottages

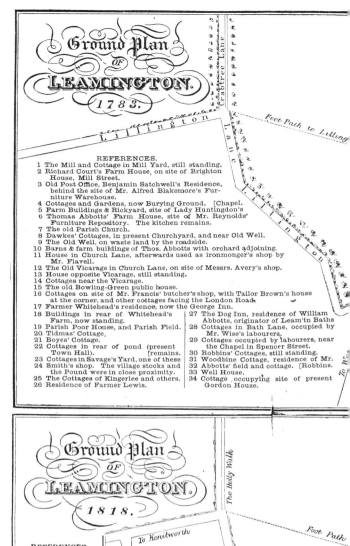

Ground Plan OF LEAMINGTON. 1783.

Crabtree Lane

Lillington

Lillington Lane

Foot Path to Litting

REFERENCES.

1 The Mill and Cottage in Mill Yard, still standing.
2 Richard Court's Farm House, on site of Brighton House, Mill Street.
3 Old Post Office, Benjamin Satchwell's Residence, behind the site of Mr. Alfred Blakemore's Furniture Warehouse.
4 Cottages and Gardens, now Burying Ground. [Chapel.
5 Farm Buildings & Rickyard, site of Lady Huntingdon's
6 Thomas Abbotts' Farm House, site of Mr. Reynolds' Furniture Repository. The kitchen remains.
7 The old Parish Church.
8 Dawkes' Cottages, in present Churchyard, and near Old Well.
9 The Old Well, on waste land by the roadside.
10 Barns & farm buildings of Thos. Abbotts with orchard adjoining.
11 House in Church Lane, afterwards used as ironmonger's shop by Mr. Flavell.
12 The Old Vicarage in Church Lane, on site of Messrs. Avery's shop.
13 House opposite Vicarage, still standing.
14 Cottages near the Vicarage.
15 The old Bowling-Green public house.
16 Cottages on site of Mr. Francis' butcher's shop, with Tailor Brown's house at the corner, and other cottages facing the London Road.
17 Farmer Whitehead's residence, now the George Inn.
18 Buildings in rear of Whitehead's Farm, now standing.
19 Parish Poor House, and Parish Field.
20 Tidmas' Cottage.
21 Boyes' Cottage.
22 Cottages in rear of pond (present Town Hall).   [remains.
23 Cottages in Savage's Yard, one of these
24 Smith's shop. The village stocks and the Pound were in close proximity.
25 The Cottages of Kingerlee and others.
26 Residence of Farmer Lewis.

27 The Dog Inn, residence of William Abbotts, originator of Leam'tn Baths
28 Cottages in Bath Lane, occupied by Mr. Wise's labourers.
29 Cottages occupied by labourers, near the Chapel in Spencer Street.
30 Robbins' Cottages, still standing.
31 Woodbine Cottage, residence of Mr.
32 Abbotts' field and cottage. [Robbins.
33 Well House.
34 Cottage, occupying site of present Gordon House.

Ground Plan OF LEAMINGTON. 1818.

REFERENCES

1 Assembly Rooms
2 Bedford Hotel
3 Royal Pump Room
4 Robins's Baths
5 Ld Aylesford's Well
6 Theatre
7 Church
8 Bath Hotel
9 Original Baths
10 Wise's Baths
11 Albion House
12 Crown Inn
13 Read's Baths
14 Smart's Baths
15 Meeting House
16 Blenheim Hotel
17 Royal Hotel
18 Elliston's Library
19 Poor House
20 Post Office
21 Mill
22 Regent Hotel

The Holly Walk

To Kenilworth

Foot Path

New Road to Warwick

Cross Street

Upper Union Pe.   Union Parade

3. Leamington in 1783 and in 1818, from *Spennell's Directory*, 1890.

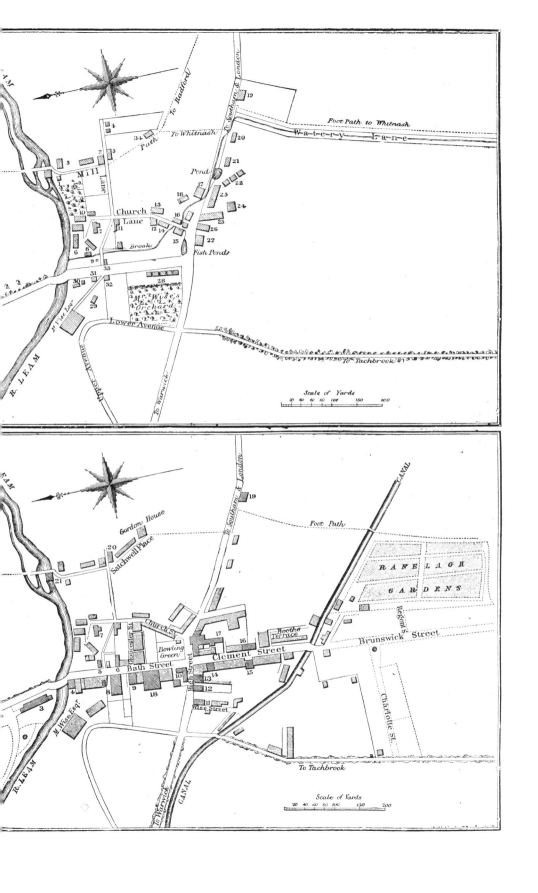

were replaced by the old burial ground and the chapel built by Lady Huntingdon's Connexion; this is still a place of worship, but for another sect. The parish church has been greatly altered and enlarged, but the old vicarage, Mr. Flavel's house and other dwellings nearby, as well as the original well-house, have all gone. In the High Street *The George Inn* survives, refurbished and renamed, while *The Bowling Green Inn* has been replaced by a garage and *The Dog Inn* has disappeared. The oldest buildings in the town are probably the outbuildings and cottage behind the former *George Inn*, structures which despite changes are basically as when first built, as are the three small cottages in Church Street. These cottages, nos. 15, 16 and 17, no doubt the oldest buildings still inhabited in Leamington, are timber-framed. Their construction was revealed during recent repairs when some of the old framing in the front walls was uncovered for the first time in many years.

The 1783 plan also shows the bridge across the Leam, replacing the ford and forming part of the lane to Lillington which later became the lower part of the Parade. This bridge was the vital connection between the old village on the south bank, with its mineral springs, and the New Town. The first bridge often needed repairing, according to the Quarter Sessions records, and was a frequent cause of local disputes and court cases. The first reference, during the reign of Charles I, shows that after repairing the bridge at a cost of 47s. there was difficulty in obtaining payment, so the cost was imposed on the inhabitants of the hundred of Knightlow, in which Leamington then lay. In 1651 several townships in the hundred were summoned before the Sessions, having refused to pay for repairs, and more repairs were needed in 1669, 1679, 1684 and 1697. In 1709 work was carried out by Edward Willes of Newbold Comyn and the Sessions ordered that he be 'reimbursed for certain monies expended by him on the bridge'. Keeping the bridge in repair was clearly a burden on the poorer people in the village.

Chapter Two

The Battle for the Springs

Once the residents of the old village had seen the fortunes being made by people in Bath and Cheltenham they realised the advantages of developing the mineral spring at Leamington Priors. Unfortunately for local speculators, the only known spring was on the land owned by the Earl of Aylesford, the lord of the manor, who was not interested in the financial gain to be made from developing it commercially. Early in the 19th century, in fact, the earl turned down an offer of £1,000 for a building lease of the site made by Dr. Holyoake of Warwick, making it clear that the spring was to remain available free of charge to all the poor people in the parish. Accordingly the other landowners in the area around the village began searching for another spring.

One was found almost too late to ensure the prosperity of the town, for without the Napoleonic Wars, which made it difficult to visit continental spa towns, visitors might have been unwilling to risk coming to a new and unknown spa when Bath and, to a lesser extent, Cheltenham were already popular. One thing in its favour, however, was the quantity of the mineral water available once new springs were found and commercially exploited; in spite of its lack of social advantages Leamington succeeded in establishing itself as the last of the spas in the easily accessible south of the country.

Since the search began for a second spring, one which would be beyond the control of the Earl of Aylesford, eight saline wells have been found in the southern part of the present town. These were all near the Leam and most of them south of it. Nowadays it is known that saline water would be found in varying quantities if a well were dug deep enough almost anywhere south of Dormer Place. While the first spring was a genuine one, where water issued from the ground in a natural way, the other so-called 'springs' were wells from which the salt water was pumped up for use. These wells penetrate to a deposit of saliferous marl which lies under the southern half of the present town, separated by a geological fault from the sandstone found under the north of it. The line of the fault runs roughly along Dormer Place and Newbold Terrace. In the early 19th century the line of this fault was not known nor, of course, its importance understood, and unsuccessful attempts were made to find saline water north of it.

Public attention was drawn frequently to the need for better bathing facilities at Leamington after the medicinal value of the spring had once more been promoted by Dr. Russell in a treatise on sea water and salt springs written in 1765. Although there is no clear evidence of how the mineral water from the first spring was used, Moncrieff, in one of the early guides to the town, said that near to the spring was a tub, placed in a ditch, which was used for bathing and for the immersion of sufferers from hydrophobia. He goes on to say that it was used

more in the cases of hydrophobia than any other; a regular dipper, Thomas Dilkes, having been engaged from the beginning of the eighteenth century for this express purpose. Of the persons thus cured of that dreadful disorder, an annual register was kept, attested by the dipper on oath, from these registers, it appears that from June 1778 to 1786, eight years, no fewer than 119 persons, who had suffered from the bite of mad dogs, had been effectually cured by immersion in the water. This Thomas Dilkes, the dipper, was quite a character in his way; so jealous was he of the water, that he declared, if ever he should meet with a failure, he would not dip anyone again, and, on a patient being brought, whose case was more than commonly desperate, he obstinately refused to perform his office, so that the friends of the sufferer were obliged to undertake it themselves, and were luckily successful, for says my authority, though the man was absolutely raving mad at the time he was brought, he very soon afterwards perfectly recovered.

The name Thomas Dilkes does not appear in any of the surviving records, so Moncrieff's account may merely be a folktale. But as Thomas Dawkes, who kept the earliest records of the use of the spring, lived near the site, it is likely that he was the regular dipper and that the name 'Dilkes' is an error.

Early visitors noted that when the villagers realised the commercial value of the waters they collected them in a tub instead of letting them drain away into the ditch. The tub is reputed to have belonged to a local butcher; a clothes-horse, with a blanket, gave some privacy and the bather had to provide his own towel. A charge of one penny was made for each bath, and if two visitors arrived at the same time to use the tub one had to stroll around until the other had finished. As no changing accommodation was provided the bathers had to come wrapped up ready for their bath. There were some who suspected that the water might well have been used more than once, so primitive were the arrangements in contrast to those at Bath and Cheltenham.

The discovery of a second source of mineral water by Benjamin Satchwell and William Abbotts on 14 January 1784 was of great importance – from that date Leamington dates as a spa. Although Abbotts had sunk several wells in an effort to find water, tradition says that the two friends were walking across a piece of land near the lane to Lillington, later to become known as Bath Street, when they found the spring; it was by chance that it was on land owned by Abbotts himself. Abbotts, landlord of *The Black Dog*, one of the two inns in the village, had been left some property by an uncle. On this land the friends noticed spring water welling up into a pool of stagnant water in a ditch, and on tasting found it to be saline, similar in every way to the original spring. There was jubilation in Leamington as the village now had a source of mineral water not controlled by the lord of the manor but open to commercial exploitation.

Sceptics might ask how it was possible for a second source of saline water to be discovered like this after being unnoticed despite intensive searches – Abbotts himself had already sunk several wells without success. As the weather was cold, however, the ground was probably frozen and the salt water would be all the more noticeable by remaining liquid rather than becoming ice like fresh water. In support of this theory it should perhaps be mentioned that *The Gentleman's Magazine*, published every month from 1731 until early this century, gave details of the weather experienced on each day of the previous month. The issue for February 1784 shows clearly that the weather was freezing in most of January.

In the 1780s promotion of the waters for treatment by cold and, less frequently, warm baths was begun in a modest way. Leamington soon received a fillip from the interest in its waters of Dr. Kerr of Northampton. Contemporary writers suggest that it was thanks to him that Leamington spa water became known as so beneficial in the early days of the spa as it was his 'sagacity that first clearly penetrated its valuable qualities and whose powerful recommendations first led to a fair and reasonable trial of its medical virtues'.

It took a long time for the village to develop to suit its new role. Dr. Kerr's patients usually stayed at *The Black Dog* or *The Bowling Green* inns, which had become well known by 1785. There was really nowhere else to stay then, and the situation was little better in 1808. William Charles Macready, a visitor in that year, wrote:

The summer months in Birmingham were diversified by a short stay in Leamington, then a small village consisting of only a few thatched cottages – not one tiled or slated; *The Bowling Green* being the only one where moderate accommodation could be secured. There was in the progress of erection a hotel of more pretensions, but which had some months of work to fit it for the reception of guests. We had the parlour and bedrooms of a huckster's shop, the best accommodation of the place; and used each morning to walk down to the spring across the old churchyard, with our little mugs in our hands, for our daily draft of Leamington waters.

After discovering the mineral water rising to the surface, Abbotts sank a well and found saline water about 25 ft. down. At Dr. Kerr's suggestion he erected a bathhouse above the well, which was on the corner of Abbott Street and Bath Street. Contemporary engravings show a small, plain, single-storey, lean-to building, unlike the elaborate pump-rooms erected over the later wells, but it should be borne in mind that Leamington was not then established as a spa, so Abbotts was not so sure of success as later well owners. According to Dudley, accommodation was 'rude in the extreme. There was one reservoir for warm salt water and another for cold', with no other amenities beyond a small bath for children, but its popularity grew as Dr. Kerr continued to send his patients there for treatment.

Abbotts died on 1 March 1805, aged 69. His wife carried on the business until April 1806 when she transferred both *The New Inn*, later to be called *The Bath Inn*, and the adjoining baths to her son-in-law, William Smith. She continued to superintend the baths for many years while Mr. and Mrs. Smith looked after the inn. After the baths were enlarged in 1815 local poor people were treated at a nominal charge. In 1826 the old structure was demolished and 'a new edifice, more in accordance with the changed condition of the town, erected on the site', with eight baths for both hot and cold bathing as well as a similar number of shower-baths. The first douche bath was also fitted as were both a vapour and a hot-air bath.

The business was taken over by Mr. John Goold, who renamed the baths Goold's Original Baths and Pump Rooms and described them as saline and sulphureous. Dr. Granville in his *Spas of England*, published in 1841, described the establishment in some detail. He particularly praised the suite of bathrooms, which were 'fitted up in a style worthy of a private gentleman's residence, being well papered and carpeted', each of the eight baths being fitted with a shower. He considered them superior to those of the Royal Pump Rooms. There was also an invalid chair to enable cripples to bathe, and a large plunge-bath.

The baths changed hands again several times. Ten years later a Mr. and Mrs. Gardner were in charge and in 1858 Mr. Wood, who had previously managed the Victoria Baths, became the tenant. Within three years the property was acquired by a Birmingham company, Messrs. Stocks and Co., and it was run by White and Locke, the Leamington auctioneers. In 1867 the baths were demolished to enlarge the shop of Messrs. Francis and Son. The family continued in business there until 1984 and their premises survived until 1987, although much altered and with no trace of the old well. *The Bath Hotel*, formerly *The Bath Inn*, was demolished in the early 1960s.

Abbotts' baths were so popular and consumed so much water that the water-table was lowered. This affected the original spring, for its supply almost failed in 1800. A small pump was needed by 1815. In 1803 the Rev. James Walhouse, a resident of the village, proposed raising a public subscription to erect a building over the spring, which was suffering from neglect. When the Earl of Aylesford was asked for his consent, he built a small stone house there at his own expense. To ensure that the poor continued to have free access to the water the building had no door or gate. Two channels led from the basin into which the spring flowed, one going outside the building to give a free supply to everyone, and the other inside the well-house where 'Widow Webb', the first keeper, was in charge. There was a fixed scale of fees for wealthier visitors. Considering the value of money in the early 19th century these charges were high: for one person the charge for the season was 7s. 6d.; for two members of the same family, 10s.; for the whole family, £1; for one person for a month, 5s.; and for one person for a week, 2s. 3d. Nevertheless the spring continued to be well patronised.

4. The Well House over the original spring was demolished in 1961. This view was taken after the adjacent shops were knocked down, which was in about 1905.

So successful were these improvements that in 1813 the fifth earl had the original well-house demolished and a new structure erected. This was again improved in 1828 and in turn replaced by an even larger building in 1891. This building was demolished and the site cleared in 1961; it is today marked by a memorial plaque in front of the parish church. The houses around the original pump-house were removed to expose the new west front of the parish church after its completion in 1902.

Mr. Squiers, the attendant of the new pump-house in 1813, later became famous for the manufacture of Squier's Mineral Salts and the original Spa Water Toffee. After his death the property was for several years managed by his wife and daughter and later these salts were made by William Smith, one of Abbotts' grandsons. In 1821 he manufactured what were then claimed as 'the genuine Leamington Salts' at the pump-rooms in Bath Street. About 1836 he sold the sole rights to Mr. Herring, 'an ingenious chemist in Bath Street, in whose laboratory [in 1841], open to public inspection, the process is going on daily'. Herring condensed the water by boiling, then evaporated it slowly in zinc pans. The salts were no longer made after 1900, but the toffee was made until the last war.

Some time after Squiers' death the pump-house over the original spring was taken over by Mr. Thomas Hancock. In addition to selling the water he used the building as a bazaar, offering all sorts of goods to visitors. In the 1890s Spennell's *Almanack and Directory* stated that 'water may be taken free in small quantities from the pump erected outside the building, wine bottles filled within for 1d. each'.

In 1790 Mr. Wise sank a well on his property in High Street and found water at a depth of 42 ft. Wise, unlike Abbotts, was a wealthy man and after the success of the first two 'springs' knew that he was unlikely to lose money if he discovered saline water. The baths he erected on the north-west corner of the junction of Bath Street and the High Street were more imposing than the earlier bathhouse erected by Abbotts.

At first known as Wise's Baths, they originally had two cold baths and two hot, each with a dressing-room. There was a boiler to heat the water with a prominent chimney-stack clearly seen in early engravings of the baths and Bath Street itself. In 1800, as the number of visitors increased, the baths were enlarged and improved by building a new pump-room in front of the original building. At this time the High Street was widened. The baths were then entrusted to Mrs. Curtis and became known as Curtis' Baths. In 1815 further improvements made more baths available, giving seven baths for ladies, four for gentlemen, one for children and one cold bath. The Baths continued until 1847 when, along with *Copps' Hotel*, the building was demolished to make way for a railway bridge across the road junction.

It soon became obvious to medical practitioners that there was a plentiful supply of water at Leamington, both for drinking and hot and cold bathing, unlike at Cheltenham where the supply was restricted to drinking only. One contemporary critic expressed the view 'that the water at Cheltenham was a mere trickle that needed pumping from the ground, while at Leamington Priors there was enough to float a man-o'-war.' Success was encouraged by the publication in 1794 of an article by Dr. Lambe in the *Memoirs of the Manchester Philosophical Society* in which he pointed out that the waters at Cheltenham and Leamington Priors were almost identical. In particular he noted the presence of iron in the Leamington waters. Dr. Lambe 'practised as a physician, with great reputation and success at Warwick' and although he was thought by his contemporaries 'to be somewhat eccentric in practical views, he was not the less a scientific man, an intelligent observer of nature and an accomplished physician. He was, moreover, one of the most elegant medical writers of his day'.

The mineral waters of Leamington may be divided into three types: saline, sulphureous and chalybeate, each containing varying amounts of oxygen, nitrogen and carbonic gases, while the sulphureous wells also contained sulphuretted hydrogen, sodium sulphate, sodium chloride, calcium, magnesia and some silica, peroxide of iron and traces of iodine or bromine. The main minerals are sodium chloride, magnesium sulphate and calcium sulphate, perhaps better known as common salt, Epsom salts and gypsum. In addition a little iron carbonate is also found in the strongest waters, this sometimes being enough to cause some ironing of containers. The well in the High Street contained five times as much iron as the other wells and as a result was known as a chalybeate well.

Lambe was followed by Dr. Amos Middleton, whose *Analysis*, first published in 1806, was illustrated 'with cases to prove their efficacy in the cure of Scrofula and Scorbutic Humours, to which are added instructions for cold and warm bathing'. This was the most practical work on the subject written for the general public, or at least those who could afford to 'take the cure' at Leamington. His were among the first of such rules. He prescribed drinking large quantities of saline water several times a day and also taking hot or cold baths several times a week if not daily. To allow this a spa needed copious supplies of saline water.

The fourth well, originally known as Robbins' Well, was sunk on the south side of the bridge in 1804; it had water at a depth of just over 25 ft. These baths opened on 5 July 1806 and were later renamed 'The Victoria Baths' in honour of Princess Victoria. The building was later rebuilt as part of the present Victoria Terrace. The first establishment was a lavish affair, with six marble-lined baths, each with a dressing-room, and there was a large cold bath, a children's bath, and reception-rooms for taking the waters. According to guidebooks of the period the saline water was raised by a horse-driven pump, an object of

5. Victoria Terrace in 1864. Designed by William Thomas in 1837, the ground floor of the houses was later altered to form shops. When the terrace was built the right-hand section was occupied by the Victoria Baths.

6. Victoria Terrace, *c.*1909.

Victoria Terrace,
Leamington Spa.

great interest to all visitors. In spite of these attractions, however, Mr. Robbins lost money and had shortly to sell the property.

A second baths were erected here in 1838, built as part of the improvements carried out to the south bank of the river just before the new bridge was completed. Almost nothing remains of these baths, just a few fragments of the original building hidden away among the many later alterations to the existing structure. The baths had their entrance at the north end of the terrace, the main front being toward the Leam. This façade was 112 ft. long with a colonnade of the same length. The internal arrangements were in a classical style with a large, well-proportioned pump-room and, in 1850, a 'superb fountain from Messrs Austin's Repository in London' was installed. After having a number of different owners, however, the baths succumbed to competition from the pump-rooms across the river, and closed.

The fifth well was dug in 1806 on the southern edge of the village, the water being 60 ft. down. It lay almost opposite Wise's Baths, between *The Crown Hotel* and Clemens Street, on the site now occupied by 12 High Street. Naturally a bathhouse was erected as soon as possible, although this was only a small establishment with one cold bath, three hot baths and one for children but litle else. These, Read's Baths, were owned and operated for several years by the Rev. Read, the Baptist minister in Warwick. With each of the several changes of ownership the name also changed; in 1832 the best known owner, Mrs. Lee, took over and from then it was known as Lee's Baths.

In 1841 Dr. Granville, when visiting Leamington, preferred the water at this bath as it came up quite clear, free of iron and contained sulphur. Although rather doubtful of some of the claims made for waters in Leamington, he felt this well was less likely to be polluted than some of the others in the town. He also described how one proprietor was ruined by the cost of litigation against the owners of a rival bath, whose new well diverted his water. When Mrs. Lee bought the property, however, she deepened the well and found sulphurated water again. In 1861 the owner, James Hudson, installed the first Turkish baths in the town and renamed the business The Royal Leamington Spa Turkish Baths. The venture lost money, however, and the baths were finally closed. Although no trace of it now exists, a drinking fountain remained on the premises for many years.

The rival well, known earlier as Smart's Baths and later as The Imperial Sulphuric, Medicinal, New Marble Baths, better known as The Imperial Fount, was discovered in 1817 on the west side of Clemens Street. The establishment contained an assembly-room and a library besides the usual baths, but it did not last for many years. Besides the cost of the lawsuit it was really too far from the New Town on the north bank of the river. After it closed the building was used as a carriage works.

Another 'spring' was discovered in 1818, according to Moncrieff's *Guide to Leamington Priors* of that year, at the southern edge of the town. A sumptuous suite of baths, to be called The Grand Spa, was talked of, with several streets to be laid out around it. One of these streets, Charlotte Street, still exists, but lack of interest in the building plots because of the competition of the New Town meant that the baths were never built.

Today the only supply of saline water is at The Royal Pump Rooms, built on the site of the sixth well. When the New Town was started in 1808 on the north bank of the Leam, the first houses were built as a terrace on the west side of the Parade, well above the floodland. Mr. Greatheed, the landowner, soon realised that these houses were isolated from the existing baths in the old village and that for the development to succeed he needed to find a saline well nearer at hand.

His early search in 1808 on the high ground to the north of the Parade was expensive and fruitless. In October 1810 salt water was found near the river, but the flow was inadequate.

7. A view of Leamington from the mill, drawn in the late 1820s. It shows the 'new bridge' finished in 1809-10, with the Royal Pump Rooms to the right and the Victoria Baths to the left. The parish church has its spire, built in 1825.

Not until September 1811 after another attempt on the same land could Greatheed write in his diary:

> The flow is more copious, sufficient for the supply of an ordinary pump constantly going and [as] full of salt, or more so, as Robbins' well. On plugging the bore the salt water is within ten feet of the surface, that is above thirty feet from the bottom.

Within three days Greatheed was talking to Mr. Tomes and Mr. Parkes, both from Warwick, about baths in Leamington 'on a handsome scale in which I am deeply concerned', but it was not until late in 1812 that Greatheed, Tomes, Parkes and Mr. Tancred, also of Warwick, felt sure enough to form a syndicate to build a pump room and baths. Even then the supply of saline water was erratic and as late as October 1813, when the buildings were under construction, a further well was sunk.

The New Pump Rooms and Baths, the original name, were opened in July 1814. They were acclaimed as the best in the country, a claim which is certainly open to doubt, but the establishment was extremely popular. So great was the demand for treatment there that the building was found to be too small. It was extended almost immediately, not really being complete until 1816. The building was of stuccoed brickwork, 106 ft. long and 30 ft. high. On three sides it had a colonnade of Doric pillars standing in pairs. These were each of one piece of stone, turned to shape by Mr. Fox, a well-known engineer, at his works in Derby and transported by canal barge to Guy's Cliffe Wharf, near Warwick, from where they were brought by cart. After erection each was coated with Roman cement and given a fluted finish. The roof was in the cottage style, described by *The Warwick Advertiser* as 'remarkable for its taste and simple elegance'. The pump had an ornamental pedestal, a basin of Derbyshire marble and was enclosed by a mahogany balustrade. The pump-room was lit on one side by seven windows, the intervals being filled by Doric pilasters, and it was heated by two chimney-pieces of Kilkenny marble. Either side of the pump-room were wings, 30 ft. in length and 20 ft. high, which formed the principal entrances into the public baths. In 1814 there were 17 hot and three cold baths.

Others were more critical than the *Advertiser*. The Rev. Field, writing a year after the baths were first opened, considered the roof 'low and heavy, and admitting of no relief'. It was 'considered by some, as not happily chosen; and the introduction of a ponderous square pillar, between two round ones, in the colonnade, is still less admired by others'. Another contemporary thought it too near the road to be appreciated, but that it appeared 'strikingly grand' from the fields a small distance away. Certainly the low classical building was not universally admired. Dr. Granville, in 1841, thought its general effect spoilt by its lowness and commented:

> Still to make good the claims that its proprietors at Leamington set up for it, of being a building 'excelling all baths in England and rivalling the thermae of the ancients', one would have expected something better than four naked walls in the interior of the [pump] room, distempered over with a deep peach-blossom coluor; having on one side high chimney pieces of painted wood, and pilasters similarly painted, to imitate Sienna marble; with a plain white-washed ceiling, from which hangs pendant an ordinary chandelier, serving to light up at night four casts of statues in different parts of the room, besides the large counter at the upper end of it, at which the water is distributed in the morning.

He also dropped veiled hints that the saline water in both Robbins' Victoria Baths and the Royal Pump Rooms was possibly polluted by river water, their wells being only a short distance from the Leam into which most of the town's sewers discharged.

Mr. Greatheed's journal relates the numerous difficulties which had to be solved before the new pump-room was opened. Not the least of these was an adequate supply of saline water. In September 1812 C. S. Smith, the architect, and Mr. Binns, the bath-maker, estimated that the proposed 'fifteen baths, each used six times a day, giving ninety baths, will require seven thousand gallons and upwards besides the cold baths which require an enormity of water'. The baths finally installed contained, in the case of the hot, upwards of 350 gallons and the cold, when full, 1,554 gallons. To raise this vast quantity of water from the well a two horse-power steam-engine was used.

In October 1812 the proprietors of the baths met Mr. Parkes and Mr. Fox to discuss equipment for pumping and heating the water. On 27 September 1813 Greatheed saw the steam-engine working for the first time. He seems to have thought little of such inventions and did not say who had made it. Parkes, a friend of several of the syndicate, had already installed a Boulton and Watt steam-engine in his factory, and so it is possible that the engine used in the baths came from the same source, Fox being responsible for its installation. There would have been nothing unusual in this since Boulton and Watt supplied pump parts, leaving the installation to be done by the users.

Greatheed does not mention Boulton and Watt in his journal, but there is evidence that they provided at least some of the equipment used at the Pump Rooms. Eleven small drawings in the Boulton and Watt Collection, Birmingham Reference Library, made in February and April 1815, are survey notes and measurements for the installation there of two new boilers and a large cistern for heating saline water. These were necessary to cope with the extra demand for hot water once the baths had been extended. A plan of the existing boiler and mangling-room on the south side of the building shows the two original boilers and the space between them into which the new ones were to fit. The new boilers were the same size as the older ones, which suggests the firm may also have built the originals. Another drawing is for a 'washer', part of a pump for forcing water to the pump-room, indicating Boulton and Watt may have built the steam-engine, too. The drawings also show that the well was not in the building, but lay 50 ft. from the colonnade towards the river. The collection includes too a bill from the company 'for work done for the proprietors of the Leamington New Baths' costing £704 12s. A postscript gives the news that Mr. Murdock's leg was healing well; William Murdock, the inventor of gas lighting, worked with Boulton and Watt at that time. Samuel Smiles recorded that Murdock was badly injured when a cast-iron plate fell on his leg while he was erecting apparatus for heating water for the baths.

When finally completed the gardens around the pump-rooms occupied the same area as at present. There were several acres north-west of the building beside the river, and to the south a promenade along the course of the Leam. According to a description in *The Leamington Spa Courier* a few years later, this turned up a circular path through a row of trees, following a spacious walk on the opposite side of the gardens.

The final cost of building and furnishing the baths was given by Greatheed as £18,024. This was a very substantial sum, although not as great as the £25,000 quoted in many contemporary accounts, and it was hardly surprising that the syndicate sought to offset it. Before the baths opened they investigated a scheme to turn the extra power and heat at the premises to profit by manufacturing mineral salts. 'Thompson of Cheltenham gains hundreds a year by a similar plan. We are immediately to consult Fox on the subject' wrote Mr. Greatheed, but the scheme was not carried through, perhaps because of competition from the owner of Abbotts' Baths. Despite the high costs the charges for bathing and drinking the waters were not at first set higher than those of the other baths. They were still high in real terms, of course, yet the new building was so attractive that visitors resorted to it in large numbers.

In these early days the pump-room was well patronised and proved a very profitable investment to the original proprietors, but by 1848 other spas, particularly on the continent, were attracting visitors and the fashion for 'taking the waters' was declining in favour of sea bathing. Gradually the members of the original syndicate either died or sold their shares to the Hon. Charles Bertie Percy, who had married Mr. Greatheed's granddaughter and lived at Guy's Cliffe after Greatheed's death in 1826. As a result he became sole proprietor and in 1860 decided to close the establishment, demolish the building and sell the land.

A public meeting was held at *The Regent Hotel* at which it was decided to raise a fund to purchase the pump-room and grounds, improve them and so preserve them. The scheme received little public support and the promoters admitted defeat the following year. Dr. Jephson and a number of other influential local people then formed The Leamington Royal Pump Room Company Limited and issued a prospectus for a joint-stock company with a capital of £8,000 in £5 shares. These were all taken up and the property was purchased for £8,500 in October 1861.

Improvements costing over £17,000 were carried out, including replacing the original cottage-style roof, and new baths were installed. But after struggling for several years without paying any dividends, the company sold the property to the Local Board of Health in 1868 for £15,000. Thus it came into the hands of the local authority, the forerunner of the Royal Leamington Spa Corporation and Warwick District Council.

In 1875 the Pump Room Gardens were first opened to the public free of charge. During 1885-6 the Board spent a further £4,000 on improvements and renovation, including adding new baths and a tower at one end of the parade elevation. The work was completed in 1887 when the pump-room and baths were reopened by the Speaker of the House of Commons, the Right Hon. A. W. Peel, M.P. for Warwick and Leamington Spa. The large swimming-bath was added a short time after at a cost of £2,500. A new annexe was built on the river side of the building in 1910 and other improvements were carried out in 1926, costing over £15,000. The Pump Rooms continued to be a feature of the life of the town for many years,

8. The Royal Pump Rooms in 1864, showing the buildings after the 1861 alterations carried out by the Local Board of Health, when the tower was added.

9. The interior of the Royal Pump Rooms early in the 20th century.

but the number of visitors coming to 'take the waters' has declined, particularly since the First World War.

During the Second World War the Pump Room and annexe were occupied by a government department engaged on camouflage work. The tower was removed in 1950, which restored the building to something like its original appearance although the wings at each end have gone. The completion of this work was delayed due to shortage of materials, but it was finished in 1953 to commemorate the coronation. The pump-room and particularly the baths still function as a treatment centre supported by the National Health Service, and it is the only spa in England offering this service through the N.H.S. The property and equipment, which are the responsibility of the local authority, now need extensive modernisation, however, so once again the future of the building is in doubt. At the time of writing a private syndicate is promoting a scheme to extend the Pump Rooms and Baths by building over part of the original gardens, although there is local opposition to the loss of this long established and well-used public open space.

Chapter Three

The Old Village

Until the beginning of the last century Leamington Priors was a small village on the south bank of the Leam, while on the opposite bank open farmland sloped up from the low-lying ground by the river; the only building north of the Leam was Mr. Willes' house at Newbold Comyn, then outside the limits of the parish. The development of the village into a spa town brought dramatic changes.

The oldest known street plan of Leamington is dated 1783. At that date the village had one main street, later known as Bath Lane and now Bath Street. Bath Lane was part of the old road from Whitnash to Lillington which, north of the river, became the lower section of the Parade. It ran south from the bridge to meet the turnpike road from Warwick to Daventry. The turnpike became known as the High Street about 1815. Besides these principal thoroughfares there were several lanes east of Bath Lane.

In 1783 there were a few cottages along the west side of Bath Lane owned by Mr. Robbins and Mr. Wise and occupied by their workmen. Wise himself lived in a large house just west of the lane, and near to the entrance drive was Abbotts' field and cottage. These became the site of the second saline well and *The New Inn*. Wise's house was later altered and extended and some of the original building now forms part of the present *Manor House Hotel* in Avenue Road. This street takes its name from the Upper and Lower Avenues marked on the 1783 map, described in 1815 as 'beautiful plantations, forming a bold semi-circular sweep'. Wise's orchard extended alongside Bath Lane to the turnpike road, and in it he found another saline well in 1790. On the east side of the lane was the original saline spring, near Mr. Dawkes' cottage. Open ground lay southwards from there to the village pond on the corner of High Street.

East of Bath Lane, Church Lane (the modern Church Street) led past the church to *The Bowling Green Inn* and the village green. Behind the church, in Mill Lane (now Mill Street), was the village mill, Benjamin Satchwell's cottage, which was the first Post Office, cottages and a farm. On the south side of the High Street was *The Dog Inn* where Mr. Abbotts originally lived and on the north side was a farmhouse where *The George Inn* later stood. Around it lay cottages, shops, the smithy, the stocks and some outbuildings mostly owned by a farmer, Mr. Whitehead. A second pond lay in the street to the east, and more cottages. Beyond them was the parish poorhouse. In all there were about fifty cottages and three farmhouses.

Some of the first development in Leamington took place to the south of the village. Two new streets were laid out running southwards from the High Street towards the Birmingham-Napton canal, opened in 1795, along the line of lanes to Whitnash and Bishop's Tachbrook. These roads were Tachbrook Street and Clemens Street.

Clemens Street, laid out in 1808, was the first of the 'modern' streets of Leamington although it took some years to complete. It was the work of John Webb, a Birmingham builder. An advertisement in *The Warwick Advertiser* in that year states that 'A new street is laid out and begun on this year leading from the village to the canal, and there is great probability of it being completed in the course of another summer or two'. It also mentions that brick kilns were opening nearby and that, as the canal went through the land, building materials were easily conveyed to the site. The kilns were in Court Street and Grove Place, afterwards narrow courts of houses; Court Street leads off High Street and Grove Place leads off Ranelagh Street.

The first houses built in Clemens Street were on the west side near the site of the present railway bridge; the very first house was probably on the corner of Clemens Street and High Street, facing Bath Street. It was demolished when the railway was constructed between 1847 and 1850. Mr. Olorenshaw is known to have purchased a house on this corner from the Rev. William Read in 1809. Here Olorenshaw provided a 'commodious Reading Room and Circulating Library', which according to contemporary accounts was 'carefully adapted to the usual tastes of watering-places, in a tolerable collection of voyages, travels and above all – novels'. He also sold jewellery and stationery.

The west side of the street was built up before the east. James Bisset, who settled in Leamington in 1812 and built a picture gallery in Clemens Street, recorded that 'there was not a house beyond my gallery, which was the only building on the east side of the street'. In 1812 a boarding house, later called *The Stoneleigh Hotel*, appeared on the west side, followed in 1813 by Booth's Terrace adjacent to the canal; although much altered these buildings still stand. By 1842 the hotel had been converted into several small houses. Houses were built by Benjamin Satchwell and later a chapel appeared. Among the largest buildings in the street was Smart's Marble Baths, opened in 1817 on the west side near the railway bridge.

By 1818 Clemens Street was finished. *The New Hotel*, later renamed *The Blenheim Hotel*, *The Royal Hotel*, Elliston's library, Booth Terrace, a chapel and Smart's Marble Baths were all shown on the plan of that date. One side of the street was taken up by a range of houses, complete with decorative iron-work balconies, concealing a considerable number of smaller houses cramped around poorly-lit courts. Many of the terraced houses have survived in much altered form as shops, but all the courts were swept away during slum clearance. On the other side of the street there were in 1815 some shops, another new hotel not yet occupied, Probett's Mews, 'capable of holding fifty horses and half as many carriages' and 'a range of uniformly built houses which formed Clemens Place'. Stephen Probett, who had previously managed Lord Middleton's stables, opened the mews in 1813 but just over 18 months later he was bankrupt and William Merry took over the business. Eventually the buildings were used for other purposes as trade in the old village declined in the face of competition from the New Town.

Buildings were also constructed to the south of the canal bridge. Springfield House in Upper Clemens Street, now called Brunswick Street, was built in 1819. It was sold by auction in 1833, being described as 'with a shrubbery at the top of Brunswick Street, a dwelling house with stables and being 1984 sq. yds. in area'. Some years later it was demolished and the site built upon again. To the right of the bridge was 'the occasional residence, in the cottage style, of William Moody of Beaudesert', and beyond was 'the busy navigation wharf, chiefly filled with coal'. This was Hiorn's wharf, later purchased by Mr. Stanley. East of Brunswick Street were two other streets newly laid out in 1818: Ranelagh Street and Regent Street, later renamed Aylesford Street. Many of the houses here and in the adjacent streets are late Victorian in date, so the 1818 development was obviously never completed.

These two streets led to The Leamington Nursery and Pleasure Grounds, later called The Ranelagh Gardens. These ten acres planted with trees, shrubs and flowers were laid out in 1811 by a Mr. Mackie. He opened them to the public as the town's first public gardens or pleasure grounds, modelled on the famous Ranelagh Gardens in London. In 1813 Mackie was joined by a Mr. Brown and a year later the property was sold to Mr. John Cullis, who is reputed to have planted with his own hands the original trees forming Linden Avenue on the north side of the Pump Room gardens. Under his management the gardens

10.   Clemens Street in 1822 showing Rackstrow's *Blenheim Hotel*.

11.   Eastnor Terrace, demolished in 1852 to allow the present railway station to be built. A view published about 1843.

became a very popular venue for visitors, but with the opening of the Jephson Gardens on the north side of the river the Ranelagh Gardens fell out of favour. Cullis died in 1849 and after several years the gardens were closed.

The Rev. Field described the gardens in rather patronising manner as

> extensive flower and fruit gardens occupying a space of nearly ten acres, but not laid out at present with much taste, in which are large hot houses and green-houses for which a botanical collection is said to be preparing. On these must rest their claim to the high-sounding name of Ranelagh Gardens, which they have lately assumed; it must however be allowed they have already opened a source of amusement to the visitors to Leamington, at once pleasing, rational and healthful.

The attractions of the gardens can hardly be visualised now for the site is covered by Messrs. Flavel's factory, a public recreation ground and streets of houses. All that remains is the name, preserved in Ranelagh Street, leading to the factory, and Ranelagh Terrace, beside the canal. This terrace was built in the 1820s while the gardens were still open, and was originally laid out as an avenue to a villa at its west end. This house was demolished by 1857, and today the few other original houses that remain there are only an echo of the elegant Regency buildings that once existed in this part of the town.

On the west side of Brunswick Street is shown on the 1818 map another newly laid out street called Charlotte Street. The quality of the surviving terraces demonstrates that this was intended to be a very fashionable address. When building land was first advertised here in 1817 there was little response, however. Interest was stimulated by the discovery of a saline well on the south side of the street in 1818 and its presence was pointed out in adverts of 1821. A 'Grand Spa', never built, was proposed on the site. Speculators were encouraged to acquire land here and in Brunswick Street from the landowner, Thomas Read, and they agreed recklessly to covenants in their 99-year leases that each house must cost between £800 and £1,000 to build and that no house could be used for commercial purposes. Between 1818 and 1825 some 15 houses were built, but then development stopped, blighted by the popularity of the New Town.

In this part of the town some houses remained empty for years. James Bisset, writing in 1830 about the house he owned in Ranelagh Street, commented: 'It has been built upwards of seven years, at a cost of above a thousand pounds and never been inhabited although in a pleasant part of the town', while a house which he had formerly let for £50 a year now brought in only 25 guineas. Dr. Granville observed in 1841 that 'to the westward of the High Street on the border of the Warwick Road, a row of lofty houses rear their pretending heads, in imitation of those in Brunswick Square in Brighton or in Kemp Town, but look in vain for dwellers', a general picture of the older part of the town at this period.

In 1810 Wise Street was laid out between Clemens Street and the Tachbrook Road on land owned mostly by Mr. Wise but partly by Mr. Robbins. By 1815 the street had almost reached its present length. All the original houses have now gone, but it was then quite a desirable address. In 1822 Wise sold the land between this street and the canal to the Leamington Priors Gas Light Company for the construction of the town's first gasworks. Later came Victorian terraced housing.

Although they are not shown on the 1818 plan the first houses in the Tachbrook Road were built in the early part of the 19th century on the corner where this road met the High Street. The development can be dated by a notice in *The Warwick Advertiser* of 15 September 1810 advertising this land for sale. Eastnor Terrace, as first built in 1838, was an impressive range of houses. It had to be demolished in 1850 to allow the Great Western Railway station to be erected on the site; however the existing terrace was built from the salvaged materials. The terrace was named after Lord Eastnor, who owned the land. He lived north of the river.

No other building took place towards Warwick beyond this junction with High Street until recent times. But south of the canal, up the Tachbrook Road, terraces of houses were built in the late 19th century and development continued into the 20th. Tachbrook Road was also the site of Shrubland Hall, built in 1818 for Matthew Wise, who then moved from his house near Bath Street. The new mansion was a stuccoed house of two-and-a-half storeys with a bow window in front, rather like Dr. Jephson's house, Beech Lawn, in the New Town. When Charles Wise died soon after the First World War the house became a private school and remained one until 1939. It was demolished in 1948.

A limited amount of new building also took place along the High Street. Approaching Leamington from the west, noted the Rev. Field in 1815, one passes on the left Matthew Wise's seat, then 'on the right appears the first of the new erections, Albion House, a singular structure built in a sort of mock Gothic Style, rather fanciful than tasteful – but affording within three comfortable dwellings'. Albion House, built in 1813, was near the canal at the back of Wise Street. After its demolition it was commemorated by a canal-side terrace known as Albion Row, which stood until the 1950s. A short distance along was *The Crown Inn*. Built about 1808 as a vicarage, it was used as a school and then in 1815 was extended, altered and opened as an inn by Joseph Stanley. Next to it stood Olorenshaw's shop, and opposite, on the corner of High Street and Bath Lane, Wise's Baths, opened in 1790.

East of Clemens Street there was also some new building. A terrace built in 1810-15 was described in the latter year as 'Barford Buildings, a row of houses small, but very snug'. They were so named, presumably, because some of the land was originally owned by the parish of Barford. Other 'new and good houses' were interspersed among the old cottages on this side of the village and a few small terraces were built which can still be identified although much altered. None were of such high quality as the houses being built north of the river, however. The new houses did not spread beyond the limits of the original settlement; the expansion along what is now known as the Radford Road is largely late-Victorian or Edwardian in date, there being only a few older houses. But in 1832, on the site of the old poorhouse just beyond the edge of the village, a new hospital was constructed, now called The Warneford Hospital.

The most important building in the High Street of the early 19th century was the new Town Hall, built in 1830 and used for the first time on 27 June 1831. It has survived although converted to other uses. The narrow courts and streets built behind the Town Hall near the canal and the railway line largely date from the period 1830 to 1870. Inevitably they became overcrowded slums and were described in lurid detail in the Public Health Report on sanitary conditions in Leamington Priors compiled in 1850. In spite of the bad condition of many of these houses a large number survived until the slum clearance programmes of the 1930s to 1950s.

Change also took place in the northern part of the village. The Rev. Field, generally an accurate observer, wrote in 1815

> as most of the cottages, which once composed the whole of this small and humble village, still remain, it is easy to compare together its former and its present state; and to perceive in every part a change so great, as almost to entitle even the Old Town to the appellation of 'New'. In the central part of Church Street, are several good houses, recently finished, forming a strong contrast with the thatched roofs, and mud walls, amid which they rear their modern and shewy fronts.

Moncrieff's *Guide*, first published in 1818, described albeit with hyperbole the period just before that year as one when

> Improvement became the order of the day; every cottage made haste to look like a house and every house offered a lodging. Tradesmen, builders, speculators and others, all rushed to consult the capabilities of the place . . . buildings sprung up like mushrooms, houses grew in the streets, and the streets into a town . . . the tools of the carpenters went merrily in winter, and every summer presented some fresh claim to the favour of the public.

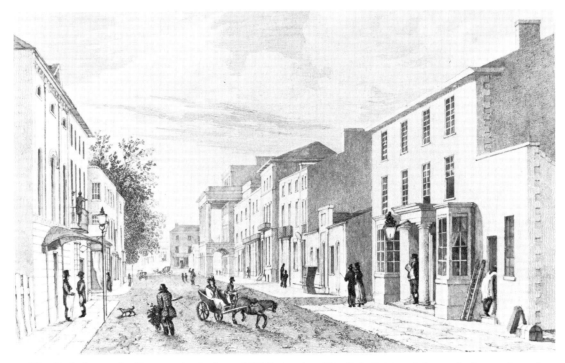

12.   Bath Street, looking south. A view of 1822 showing *The Bath Hotel* and, beyond, the portico of The Parthenon. Opposite the hotel is the theatre.

Much of this was infilling, however, since before he moved to Shrubland Hall in 1818 Mr. Wise was reluctant to sell land for building near his house.

From property deeds we know that by 1813 the High Street, Gloucester Street, Bath Street, Mill Street and Clemens Street were laid out but only some of the frontages were built up. On the west side of Bath Street were, among other buildings, Abbotts' Baths, *The New Inn* (later *The Bath Hotel*) and, near the river, Robbins' Baths. Also in Bath Street opened in 1821 Elliston's Library, later called The Parthenon. This building survived almost unaltered internally above ground floor level until destroyed by fire in the late 1960s. Apart from these most of the early developments in this street were residential and many of the larger houses shown on the 1828 plan of the town had gardens on the street; the 1818 map was incorrect in showing the street frontage as wholly built up. Leamington's first market opened in Bath Street behind *The Bath Hotel* in 1813. It was replaced by a new one in the New Town, opened in 1828; this took the name Covent Garden Market.

On the east side of Bath Street the Earl of Aylesford replaced the first building over the original spring with the Well House in 1813. There were houses on the corner of Church Walk and Gloucester Street, and between them an inn. The first, small, theatre was built in 1814 facing Abbotts' Baths. It was opened by Mr. Sims, taken over by Mr. Elliston and he was followed by Mr. Bennett. It lasted until 1826, then being known as The Old Theatre. The building was acquired by a wine merchant and is now, much altered and extended, *The Chair and Rocket* public house. Adjacent to the village green was the first *Bowling Green*

Hotel, which was replaced in 1825 by another building on a piece of land opposite called the Town Close. This new inn was originally called *The Bowling Green Commercial Inn*; it was later re-opened as *The Guernsey Temperance Hotel* by Mrs. Meeks. The new name was taken from the title of the son of the Earl of Aylesford, Lord Guernsey. The site is now occupied by the Guernsey Garage.

Gloucester Street was laid out in 1806 on one-and-a-quarter acres of land sold by Mr. Willes to Mr. William Freeman, gent., of Hidcote in Gloucestershire, who was a speculative builder. The first house was built that year; by 1812 several houses in the street were being used for commercial purposes, the one on the corner of Bath Street being a hardware shop. In 1814 James Bisset used the drawing room of a house there as a museum. Church Street had also been started by this time and a track led eastward to Satchwell Place and Gordon House, both of which still exist, and the first post office. Satchwell Place, several houses towards the end of George Street, was built in 1807 by Mrs. Hopton, Satchwell's daughter; Gordon House was built by the Duchess of Gordon as a residence during the season, as she was a regular visitor for many years from 1810.

The first Leamington post was established by Benjamin Satchwell soon after he settled in the village. Satchwell was the local shoemaker, an amateur poet, Leamington's first chronicler and the man who discovered the second mineral spring with William Abbotts. In 1783 he became the keeper of the mail-bag at his cottage on the corner of what is now Mill Street and New Street. A new post office was later built in Mill Street, near this cottage. When Satchwell died in 1810 his eldest daughter took over the post; in 1816 she married a Mr. Hopton who managed the post office until 1826, at the same time running *Hopton's Boarding House* in nearby Satchwell Place. Hopton probably gave up the postal service when he went to live in Clemens Street,

13.   The original post office, in a cottage on the corner of what is now Mill Street and New Street.

for in 1826 the house in Satchwell Street was to let, together with 'the thatched cottage lately occupied as a post office'.

At first the post arrived at midday and outgoing letters had to be taken at 2.15 p.m. to the Warwick post office. In July 1818 a new mail-coach began running from London to Warwick via Leamington, an innovation designed to give a better service to the 'increasing and flourishing Spa'; it allowed letters to be delivered in Leamington between 9 and 10 a.m. and replies to be posted until 4 p.m. This was the first real improvement in the service started by Satchwell and was largely due to pressure exerted by Charles Mills, M.P. for Warwick.

In May 1829 the townspeople petitioned the Postmaster-General for an independent local post office, and after a first refusal the request was granted in 1830. The business was then transferred from Mill Street to 29 Bath Street where the postmaster, George Bevington, occupied part of Messrs. Beasley and Jones' chemist's shop. Postal charges were still so expensive that only the wealthy or those with urgent business could afford to use the service, so letters were not very numerous. The penny postage system introduced by Sir Rowland Hill in 1839 brought about a change; the increased business it created made larger premises essential, so another move was made, to 41 and 43 Bath Street. In 1846 a new post office was opened lower down Bath Street, nearly opposite The Parthenon. It had an entrance portico of six columns, surmounted by a parapet and balustrades and displaying in the centre the Royal Arms, letter-boxes on either side of the door and, in the window, a large clock showing the standard Post-Office time. This building was demolished in 1872; the present post-office building on the corner of Priory Terrace opened in March 1870.

14.   Spencer Street in 1914.

Eighty-one people in the whole parish paid rates in 1813 and 175 the following year. The homes of ten of the latter were not given, but 35 of the others lived in High Street, 14 in Church Street, six in Mill End, 23 in Clemens Street (then known as Clement Street), 20 in Bath Street (owning 25 houses) and nine in Gloucester Street.

Two new roads were made in 1825: Regent Place, near the bowling-green, laid out to connect Bath Street with Church Street, and Russell Terrace, a street leading further eastward from Regent Place. In 1827, when a new bridge was constructed over the Leam east of the town and a new road, now Willes Road, was made to link Kenilworth and Southam, Russell Terrace was extended further eastward to meet the new road. The development of the town south of the river and east of the village was thereby encouraged. In the following years, 1828-36, the adjacent roads Priory Terrace and Leam Terrace were laid out. In the 1840s Leam Terrace was extended beyond Willes Road. In 1838 St Mary's church was built in the fields south of the Radford Road, on the edge of Sydenham farm. St Mary's Road and St Mary's Crescent, laid out in 1838-50, still contain many of the original villas, including some interesting examples of the Victorian 'Gothick' style. Other

15. All Saints' church and the bridge about 1826. This view shows the original Victoria Baths and the church with its new tower and spire.

16. The Victoria Bridge, c.1920.

THE VICTORIA BRIDGE, LEAMINGTON.

streets of smaller houses, like Gordon Street, New Street and Plymouth Place, were laid out in the late 19th century behind the Regency streets. Gaps in the older streets were filled in with detached Victorian villas, in contrast with the fashion for building uniform terraces typical of the previous era.

In the heart of the village further changes took place. Spencer Street was laid out in 1832-9, leading west from the original spring. Its first important building, a chapel, was erected in 1836. Although he had no connections with Leamington the street was named after the Rev. Thomas Spencer, a Congregational minister drowned in the Mersey; the name was chosen by the first minister of the chapel. To the north, opposite the church and fronting Bath Street, is Victoria Terrace. These houses were completed in 1836, when Bath Street was widened.

The widening of Bath Street by some 29 ft. in 1836 was part of an improvement scheme which also involved widening the bridge across the Leam. The bridge was a vital link between the two parts of Leamington. It was plainly too narrow for the increasing numbers of fashionable visitors coming to take the waters in the early 19th century, and if the proposed new town on the north bank was to succeed it had to be improved. As a result it was largely rebuilt in 1808-9 by Henry Couchman junior, just as the first houses were being built north of the river. The finished bridge was described at the time as 'a very handsome stone bridge in the Gothic style'. This work was mostly paid for by Mr. Edward Willes and Mr. Greatheed, who owned the land north of the river and who therefore would gain most benefit from development there. The stone was bought by the county from a quarry on Mr. Greatheed's property, however, which he thought would 'probably put £200 in my pocket unexpectedly'. At the same time the county laid out the road from the north side of the bridge to line up with the new Union Parade.

In the 1830s, when local people again felt that the bridge needed to be widened, the County Quarter Sessions, who controlled the structure, refused to meet the expense. The paving commissioners, however, decided they were empowered to do the work themselves under the Leamington Priors Improvement Act of 1825. They chose to widen the bridge on the east side, making the width between the balustrades 40 ft. The opportunity was also taken to improve the flow of the river, as between the mill and the bridge the Leam was little over half its present width, the banks were overgrown, the flow in summer almost non-existent and the water polluted with sewage and debris of all kinds.

Dr. Jephson started proceedings by laying the foundation stone on the north-east abutment on 14 August 1839. The bridge was finished eight months later and the inscribed, final coping stone was laid on the Queen's birthday. The inscription read:

> This stone was laid by Henry Jephson M.D. on the 25th May 1840 in commemoration of the extension and improvement of this bridge and in celebration of the Birthday of Her Most Gracious Majesty Queen Victoria.

Its structure was designed by Mr. J. G. Jackson, a local architect, and built by Mr. Green. After its completion the workmen were entertained at *The Angel Hotel* and the Commissioners and their guests dined at *The Bath Hotel*. Eight years later it was again found necessary to widen the bridge, though slightly, and this was done on the west side. The footpath was supported alongside the bridge on projecting iron beams and brick trimmer arches, and now formed a continuous path between the Pump Room and Victoria Terrace, which it had not been possible to make before.

Further repairs have been needed since then, most recently in 1984 when the balustrades were largely replaced. Perhaps the most anxious time in the bridge's history was on 22-23 May 1932 when during floods the River Leam rose to over 12 ft. above normal. Heavy tractors and a motor lorry had to be parked and stone slabs laid on top of the arches to prevent them moving and possibly collapsing when the water rose above their tops.

Chapter Four

The New Town

The development of the north side of the Leam was in marked contrast to that of the south: between 1808 and 1840 the 'New Town' was successfully built there. Almost all this new town was built on 65 acres of farmland opposite Victoria Bridge, owned by Bertie Greatheed and leased to Mr. Perkins, a farmer from Warwick. Later developments took place on the adjoining land: that to the east belonging to Edward Willes, who also owned some to the west, and that a little further away across the Bins Brook, the parish boundary, belonging to the Earl of Warwick. In 1809 the Earl was a bankrupt whose estates were in the hands of trustees. Lillington Lane climbed northwards from the River Leam and halfway up the slope it was crossed by another right of way, a lane leading westwards to Warwick from Lillington and Cubbington. Lillington Lane was renamed Union Parade, a name chosen because the road formed a 'union' between the old and new developments; the name was abandoned in 1860 in favour of The Parade. The other street was first called Cross Street, then renamed Regent Street after the Prince Regent's visit to the town, but for a short time it was known as Lower Cross Street, and the newly created Warwick Street, higher up the slope, was known as Upper Cross Street. According to Mr. Greatheed the latter's name was changed to Warwick Street as early as 1813. The extension of Regent Street westwards was later known as Wellington Street and was renamed Church Hill many years later.

The first house in the New Town was not *The Golden Lion* as stated in Richard Hopper's *History of Leamington Priors* (1843), but was on the north-western corner of the crossroads; it is now a shop. The Rev. William Field wrote in 1815:

> it would be ungenerous, if not unjust, to disappoint, the fair and laudable ambition of an honest and industrious professor of the masonic art – who has sent for insertion in these pages the following notice, which we willingly give, nearly in his own words . . . as a record of an interesting fact.
>
> George Stanley, mason of Warwick, laid the first brick of the first house erected at New Leamington, October 8th 1808. This first house which was built by Mr Frost of Warwick stands at the corner of Upper Cross Street, opposite the Assembly Rooms . . .

Bedford Street was originally named Frost Street in the builder's honour.

In fact the site was on the corner of Lower rather than Upper Cross Street. It can be identified on a plan of 'Building Land in the New Town of Leamington Priors' drawn in 1822 by John Kempson, a local surveyor, which showed all the sites in the lower part of the Parade then sold by Mr. Greatheed as well as much of the rest of his estate. It was a plot measuring 63 yds. by 12 yds. Reference to Greatheed's account book shows that the land went for £189, the fifth plot to be sold.

In *West's Directory* of 1830 Frost's building is shown as a private residence, but three years later it was being used by John Baly, a linen and woollen draper from Warwick. It is doubtful whether the present store on the site conceals any of the original building as it has been altered so many times. The rendered front, with its foliated capitals and cornice, which survives above ground floor level, is obviously not original as the house was brick fronted like the other buildings erected about the same time lower down the Parade. Moreover it does not correspond in any way with a view of the house shown in a sketch of the Assembly Rooms and adjacent buildings made by a visitor to *The Regent Hotel* in 1828, now in the collection of Leamington Art Gallery.

Among the other very early buildings were *The Golden Lion* inn, whose exterior appears to be still largely unaltered, and the two adjacent houses; these three were on the north side of Regent Street just to the east of the Parade. At some time the houses were altered to become shops; both survived until 1985 when one was demolished and rebuilt as offices with a replica façade. The inn was certainly the first building in that part of Regent Street, built on the rear part of a vacant site facing the Parade and owned by a builder from Warwick, William Pratt. Bisset's *Guide* of 1814 describes *The Golden Lion* as 'a common public house', which, as it was only about 30 yds. from the first houses on the Parade, suggests that from the very start there was no overall plan for the development of the new town and that Mr. Greatheed placed no restrictive covenants on his land when selling it for building. Greatheed sold the site, 1440 sq. yds., to Pratt, a joiner, and John Russell, banker, also of Warwick, for £360 some time before 1810.

The development of this important site was rather a haphazard affair. Mr. Pratt obviously found it difficult to dispose of the land and buildings erected on it, as part was sold by auction in June 1812. The lots consisted of 'a new built dwelling house, the *Golden Lion* inn, Cross Street, occupied by Mr. Miles. Two houses and building land adjoining'. This plot was said to be suitable for building three houses. It lay on the corner of Hill Street, which was renamed Satchwell Street some time before 1822. In 1817 Pratt disposed of some more to a Mr. Abraham Blick; the bank facing the Parade and the adjacent chemist's shop in Regent Street were built a few years later. The chemist's shop has served the same purpose since it was constructed; part of the bank was originally a house with its entrance in Regent Street. It was known for some time as Gloucester House, after being occupied by the Duke and Duchess of Gloucester during a visit to the spa in 1822. It was later altered and a new entrance provided to house a bank in 1834 and, although still occupied by a bank, it is known as the 'Old Bank' building.

Before many new buildings could be erected in the New Town the roads and culverts had to be provided. Some idea of the expenditure involved between 1810 and 1823 as Mr. Greatheed laid out his land for building purposes may be gained from the account book drawn up by his executors after his death in 1826 for an audit and payment of tax. It is known as the '1828 Audit' and was compiled by Charles Bertie Percy, his son-in-law, and John Tomes, his solicitor and financial adviser. This book, now in the County Record Office, shows that land sales produced just over £50,000 while developments, extra land purchases in Leamington and other expenditure amounted to a sum of about £34,000, although this may include some items not strictly connected with the New Town.

The earliest payments include those in connection with Justices' orders 'for stopping up old tracks and directing new roads at Leamington', presumably concerning existing public rights of way. Large sums were also paid during 1809-12 for laying out and gravelling roads, constructing culverts, staking out sites and setting out levels. The large amount of £6 10s. was spent during one period in 1810 for 'surveyors and men eating and at different times when planning, measuring and staking out land in lots', and John Kempson, the surveyor in charge, was paid in that year £183 9s. 9d. for survey work, a considerable sum. £3 1s. was also paid to Mr. Sharpe for advertising and printing. In 1812 Greatheed spent £23 1s. 6d. entertaining the 'Building Society', which built the first terrace of houses on his land and over £10 went in entertaining other possible purchasers during the early years of the development.

The first few buildings in Regent Street were followed by a terrace of 20 plain, brick-fronted, three-storey houses on the west side of the Parade. These extended southwards from near Regent Street and ended at *The Bedford Hotel*. The brick fronts of most of the surviving houses, which unlike the buildings lower down the Parade are not stuccoed, can be seen above the modern shop fronts. They were built by a group of Warwick businessmen, members of a syndicate formed by Mr. Tomes, the solicitor, and Mr. Parkes to build a terrace of houses to rent to visitors. It was never intended that the members should live in the properties themselves. The first reference to this 'Society' made by Mr. Greatheed was when he wrote on 29 August 1808 that 'Tomes and Parkes came about Leamington business, a club of friends have subscribed £10,000 for building purposes and will pay £1,200 per acre'. Two days later he noted that the fund was then £16,000 and would eventually raise £20,000 and 'the Society have purchased under 3½ acres for £4,000, the interest at 5pc begins next Lady Day', while his account book confirms that the group in fact paid £4,090 for the land. On 3 September *The Warwick Advertiser* reported

> that subscriptions of £20,000 [have been] entered into by several Gentlemen of this Town, for building an elegant range of houses at Leamington . . . forty houses have already been subscribed for, which are to be immediately erected on the land of Mr Greatheed which is most advantageously situated, and now allotted out for sale for the purpose of building upon.

Though the first report in *The Warwick Advertiser* stated that 40 houses were to be built, only 20 were in fact completed. Although the society bought most of the land on the west side of the Parade between Dormer Place and Regent Street, after the first houses were built the other plots were developed by individuals. Work on the site began before 1810 and by 8 March of that year the paper announced a 'ballot by members of the Society for the first eight houses already built'. The 'Leamington Building Society' was not a building society in the modern sense, but a group of businessmen who pooled their resources to borrow jointly money to build houses to rent. There was eventually to be one house for each share, a ballot deciding in what order the shareholders should have the houses as they were finished. The last ballot was held on 13 November 1810. The original shareholders included an auctioneer, a baker, a banker, a builder, a timber merchant and builder, a clergyman, a coal dealer, a farmer, a grocer, a hatmaker, an innkeeper, an ironmonger, three manufacturers, a miller, a physician, a postmaster and undertaker, a printer and bookseller, and three solicitors. Some of the shareholders held several shares, others had only part of one.

Little precise information is available about how the Society worked, only brief reports in *The Warwick Advertiser* and details recorded in Greatheed's journal. Members entered their names for one or more shares, or part of a share, and as money was required for building a call of so much per cent was made by the management committee. According to the newspaper 10 per cent a share was required on 15 July 1809, to be paid to the treasurers Tomes and Russell. Further payments were requested: 5 per cent in October 1809, 5 per cent in December, 10 per cent in February, June and October 1810 and again in February 1811. Shares were sold by some members presumably unable to meet payments or wishing to make a profit on the money already invested. The average cost of each house was about £500, and the Rev. Harry Williams drew the first house in the first ballot. Three of those receiving houses in this ballot were not among the original subscribers, so already since the start of the project some shares had changed hands.

Greatheed wrote that by June 1810 Rev. Williams' house was furnished, and he had commented on 16 March 'the job of furnishing thickens around Harry, and pots, featherbeds and pans, begin to dance before his troubled mind'. The house was let for the season to the Bishop of Kilmare, perhaps the first visitor to stay in the New Town, for £150 a year, giving a return of at least 20 per cent on the capital invested, rather than 5 per cent, the average rate at that period. John Tomes' house was also let during the season, for eight guineas a week, giving an income of about £130 for the four month period. On the other hand *The Warwick Advertiser* reveals that a number of these houses were sold in the summer of 1811, so perhaps the initial investment was not so profitable as first appears.

These first houses were plain ordinary brick houses of under 900 sq. ft. in area, of the type classed as 'third rate' under the London Building Act of 1774. They had no pretensions to grandeur, probably being copied from one of the standard builders' pattern books then

17. Union Parade. The first houses to be completed stand on the west side, *The Regent Hotel* stands on the east and beyond it is the 'Old Bank' building, at that time a house, on the corner of Regent Street. The trees in the foreground mark the site of Denby Villa and later the Town Hall. Published by John Merridew of Warwick in 1822.

18. Union Parade about 1850. The houses on the west side have already become shops, and just beyond *The Regent Hotel* the coach office has been established, projecting slightly across the pavement; this building was demolished in the late 1970s. The carriage turning into the hotel is thought be Dr. Jephson's.

widely available. Such books were certainly in Mr. Greatheed's own library at Guy's Cliffe. The houses were also similar in design to houses built slightly earlier in Warwick and other neighbouring towns during the 18th century, such as those in Church Street, Warwick, where Mr. Sanders, a builder, lived. Mr. Treadgold, a London surveyor, may have been the designer, for on 5 November 1808 a notice appeared in *The Warwick Advertiser* as follows:

> Persons desirous to contract for building about thirty houses at Leamington, near Warwick, may apply to Mr R. Sanders, Surveyor, Warwick, or at the office of Mr Treadgold, Surveyor, Farm Street, London, where plans may be seen and every particular known. Builders to put in offers by 21 December and to offer not less than a block of four.

Miss Berry from London, who was a guest at Guy's Cliffe in 1810 just after the houses were completed, wrote: 'The houses now building are in rows like any street in London, and are in the worst possible taste'. But she was a friend of Horace Walpole and an admirer of the fashionable new 'Gothick' style of architecture. When the houses were sold in 1811 the advertisement was for 'part of a handsome new street, built uniform, front palisaded and flagged, contiguous to the elegant Public Rooms which are building'. The construction of the Upper Assembly Rooms followed soon after that of these houses, on a plot left vacant for the purpose by the Leamington Building Society when planning them.

The Rev. Field's description of the development in 1815 is worth quoting at length.

> Entering the 'New Town' – Union Street first appears – uniformly built – in one straight line. The houses are lofty and handsome, furnished with light iron balconies and finished in the usual style of modern elegance. The whole appearance, indeed, as an ingenious observer once remarked, is exactly that of the modern streets of London removed, as if by invisible agency, and placed among the fields of Leamington. To every house a garden is attached; and though the plan of the interior seems not to have been well laid, at first, yet subsequent alterations and additions have rendered most of them commodious dwellings. A fine broad pavement before this whole range, extending from one extremity to the other in a length of about four hundred yards, forms a noble promenade . . . towards the centre of Union Street, is the 'Bedford Hotel'; of which the exterior presents a uniform and handsome front.

Cross Street, he noted was 'only part formed', and although a considerable number of houses were already built, most of them were of second or third rank.

This standard type of house was even adapted for use as the first hotel, *The Bedford Hotel*. Three houses in the middle of Union Parade were joined together for the purpose. These were once thought to be the houses purchased by John Russell, the banker, with his three shares in the building society but recent research by Mr. Arnison has revealed that although Kempson's plan of 1822 shows the whole of the site as being owned by Russell, a third share of it was actually owned by Dr. Amos Middleton. The hotel opened in 1811 having cost about £5,000 to build and furnish, while the 1,260 sq. yds. of land cost 5s. a yd. It was demolished in 1857 and replaced by a bank; the land is still occupied by a bank, but one of more recent date.

It should be stressed that all the terraces in the town centre were originally constructed for residential purposes of one kind or another, either as private houses, lodging-houses or a few as hotels. The number of shops was quite small until the character of the New Town started to change in the middle of the 19th century and houses became business premises with shop windows inserted into the ground floors. Many of the buildings seen today are not as originally designed, therefore, and although the upper façades have not changed as much as those at ground level, in all cases the interiors have been altered beyond recognition. Moreover a considerable number of the properties in the present Upper Parade have been rebuilt as 'replicas'.

By 1811, 120 new houses had been built in Leamington, both north and south of the river, and another 40 were under construction. By 1814 there were 20 houses on the west side of the Parade south of Regent Street, 12 to the north and about 24 in Regent Street. The 1814 rate book also lists three brickyards. During the years 1808-18 most of the building activity was centred on the Parade and Regent Street, almost all south of Warwick Street. Although a number of the adjacent streets had been laid out on the present gridiron plan, most of this land was not built on until the landowner, speculators and builders were convinced that the houses built beside the Parade were a profitable investment. Any doubts they might have had were dispelled by the success of *The Regent Hotel*, opened in 1819 and then one of the largest hotels in Europe.

Building activity slowed down about 1814, but its revival in the 1820s resulted in an Act for the Paving, Flagging, Lighting, Cleansing and Watching of Leamington Priors, a private Act of Parliament promoted by influential townspeople which received the royal assent on 10 June 1825. The first paving commissioners were then appointed and ensured some control over the new developments then taking place.

19. Lower Parade in 1864. The corner shops near Dormer Place are now a bank, but the elevation above ground-floor level is almost intact. Next to it is the first of the New Town's commercial buildings, the offices of one of the first estate agents Messrs. Locke, later Locke and England, who occupied the building until recently.

Already a large number of streets were laid out, and more soon followed. Buildings had been constructed in most of them, but there were plenty of gaps in the frontages for later developers to fill in. The deeds of the earlier structures allow the streets to be dated approximately, although some individual houses may have been erected a little before the dates given below. Lower Union Parade and Regent Street were begun in 1808; Dormer Place to the south of the Parade, originally known as The Mall, was laid out by 1822; east of the Parade, Satchwell and Park Streets were begun by 1822; north of Warwick Street, Kenilworth and Oxford Streets followed in 1822-6 and Newbold Street was started about 1826. To the west, in the Quarry Field area owned by Edward Willes, Portland Place and Street were begun in 1823-4; Grove Street in 1828; Clarendon Place in 1825; Dale Street in 1832; Clarendon Crescent about 1825; Wellington Street, the extension of Regent Street westwards across the parish boundary up what is now Church Hill, in 1832.

The east side of the Parade north of Warwick Street was started in about 1824 and the west side in 1827, both frontages remaining incomplete until the early 1830s. North and west of the Parade, Binswood Crescent was started in 1825 but never completed; Milverton Crescent was begun in 1827; Beauchamp Terrace at the top of the Parade was started in 1829, Beauchamp Square in 1822-5 and Bertie Circus (Clarendon Crescent), in 1825. The last, too, was not completed until many years later, and then not in its original form of a 'circus'. The first land in Clarendon Square was sold in 1827, but it was not finished until 1838-9. The 14 houses on the east side, all 1829-39, cost about £1,500 each to build, very expensive for the time. Binswood Avenue, 1831-3, and Lillington Avenue, 1833, comprised the northern limit of the town at that period. Holly Walk and Brandon Parade date from about the same time, the farthest part of Upper Holly Walk not being completed until much later in the century.

Near Victoria Bridge, Union Promenade, now known as Euston Place, was built in 1834 but destroyed by fire on 7 November 1839. It was rebuilt in its present form, except for the usual alterations to the lower floors to make shops or offices. Nearby Hamilton Terrace dates from about 1833-4 and in the following year Lansdowne Crescent and Circus were started. Newbold Terrace was laid out around 1828 but not completed for many years and then to a different plan. By 1834-8 the limits of the 'Regency' town were established. All the streets were laid out as far north as Binswood Avenue and Rugby Road, as far east as Clarendon Street, and as far west as the Dell in Warwick Street. The latter is now marked by blocks of flats in New Brook Street.

After 1834 builders filled in the gaps left in earlier developments rather than creating new ones. As a result the less fashionable streets, providing small houses for the tradesmen and poorer people, were laid out behind the wider thoroughfares. Such streets included Augusta Place, Windsor Street, Russell Street, Tavistock Street and Bedford Street, all dating from the late 1830s.

The dramatic expansion of Leamington during the early 19th century, and in particular the decade 1820-30, can be seen from the census figures reproduced in the table below. The population grew from 315 in 1801 to 2,183 in 1821, 6,269 in 1831 and 12,812 in 1841. Meanwhile the total housing stock increased from 481 in 1821 to 2,607 in 1841. Herein lay a problem. Dr. Granville commented in that year, when the census showed there were at least 250 unoccupied houses, 10 per cent of the complete houses in the spa, 'here among the villas and these rows of larger houses, signs of more house-room than people can require, stare you in the face'. Population growth was rapid but not constant, and when it slowed house-building tended not to slow at the same time. A surplus of houses was created at certain times and builders were bankrupted as a result.

20. Waterloo Place about 1843. The terrace, begun in 1829, was named in honour of the Duke of Wellington's visit to Leamington in 1827. Mr Bradley's house, at the end facing Clarendon Place, was demolished in the 1970s and the 'replica' elevation erected conceals a block of modern offices.

21. Houses in Binswood Avenue, built in 1835-6, being demolished in 1911 to allow the present Edwardian-style houses to be erected.

The Population of Leamington in the 19th Century

Year	Popn.	Popn. increase	Year	Popn.	Popn. increase
1801	315		1851	15,723	22.72
1811	543	72.38	1861	17,402	10.68
1821	2,183	302.03	1871	20,917	20.20
1831	6,269	187.17	1881	22,976	9.84
1841	12,812	104.37	1891	23,124	0.64

In the period 1785-1849 building developments in Leamington followed the same long-term fluctuations as were apparent in the rest of the country. Several studies of these fluctuations have been made in recent years, based on figures showing payment of the tax on bricks in England and Wales during that period. From these figures the annual production of bricks can be worked out quite precisely. They show that there was a boom in house building from about 1808-10 until 1815, followed by severe depression in 1816. This depression lasted a few years and then there was a gradual increase in construction leading up to a boom in 1822-6. Another depression and recovery followed, leading to another peak in 1835-6. There was no marked slump after this until well after 1840.

These peaks and troughs in house building are evident in the development of the New Town of Leamington. The earliest houses date from 1808-10. After the boom period there were few large developments until the 1820s, and where developments were started the original layouts were frequently not completed – the developers or builders often went bankrupt because they could not dispose of the newly-built properties. After 1830 a relative boom took place, lasting until about 1836. This was when such schemes as Clarendon Square were undertaken. The failure of The Leamington Priors Bank in 1837 badly hit the development of the town, however. It removed a source of finance for building projects, but more importantly it caused many of the shareholders to become bankrupt, particularly those involved in the development of the town. In 1839, in order to try to pay its creditors, the bank held a compulsory auction sale of all the property owned by its shareholders, whether the buildings were completed or not. This sale was a financial disaster from which the town did not recover for many years. The development of the Regency town almost ceased that year, and there was no building work on anything like a large scale until Victorian-style villas began to appear on the outskirts of the town about a decade later.

The Regency terraced houses were mostly stucco-faced and, in contrast to the county town of Warwick, there were no stone-faced buildings in the spa before the late-Victorian period except for odd buildings such as the parish church. Leamington's houses range from those with simple pilasters and moulded cornices put up between 1815 and 1825 in terraces like those seen along both sides of the Upper Parade, north of Warwick Street, to others of more elaborate design built in the 1830s along Warwick Street to the west of the Parade or along the west side of Clarendon Square. The more important terraces of these later years had recessed central portions framed by projecting end-pavilions with moulded columns typical of the work done slightly earlier in London by John Nash and other metropolitan architects. At the same time the crescents were laid out, and also an unusual design which cannot be classified with any particular group: Lansdowne Circus. This road was constructed in the early 1830s as a development of pairs of semi-detached Regency-style houses. It is unique, for the writer knows of no similar example in this country. Finally, detached villas were built in the later Victorian period on the outskirts of the town, ranging in style from Italian to Gothic and even including an example or two of Egyptian work.

One of the problems facing the developers of Leamington was that of communications with Warwick, where a lot of the better shops were. Good roads were very important to spa

22. Euston Place. A view published in 1843.

23. Hamilton Terrace showing Denby Villa on the right. Although all the houses have been converted into offices, Hamilton Terrace is still externally very much as when built in the 1830s.

towns and Leamington was very fortunate in this respect. Field wrote in 1815:

> The great boast of Warwickshire has long been its roads; which are, by the confession of all, some of the best in the Kingdom, and those in the neighbourhood of Leamington are peculiarly excellent. Formed of well compacted gravel they are smooth almost as walks; ruts are nearly unknown; and little moisture is retained even after the dampest seasons and the hardest rains . . . In no direction, except in one, and that only for a few hundred yards, is he [the visitor] in danger of encountering the serious evil of sandy roads; that pest of Cheltenham – to avoid which its visitors are so often reduced to the dull monotony of driving up and down its main street.

Unfortunately the direct road from the New Town to Warwick was very difficult for wheeled traffic; presumably it was the exception Field mentioned. This lane, leading from the junction of the Parade and Warwick Street, dropped down a steep slope into the Dell, became a low-lying and muddy track where it crossed the Bins Brook and then presented a steep ascent on the other side. This was the isolated site of *The Star and Garter*, one of the oldest public houses in the parish. Carriages going to Warwick from the New Town had to cross the bridge to the old village and use the turnpike, now known as the Old Warwick Road and Myton Road.

The maintenance of Leamington's roads was in the hands of the parish vestry. The vestry had the power to levy rates for the purpose as well as for the poor and upkeep of the church. Unfortunately the sums raised were very small and the

> public work consisted in the employment of a few labourers to potter about the road spreading gravel purchased from Mr Wise and Mrs Shaw, and, here and there, putting down some bricks bought from Mr Mackie.

The limited effectiveness of this provoked in October 1818 the first of the public meetings to try to get an 'improvement act' for the town. In 1821 it was proposed to widen the lane to 54 ft., raise the roadway and bridge the stream. The cost of the work was estimated to be at least £1,000, more than two or three rates. The problem was solved at last by Mr. Willes giving land to widen the lane and by him and Mr. Greatheed building the bridge at their own expense. Local farmers were asked to provide haulage free of charge, work valued at about £150, and the final £200 needed was raised by public subscription. The bridge still stands and is crossed unawares by motorists using the busy road to Emscote and Warwick. The brook has been culverted and the Dell is a public open space, while *The Star and Garter* is still a popular pub but overshadowed by later buildings.

Chapter Five

The First Landowners, Speculators and Developers

In 1767 Parliament passed an act entitled 'An Act for Dividing and Inclosing the Open and Common Fields, Common Meadows, and Commonable Lands on the South and West Parts of the River Leam in the Manor and Parish of Leamington Priors in the County of Warwick'. This act was sponsored by one of the parish's principal landowners, Edward Willes, Chief Baron of His Majesty's Court of the Exchequer, Ireland. It provides an opportunity to examine the pattern of landholding in the parish, although the commonable lands with which it was concerned, estimated in the preamble at 990 acres, all lay south of the river or east of the area where the New Town was to be built and as a result it contains no information about the landowners on the north bank.

The first task of the commissioners appointed under the act was to have 'a true and perfect survey made of all the said open and common fields'. This survey was made by John Tomlinson and was finished by 1 October 1768. The commissioners then divided the common lands, setting out new public roads 60 ft. wide between the ditches. The award was made on 29 September 1769. The cost of obtaining the act, surveying the land, dividing and reallocating it came to £571 6s. 6d. It was borne by those receiving the land, who had sponsored the bill in order to consolidate their landholdings.

The rights of the Earl of Aylesford as lord of the manor were carefully protected. As a landowner he was allotted about twenty-one acres. This included the field between the mill and Willes Road (in all cases here the modern names and locations are given), which was land alongside the river and now almost all public open space. He was also given the farm in Mill Street, land to the east of the Warneford Hospital, now part of it, and some land south of the canal, bought as a public open space in the 1890s. Most importantly, however, he received the site of the original spring at the west end of the parish church. This he resolutely refused to sell in order to ensure free access to the water for the poor.

In lieu of the old glebe lands the vicar was allotted land beside the hospital (now the site of Camberwell Terrace), allotment gardens at the east end of Leam Terrace adjacent to the Radford Road (still used for that purpose), an adjacent meadow (now used as an open space) and the site of the original vicarage. Matthew Wise as patron of the church and recipient of the tithes due to it also received some glebe land in addition to his allocation as a major landowner in the parish. He was given land between the New River Walk (York Road) and the Old Warwick Road, the Shrubland estate west of the Tachbrook Road which abutted land already owned by the Wise family, a meadow adjoining the vicar's and Sydenham Farm near the Radford Road. In all Wise was allotted 472 acres, including the one acre bowling-green in the centre of the village.

The other big landowner was Anne Willes, widow of Edward who had sponsored the act. She obtained the land occupied by Leam Terrace, New Street and Russell Terrace, all on the south bank of the river east of the church; the Rushmore Farm; and a large island in the river opposite Newbold Comyn. This island is now part of the north bank as the channel has altered. Other landowners in the parish included John Lawrence, allotted 73 acres to the south towards Whitnash; Richard Lyndon, allocated 67 acres near the present cemetery and also awarded the windmill, formerly standing near the Tachbrook Road south of the canal; Thomas Aston, allotted one acre of land in the area now occupied by Grove Place;

and the Charities of the Parish of Barford, given land on the Old Warwick Road near Myton.

South of the river, then, the land east of the village was mostly in the hands of the Willes family and to the west was Matthew Wise's estate. In and immediately adjacent to the village the land was owned by a number of individuals. Apart from the Earl of Aylesford none held very much, but many had key sites in the later development of the town. North of the river were three major landowners: the Willes family, the Earl of Warwick and Bertie Greatheed.

Not surprisingly, some of this land changed hands in the following decades. In 1789 the Lyndon estate was purchased by the Earl of Warwick, and in 1791 it again changed hands, passing to Thomas Read, a wool merchant from Kidderminster, in exchange for land in Warwick which came into his possession when he married Mary, daughter of Samuel Clemens of Warwick in 1773. In 1802 it passed to his son Samuel Read of Harborne, and it seems likely that no member of his family ever lived on the estate at Leamington. Clemens Street was laid out across the land in 1808. As late as 1827 Samuel still owned undeveloped land in the area and about this time his brother, the Rev. William Read, the Baptist minister in Warwick, leased a site on the corner of Clemens Street and High Street where he built Read's Baths over a newly discovered saline well.

In 1800 much of the Lawrence estate was purchased by Francis Robbins and his two brothers, all local farmers. Most of this land was across the canal from the village, which made it difficult to sell for building. The Robbins had no success selling it at auction so they sold it off piecemeal. In 1803 Matthew Wise paid £4,500 for 42 acres south of the village near the Tachbrook Road and close to his Shrubland estate. Thomas Read also bought land at the end of the Tachbrook Road, adjacent to the High Street, to develop jointly with John Webb, a builder from Birmingham. Land in Charlotte Street, over the canal, went to William Hunter who built on part of it in about 1818. Other buyers included James Crump, a Coventry builder who purchased four acres, Edward Treadgold, a Leamington builder who took two acres, and John Garrard.

All that is known of Garrard is that he came from Olney in Buckinghamshire, a fact revealed by a deed. His name, and the place he came from, suggest an interesting possibility, however. An advertisement in *The Warwick Advertiser* in July 1809 offers some land for sale fronting the High Street near Mr. Wise's Baths. There are no other details except the name of the agent, Andrew Gardener, auctioneer and surveyor, of Woburn, Bedfordshire, and that he was the Duke of Bedford's own land agent. The Duke much admired and often visited the spa. His interest may have encouraged gentry local to his principal seat to invest in the growing town. As Woburn is not far from Olney it is possible that Gardener may have been trying to sell land owned by Garrard, originally purchased as a speculation. There is no evidence to prove that the Duke himself bought land in Leamington although he may have invested in the bank owned by his reputed cousin, John Russell.

John Aston, son of Thomas, is also unknown save for mention in deeds of sale. In 1810 he sold some of the land he owned in Clemens Street to John Garrard. He may also have had some land south of the High Street as his name appears on a map of that road. He died in 1815, according to Mr. Greatheed, but his name does not appear in the 1813 list of ratepayers. Land his family had bought in the district in 1702 was sold to the Rev. William Read in the early 19th century.

Other of the small-scale local landowners were William Treadgold, a carpenter and builder who helped repair the bridge in 1783, and Benjamin Satchwell. Satchwell had a cottage and an acre of ground east of the parish church. This land remained undeveloped until after his death in 1809. Treadgold was succeeded in his business during the late 18th century by his son Edward. In 1813 Edward was shown in the rate book as owner of a

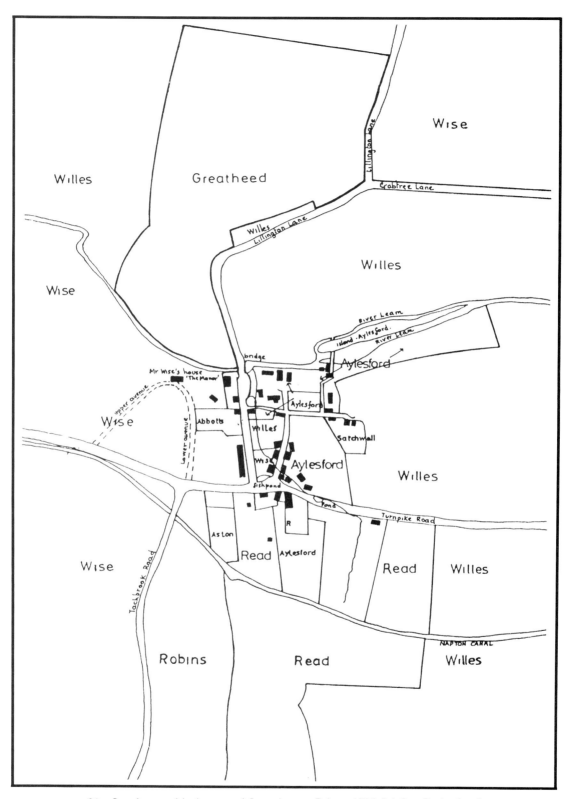

24. Landownership in central Leamington Priors, 1805-6 (after C. Arnison).

cottage and garden. William voted in the election of 1774, however, which indicates that the family owned freehold property with a value of at least 40s. a year. The Treadgolds owned and developed land in and adjacent to the village centre, particularly around Church Street.

The Willes family, the largest landowners, had possessed land in the parish since at least 1552 when they held 100 acres. When the New Town was begun in 1808 the head of the family was Edward Willes senior, a widower of 62 with a son of 21, also named Edward. The little known about him is largely due to his friendship with Bertie Greatheed, who mentions him in his journal. Naturally the journal only reveals Greatheed's view of Willes, stressing his friend's bad health and great reluctance to become involved with building projects in the spa town. He also records Willes' dislike of the increasing numbers of strangers coming to 'take the waters' at Leamington and his desire to isolate his estate from them, an attitude he maintained until his death in 1820. The Willes family's desire for privacy was well known: the guides published by both Pratt and Bisset in 1814 contained a notice stating

> that while the whole of the extensive Newbold Comyn Estate was formerly open for the free admission of all visitors to the town, many of the walks are now limited as many people had intruded on the domestic privacy of the owners as well as frequently . . . damaging the plantations.

Willes had much to gain by this policy of delaying development and keeping it at a distance, for the more successful other developers were, the more the Willes land would eventually be worth as building plots. He was wealthy enough to wait for this to happen, not being urgently in need of money like Bertie Greatheed. Moreover Willes was naturally cautious about risking his family's money, for Greatheed's journal shows that he was inclined to think that the fashion for coming to Leamington to 'take the waters' was likely to wane. Since Willes owned all the land in the parish north of the river except that owned by Greatheed, the upshot of his reluctance to allow building upon it was that the New Town was initially restricted to the area immediately north of the bridge. He was, however, prepared to sell land if it did not infringe his privacy and when he could get a good price. As early as July 1809 he sold to William Freeman for £2,000 the acre and a quarter in the village he had been allocated by the enclosure award of 1769. An important site near the original spring, it was here that Gloucester Street was laid out.

During the infancy of the New Town Edward Willes was engaged in improving his house at Newbold Comyn. Several architects were consulted by his son in the years 1821-4, but no schemes were proceeded with. From as early as 1809 he was also considering the general development of his estate, but though a number of grandiose schemes were drawn up by several different architects, none were realised. The land was finally developed in a piecemeal fashion using the road layout of one of P. F. Robinson's less ambitious early plans; this is the street plan north and east of the Parade as we know it today. Finally, deciding not to improve the house because of the encroachment of the growing New Town, Edward Willes junior moved to another house in Shinfield, Berkshire, before going to tour Europe. Apparently being interested only in the profits to be made from the sale or lease of building plots on his land, the development of his Leamington estate was left to his agent, John George Jackson, a local architect.

Other members of the family later lived at Newbold Comyn and farmed the estate until after the last war, when they left the town permanently. Part of the estate has become a reservoir, and the local authority acquired the Newbold Comyn Hills in the late 1960s for a country park and golf course. It is Leamington's largest open space, linking the heart of the town with the countryside and providing a conservation area and habitat for wildlife within a short walk of the traffic on the Parade, and is an asset for which the town should always be grateful to the Willes family because they resisted building on it for so long. The

25. Newbold Comyn, the Willes' family home; a view published about 1827.

house was demolished about the same time and a new residential estate sprang up on the
site, on the land at the end of Holly Walk in the Fernhill Drive area.

Much more is known about the other important landowner north of the river, Bertie
Bertie Greatheed. He was born in 1759, the son of Samuel Greatheed, a self-made gentleman
whose wealth came from sugar plantations in the West Indies and by marriage with a
daughter of the Duke of Ancaster. In 1740 Samuel bought the Guy's Cliffe estate, north-
east of Warwick, from the Edwards family of Edmonscote. This estate was about 400 acres,
and his wife later inherited 65 acres in the adjoining parish of Leamington Priors, the land
on which the New Town was to be built. Samuel died in 1765 and the estate should have
gone to his eldest son Peregrine after the death of his mother. But he died in 1766 and the
estate descended to the younger son, Bertie, after she died in 1774.

After Samuel's death Bertie was placed under the guardianship of his uncle, Brownlow
Bertie, later 5th and last Duke of Ancaster of the first creation. This was to result in half
of the Duke's estates descending to Greatheed and his wife when the Duke died in 1820. In
1781 Greatheed married his cousin Ann, also related to the Duke. Their only son died from
fever in Italy in 1804 during the Napoleonic Wars, having become the father of an
illegitimate daughter. This child, Anne Caroline, was adopted by Greatheed and his wife
and brought up at Guy's Cliffe. She married in 1822 Lord Charles Greatheed-Bertie-Percy,
who was given the courtesy title of Duke in 1865. The eighth son of the 1st Earl of Beverley,
he was born in 1794 and died in 1870; his wife died in 1882. The Guy's Cliffe estate
descended to the Heber-Percy family who still own its remnants.

Greatheed assumed control over the estate at Leamington Priors in 1774, and it was let
for grazing until the discovery of the second saline well in the village opposite increased

its value as potential building land. As it was separated from the rest of his estate, building on this land did not affect his house at Guy's Cliffe, so, unlike Edward Willes, he had no misgivings about new buildings threatening the privacy of his own home. Greatheed considered the possible development of his land early in the 19th century and noted its growing potential value as building plots, but nothing was done until 1808. Even then the idea was not his own but was suggested by a group of Warwick businessmen and his reluctance to risk any capital in expensive building projects meant that, with two exceptions, he took no active part in the development of his land. Certainly he was loath to become involved in 1808, having at that time no great faith in the future of the spa. He needed more money to pay for the extensive improvements then being made at Guy's Cliffe, however, including the construction of a new library wing. Difficulties had arisen as all his income but a few rents from his land at Guy's Cliffe, Milverton and Leamington came from the sale of sugar produced on the family plantation. The Napoleonic Wars made shipping this sugar across the Atlantic hazardous and his income became uncertain, resulting in periods of great financial anxiety. John Tomes, a Warwick banker and personal friend, was able to persuade him that the solution lay in developing his land in Leamington.

Apart from an occasional visit to Leamington to see what was going on, Greatheed took no active interest in the practical work of developing the land, leaving it to Tomes and Richard Sanders, a builder from Warwick. Sanders built the first terraced houses in the New Town for the building society, while Tomes provided much of the finance essential at the start of such building projects as well as mortgages for the purchasers of building plots and completed houses. Only in the building of the Assembly Rooms and the Pump Rooms did Greatheed spend any of his own money. His chief concern was for the quickest possible financial return, and in achieving it the long-term interests of his family were jeopardised by selling land freehold rather than on long leases, a practice successfully followed by developers in the rival spa towns of Bath and Cheltenham, and on the Duke of Bedford's estate in London.

The land fetched considerable sums of money. Up to the end of 1814 it was sold at a standard price of 5s. a sq. yd. for all plots, even those in the less prominent places like Bedford Street, although during a period of slump the price realised for the less popular sites fell to between 2s. 9d. and 3s. 5d. a sq. yd. Prices rose again after about 1822. Greatheed's land as a whole sold for £200-250 an acre. Exceptions to these high prices were the site of *The Regent Hotel* which was sold to Tomes and Sanders for 1s. 5d. a sq. yd., obviously a concession by the landowner for the work the two had done for him in the past, and the land on which the Pump Rooms were built which was sold for 2s. a sq. yd. since Greatheed was a member of the syndicate which built them. In 1824, shortly before Greatheed's death, Tomes purchased the rest of Greatheed's land north of Warwick Street then not developed, for £11,000.

In most cases Greatheed placed no restrictive covenants on the use and quality of any new buildings; the buyers were free to erect any type of house they thought fit. Nor, as in other spa towns, was there comprehensive supervision of building projects or any attempt by Greatheed's agents to influence the design of the new buildings. By his death in 1826 almost all the building land he owned in the town had been sold, although for many years afterwards his executors continued selling individual plots as the gaps in the street frontages were filled.

The other large landowner in the parish was the Wise family, whose land was to the south of the Leam. The Wises were descended from Henry Wise, Queen Anne's gardener. He had bought land in Warwick about 1720 before acquiring property in Leamington, but the family's Leamington estate was largely acquired after the enclosure act. Matthew Wise, head of the family in 1800, originally lived in a large house, now *The Manor House Hotel*, but later built Shrubland Hall on the southern outskirts of the village to which his family moved after his death in 1825. Although in 1796 he built a bathhouse over a saline well newly discovered on his property, not much more of his land was developed or sold for building until he died, and little before his wife died in 1830. By then the New Town was well established and the value of Wise's land as building plots had fallen as demand fell in that part of the spa. This lack of interest in selling land was probably because the family was wealthy and had no need of the financial returns to be gained by developing their estates.

At the same time as Mr. Willes began to sell his land, however, so did the Wises. In 1834 the then Mr. Wise sold 99 acres west of the village to James Hill and William Pearce, two local builders, for £23,000. They built the original Eastnor Terrace on part of it, before becoming bankrupt in 1838. Wise was the only landowner willing to allow part of the purchase price of any land sold to remain tied up as a mortgage. In the case of Messrs. Hill and Pearce he accepted £5,000 cash within a year and allowed the other £18,000 on a mortgage, rising from three to five per cent over a period of seven years and afterwards at five per cent. The builders had to remortgage the property repeatedly, however, until by 1837 it was mortgaged for far more than its value. The Leamington Bank was owed £15,000 and Mr. Wise was still owed almost all the purchase price.

The building boom continued until the early 1830s. Speculators and builders borrowed money from local banks or arranged mortgages through solicitors. It was at this period normal practice for anyone wishing to invest money to ask his solicitor to arrange the matter. Solicitors realised that the popularity of Leamington and its rapid growth could mean quick profits, so they invested their clients' money on a large scale in building projects or land purchases there. Property deeds provide evidence that building schemes attracted investors from all over the country, although, of course, a substantial percentage came from Warwickshire, Birmingham and the Black Country. The large amount of land which came on to the market when Mr. Willes began to sell parts of his estate created a glut. Prices fell and the less popular streets behind the Parade and other main streets remained undeveloped as developers bought better land slightly further away, particularly in the Quarry Field area to the west or the Lansdowne Crescent-Holly Walk area to the east. More and more building schemes were abandoned as speculators found land and houses more difficult to sell and finance difficult to find.

Many of those developing land in Leamington came from the Warwick area and relied on a local bank run by John Tomes and John Russell. These two themselves invested heavily in land in the New Town as well as lending money in the form of mortgages on land or property to many builders. A great deal of the bank's money was tied up in building projects of some kind or another. By 1834 the bank was in difficulties. In that year Tomes and Russell formed the Warwick and Leamington Banking Company, a joint-stock bank with share capital of £250,000, and in doing so they handed over their own bank in exchange for shares in the new one. The following year a second joint-stock bank, The Leamington Bank, was formed with a capital of £200,000, and in September of that year, 1835, a third bank, The Leamington Priors and Warwickshire Bank, was also started. Shares in all three were largely subscribed by local people.

The directors of both The Leamington Priors and Warwickshire Bank and The Leamington Bank tried to avoid tying up too much of their money in long-term mortgages or property ventures, making them unable to realise their capital if required at short notice. The directors of The Warwick and Leamington Bank were less prudent, advancing large sums to builders. By 1836 the bank was in serious financial difficulties. Money had been borrowed from the London and Westminster Bank, and in 1837 it asked the directors to reduce their overdraft which in June stood at just over £50,000. They could not, and news of these problems triggered off the process of winding up the bank. Since most of the bank's assets were in property this took a long time and it still owed nearly £35,000 at the beginning of 1838. As neither this nor other banks had limited liability all the shareholders became responsible for the bank's debts in the event of failure. As a result almost all the shareholders, local businessmen of all kinds including most of the builders in the area, were declared bankrupt. Those who survived could not sell their property or obtain credit to finish buildings already started, so that building in the town almost ceased.

Legal actions to recover the bank's debts led to an enforced auction, in August 1839, of the property owned by the bank's debtors. This sale was a disaster since very little of the estimated £200,000 worth of property was sold for anything like its real value. More than £130,000 was outstanding in other mortgages, the mortgagees being private individuals from all over the country, so people far removed from Leamington who had helped to finance building there also suffered financially. They included such persons as Edward Burbury, Esq., of Wroxall, Daniel Winter, attorney, of Warwick, Elizabeth Gardner, spinster, of Kenilworth, the Rev. William Wareing of Staffordshire and Mary Caldecott, widow, of Melton Mowbray.

For most shareholders the bank's failure must have been a disaster. When the Receiver of the bank auctioned its assets they included 200 properties of all kinds. The complete list, in small type, filled two columns of a local newspaper. The failure of the bank and impact on its shareholders is evident in the failure of many of the ambitious building developments in the spa, unfinished for many years and completed in the new architectural styles of the late Victorian period. Thirty of the largest builders in Leamington were declared bankrupt between 1837 and 1841. One result of the crisis was that only 55 new houses were erected in 1838-9 and in the following year only 54 were built. On average in 1841-3 just 38 new buildings were started a year.

Chapter Six

Architects and Builders

The character of Leamington was largely the responsibility of the architects and builders who put up its buildings. Most of the first architects working in Leamington were based in London; C. S. Smith was an exception. Several of these men were pupils of architects employed by the Prince Regent or the Duke of Bedford and therefore had contacts with these important patrons, but only John Nash was among the best-known architects of the age.

The first important public buildings in Leamington were designed by C. S. Smith. When he began the Upper Assembly Rooms he was an unknown young architect aged about twenty-one. He was admitted to the Royal Academy Schools in 1808 at the age of 18, and became a pupil of Sir Jeffry Wyatville, architect to George IV at Windsor. Smith may also have had some slight acquaintance with the Duke of Bedford since Wyatville made some alterations at Woburn for the Duke. Smith exhibited designs at the Royal Academy between 1808 and 1816 and again in 1828. He established himself in Warwick and almost all his known designs are of buildings in Warwickshire. It has been suggested that he was a member of the well-known Smith family of Warwick, perhaps a relative of the most famous of them, Francis, the architect of Stoneleigh Abbey. No documentary evidence has been found to confirm the relationship, however, and his early life is almost unknown.

Smith built three major public buildings in Leamington. The Upper Assembly Rooms were begun in 1811 and the building was finished early in 1813. On 27 November 1811 Smith was one of a number of people who visited Guy's Cliffe House to discuss plans for a pump-room; The Royal Pump Rooms and Baths were started in 1813 and opened in 1814. The last of the three was *The Regent Hotel*, begun in 1818 on the east side of the Parade opposite the Assembly Rooms and finished the following year. The architect's most important buildings from that time onwards were built outside the spa town, though for clients who are known to have visited it and who therefore knew his work. He is, in fact, known to have designed only one other building in Leamington, a 'cottage' for Mr. Williams, the owner of *The Regent Hotel*. It was erected on a site next to the hotel on land originally owned by Mr. Willes; this was probably the site given Mr. Williams by Willes at the time the hotel was being built, a gesture of goodwill and recognition of how the opening of the hotel would increase the value of his estate as building land. The design for this 'Gothic cottage' was exhibited in the Royal Academy in 1821, but it seems not to have been put up for seven years. *The Leamington Courier* for 11 October 1828 reported that the cottage, 'now being built', had just been inspected by John Nash who 'desired his unqualified approbation might be communicated to Mr. Smith the architect'.

The cottage, later known as Denby Villa, was built when a few such romantic cottages were appearing in the town. The first was Binswood Cottage, built in 1824 for Mr. Willes on a corner site in what became Clarendon Square. It was in the Swiss style to the design of P. F. Robinson, and survives as Magnolia Cottage. Others were the semi-detached pair of houses, complete with their curved Victorian-style bargeboards, built not long after Denby Cottage, next to the chapel in Spencer Street. All look rather strange among their more staid Regency-style neighbours.

While Smith was working on the Assembly Rooms and *The Regent Hotel* Edward Willes was considering improving his house at Newbold Comyn. He employed a number of architects, including in 1821 Henry Hakewill, but with little success since he clearly could not decide what kind of house he wanted. Hakewill, the son of John Hakewill the landscape painter, was admitted to the Royal Academy Schools in 1790. From 1809, when he was appointed architect to Rugby School, he was responsible for many buildings in Warwickshire. In 1814-16 he designed the Judge's House in Warwick and also worked for the Earl of Aylesford at Packington Hall. He is thought to have designed the building on the corner of Church Walk and Bath Street, near the west end of the church, on land owned by the Earl. The adjoining pub is also thought to be by him, and later he altered Shrubland Hall for the Wise family.

Hakewill was the first architect known to have been consulted by Willes about the development of his estate, although a plan had been drawn up as early as 1809. He produced in 1817 a plan for 45 detached villas on 23 acres of Quarry Fields, west of the Parade, laid out around a large square.

In 1821 two more schemes were drawn up for the development of the Quarry Fields area, this time by T. C. Bannister, architect and surveyor. Little is known about him save that he carried out some bridge and road works for the county in 1829. His first plan was for the area south of Warwick Street and from the Parade to Brook Street. It showed a central square with a church surrounded by streets. The second scheme was for a more conventional layout and it, or a similar plan, formed the basis of the present street plan in the Portland Street-Grove Street area. On the back of Bannister's plans is a scheme for a very different layout, showing villas ranged around a circus much like the design made by Beazley a few years later.

Samuel Beazley, 1786-1851, was a playwright as well as an architect. He specialised in theatrical design and among the theatres he designed was The Theatre Royal in Drury Lane, London. In 1816 Mr. Elliston, who had been a director of The Theatre Royal, came to Leamington to run a theatre. In 1820 he opened The County Library in Bath Street, a building designed by Beazley. The following year Beazley designed The Royal Music Hall, or The Parthenon, also in Bath Street. Both these buildings have now been demolished, but the front of The Parthenon has been rebuilt in replica. Beazley's scheme for the Quarry Fields area was for a central circus surrounded by 73 detached villas, intended to be in a variety of styles. Beazley's connection with Leamington was severed at about the time of Elliston's bankruptcy.

After selling part of his land in Quarry Fields, Willes commissioned plans for his land east and north of Greatheed's. The connection of Peter Frederick Robinson with the spa, which lasted from 1821 to 1827, began in this way. Robinson was responsible for laying out much of the second stage of the New Town's development.

Robinson, 1776-1858, was a London-based architect responsible for buildings in many parts of the country. He was a pupil of Henry Holland while Holland worked for the Duke of Bedford and for the Prince of Wales at Carlton House and Brighton Pavilion. It has been suggested that he was Holland's nephew. In 1804 he became an assistant to William Porden who replaced Holland as architect of the Pavilion. Robinson must have become known to the Duke or his agent, and this connection may have introduced him to Leamington. The Duke was interested in the spa, and one of Robinson's commissions was Clarendon Square where John Russell, reputedly the Duke's cousin, owned a house.

In 1816 Robinson visited the continent, including Switzerland. On his return to England he introduced the 'Swiss Chalet' design. He was also the author of a number of influential books on architecture, among which were *Rural Architecture or a Series of Designs for Ornamental Cottages and Villas* (1823), *Designs for Ornamental Villages* (1825-7) and *New Designs for Ornamental Cottages and Villas* (1836). The latter was published after he had ceased working

26. Bath Street in about 1846. On the left is the entrance portico of The Parthenon. The impressive portico on the right belongs to the post office newly opened in 1846.

27. Christchurch and Lansdowne Place, renamed Upper Union Parade, and later the Upper Parade. A view by J. Brandard, published by C. Elston of Leamington about 1843 showing the east side. *The Lansdowne Hotel*, at the corner of Warwick Street, has been replaced by a new store with a 'replica' front elevation, like almost all the original houses except for *The Clarendon Hotel* at the far end near the church.

in Leamington but contained at least one example of a cottage he had designed for Edward Willes and built in the town.

Copies of many of the schemes Robinson suggested for the development of Willes' land are in the County Record Office. The first scheme, dating from 1821 or 1822, was for a large circus at the head of a continuation of Union Parade – Upper Union Parade being built only between 1820-30. This plan was abandoned but in 1822-5 he produced more formal schemes, including one for Beauchamp Square with an episcopal chapel on the axis of the Upper Parade, and one for Clarendon Square to the west. Both squares were to be surrounded by a grid of avenues with long terraces of houses reminiscent of Nash's designs for the Regent's Park area of London, then under construction. In contrast to some earlier schemes Robinson not only produced designs for the elevations of the larger terraces, but of all sides of the squares.

These plans were adopted, although building was slow and Beauchamp Square was never completed. One of the architect's buildings which was finished, however, was Christchurch, the episcopal chapel in Beauchamp Square. This early example of the 'Anglo-Norman Revival' style was demolished in 1959. Robinson speculated in land on his own account for several of the plans record his name as having purchased land from Mr. Willes. These plots were all at either ends of principal terraces, enabling him to control the elevations between and ensure his designs were used by other purchasers. In the old village the architect designed *Copps' Royal Hotel*, one of the two largest hotels in the spa when it was built in 1826-7. No buildings by Robinson in Leamington survive in their original state, however, and his most important two non-residential buildings have both been demolished.

John Nash appeared in the spa in 1827. Edward Willes commissioned him to prepare a plan for the development of all the Willes estate east of the Parade, on both sides of the river. The plan Nash and his partner James Morgan produced was a romantic layout of roads with sweeping curves and areas of parkland similar to his development of Regent's Park. A few traces of an earlier grid layout by Robinson, dated 1826, were retained north of the Leam where it was obvious that roadworks had already begun, but otherwise there are no signs of the formal design the other architect had produced for the same area a year or two before.

Nash was laying out St James' Park in London and supervising the construction of Buckingham Palace at this time, but he found time to visit Leamington at least twice. His signature appears in the *Regent Hotel* register, still in the hotel's possession, in June 1827 and October 1828. *The Warwick Advertiser* of 23 June 1827 reported the progress of Nash and Morgan's plan. Two hundred and fifty acres of the Newbold Comyn estate had been laid out for building, a new bridge over the Leam designed by the pair was under construction and a number of roads were being built including Newbold Terrace. Until recently there was at either end of this street a block of Regency-style terraced houses closely resembling Nash's Regent's Park terraces. Although these houses may have been designed by Nash and Morgan, the Willes' family papers suggest that the actual building was probably supervised for Willes by John Jackson, between 1833 and 1836.

The road scheme proposed by Nash for the land north of the river bears some resemblance to the present street pattern and on the evidence of style a few of the smaller detached villas in the Holly Walk-Newbold Street area could possibly have been designed by Nash or, more likely, Morgan. The roads proposed south of the river do not match the present road system so it must be assumed that these were not started until much later. Presumably the scheme was soon abandoned, probably because it was impossible to find enough buyers for the land. Mr. Willes was forced in the early 1830s to sell individual plots, so unity of design in the houses was lost. No further involvement by Nash has been discovered.

Mr. Willes' absence from the town meant that he had to have an agent. The man he appointed was John George Jackson, an architect born about 1798 and certainly still alive in 1852. He entered the Royal Academy Schools in 1817 and later became a pupil of P. F. Robinson in whose London office he worked for many years before settling in Leamington. From the Willes' papers it seems that he came to the town because Robinson passed over him and made someone his junior a partner, but this statement should be treated with caution since it was made by Jackson himself and cannot be corroborated. It seems more likely that he first came to Leamington as Robinson's site agent and stayed on to start his own business when Robinson's connection with the town ended some time after 1827. Jackson exhibited at the Royal Academy at various times between 1817 and 1844, at the Society of British artists in 1824 and 1831, and wrote *Designs for Villas* in 1828-9.

The architect was able to obtain work on his own account from people wishing to build on Willes' land and he was paid a commission on sales he arranged. He was also involved in property deals and speculations, particularly in the Clarendon Square, Beauchamp Avenue and Binswood Avenue areas, all of which had been laid out while he was working for Robinson. For the Earl of Warwick he devised schemes for land west of the Quarry Field area, but Jackson is better known for his individual buildings such as the episcopal chapel at Milverton, built in 1833 and demolished 1883, St Mary's church south of the river, built in 1838, and the post office erected in 1846, whose exterior still remains largely unaltered although recently extended. He also provided designs for Bertie Terrace, in Warwick Place, in 1836, he was the first of several architects employed by the Rev. Craig to remodel the parish church in a continental Gothic style, and he may have designed the enlargement of the Avenue Road Railway Station for the Midland Railway Co. in 1859-60. In 1835 he acquired Strawberry Cottage, a Gothic-style cottage on the corner of Newbold Terrace, opposite the Royal Baths and Pump Room, and the following year he demolished it to erect a new house, Newbold Lodge. He was the last architect known to have worked directly for one of the original landowners in the New Town.

28. St Mary's chapel, now St Mary's church, about 1843. Designed by J. G. Jackson in 1838, the church stood beyond the town in open fields now covered by houses mostly built 1850-1900.

From 1825, when the first paving act came into force the town's paving commissioners appointed surveyors to supervise the provision of roads and drains. The first of these men was John Russell, who had served the parish vestry in the same role. In 1827 he was succeeded by Samuel Edward Nicklin. Advertisements in *The Warwick Advertiser* in July and August 1827 indicate that Nicklin had newly arrived from Cheltenham Spa. Later editions of local guides describe him as an architect and surveyor, and in 1838 he moved to a house in Grove Street where another architect, Joseph Neville, had lived from 1831, so perhaps Nicklin took over Neville's business. In 1828-9 he designed the Mill Street Chapel for the Lady Huntingdon's Connexion and in September of 1828 he was described as the architect of the proposed theatre in George Street, never actually built. He is also known to be responsible for the design of 5 Binswood Avenue, a house built on Mr. Willes' land in a street laid out about 1827-8.

After John Russell the highway surveyor retired another John Russell, perhaps his son, was in partnership with Mr. Mitchell, another architect. More is known about Russell than Mitchell. In 1814 he married in London Elizabeth Grice of Buckminster in Leicestershire; the marriage settlement and documents concerning his property are in the County Record Office. Mitchell and Russell designed the first Catholic church, in George Street in the old village, which was described by *The Leamington Courier* in 1828 as the most important building in the town by these architects. Little is known of other buildings designed by the pair except housing developments, but after Russell's death in 1839 Mitchell designed Holy Trinity Church in Beauchamp Avenue, erected in 1846.

One of the most important architects working in Leamington in the years 1830-40 was William Thomas. Although he worked for none of the original landowners he probably designed more of the larger buildings than any other contemporary architect. Many of his buildings survive and are largely unaltered externally. Thomas, described as an architect and surveyor, was born in Suffolk in 1799 and died in Toronto in 1860. He married Martha Tutin in Birmingham in 1826 and for a number of years practised as an architect there, at times in partnership with his father-in-law. He and his wife moved to Leamington Priors in 1831 and had eight children there, all baptised at the parish church.

Thomas had a varied career in the town, designing buildings, acting for developers and speculating in land and building projects on his own account. He invested quite large sums of money in property deals, successful and unsuccessful, which involved him in the failure of the Warwick and Leamington Bank in 1837. He was among the shareholders declared bankrupt in 1838 and further bankruptcy proceedings followed in 1840. In 1838-9 Thomas acted as Town Surveyor and was responsible for improvements to the street frontage in Bath Street, but his designs for rebuilding the bridge across the Leam were not chosen. Eventually, in 1843, he and his family emigrated to Canada where he became a very successful architect.

Much of his work in Leamington consisted of speculative housing schemes. His first houses were in Beauchamp Terrace (now Beauchamp Avenue) erected in the Regency neo-classical style in 1831. Their design closely followed the overall pattern set by Robinson for the street when he laid it out. The Warwick Street Baptist church and the Wesleyan chapel in Portland Street were both designed in 1834, followed by Lansdowne Crescent and Lansdowne Circus in 1835. The Crescent is a terrace of 25 houses, all five storeys high, and behind it is the Circus, eight pairs of semi-detached two-storey houses in the Regency style grouped around the private garden which is the central feature of the layout. There is also one 'Victorian Gothic' style house designed by him about the same time as the rest of the Circus, this being a detached house unlike the others in the group. In 1837 he designed Victoria Terrace, opposite the parish church. Although altered this terrace survives, the main elevation retaining much of Thomas' original mouldings and high-quality ironwork. The terrace originally included the Victoria Baths, but the building has been converted into shops and its interior completely destroyed.

Following his success in Lansdowne Circus Thomas used similar designs for semi-detached and detached villas in nearby Holly Walk. Some were in the classical style, some in the Gothic and even a few in Tudor or Elizabethan Revival styles. These houses were often covered in moulded stucco. One pair, now numbers 81 and 83, was known as Elizabethan Place; Thomas lived in number 83, which is decorated with his initials and the date 1838 in mock Elizabethan strapwork at parapet level. In New Milverton Thomas also designed several houses in a series of semi-detached pairs, all in a 'castellated' style perhaps deliberately reminiscent of Warwick Castle. The site, now part of Warwick Place, was land originally owned by the Earl of Warwick.

Many other architects lived and perhaps worked in the town, but very little is known about them other than their names and addresses, which appear occasionally in local directories, guides or newspapers, and there is little information about any buildings designed by them in Leamington or elsewhere. Among these were William Coultart, architect-auctioneer, John Mace, architect, William Watson, surveyor, and William Startin, architect. Startin lived in Bedford Street in 1832, and in Waterloo House in Warwick Street the following year. There his wife kept a boarding-house, but in 1836 she was forced to sell the property as they could not pay the mortgage. In 1831 *The Leamington Courier* mentioned Startin as the architect of Dr. Jephson's house, Beech Lawn, and he also designed Clarendon Place, a crescent just off Warwick Street. But in 1836-7 only the two ends of this classical-style crescent were built and it was never completed in its planned form.

Information about local builders and craftsmen is scanty, the little known coming from local directories, guides, newspapers, deeds and the records of bankruptcy proceedings. Although bankruptcies were quite common from the earliest years of the town's develop-ment, the bank failure of 1837 led to an unusual number in 1838. Again, picked almost at random, are names such as Philip Goldby, William Hawkins, Joseph Bateman and Edward Pinder, all responsible for developments undertaken in various parts of the town and recorded in property deeds. Those who survived bankruptcy and re-established themselves were few, but include John Toone and William Buddle, senior and junior, whose names occur most frequently in property deeds respecting the Willes estate on which they built part of the west side of Clarendon Square and almost all the original houses in Milverton and Clarendon Crescents.

During the early years of the spa, as elsewhere in the country, much substandard building was done. In an effort to combat jerrybuilding the paving commissioners introduced by-laws governing building practices. In September 1833 they issued a 'Caution to Builders' reminding them that people intending to build must give the Surveyor seven days' notice in writing before starting or be fined £5. They were also reminded firmly that party walls between houses had to be 14 ins. thick; the act specified that such walls should be carried up to nine ins. above the roof, which could not be of thatch. In 1834 the commissioners proceeded against Mr. Toone for putting up houses in Satchwell Street whose party walls were not thick enough. Toone had erected a row of buildings behind some large buildings he had built facing the Parade, to which they might be attached as coachhouses or stables. To pay the interest on the money he had borrowed to build them, Toone was going to let them as cottages or warehouses until they were added to the larger houses. He told the commissioners that if the terrace could not be treated as individual dwellings because the party walls were too thin he would convert them to one large dwelling by placing communicating doors in the dividing walls. The occupiers would be free to keep the doors closed or blocked up as necessary. He was fined only a nominal sum and the commissioners were left feeling there was a flaw in the act.

Other local builders besides Toone were fined for contravening the building requirements of the improvement act to cut the cost of their projects; nevertheless it failed to prevent poor housing being built. Toone and others put up many back-to-back houses which must have been substandard even when erected. They were built behind even some of the best houses in the town. The inspector investigating the town's request to set up a Local Board of Health condemned, in his 1850 report, houses of this kind in Kenilworth and Oxford Streets off Warwick Street, in Satchwell and Bedford Streets behind the Parade, and behind Clemens and the High Streets.

Toone was born in Stoneleigh in 1787 and died in 1875. He had business premises and a timberyard in Warwick Street, between Satchwell Street and Park Street on otherwise undeveloped land. He remained in business for nearly 60 years despite bankruptcies in 1838 and 1841, and built not only impressive terraces of houses for the wealthy, but also small back-to-back houses for the poor. The latter were not mentioned in the fulsome eulogy published by his trustees after his death, which details the better properties he built in the town. Of his 13 children four died in infancy, and of the nine survivors his eldest son emigrated to Salt Lake City in the mid-19th century and a grandson died fighting in the American Civil War. He was responsible for building part of the Parade and Warwick Street, and, with the Buddles, some of the houses in Milverton Crescent. He also built the Mill Street Chapel, the Leamington Brewery, houses in Binswood Avenue, the Methodist chapel in Portland Street (the decision to build which was taken in his house in the Parade), the Guy Street chapel and the original 'iron church' in Priory Terrace. He also laid many of the town's sewers. A parish constable, he also became a paving commissioner.

Another builder, John Fell, was as memorable for his political ambitions as for his buildings. He became mayor of the borough in 1887, having stood unsuccessfully as a Tory candidate for West Worcester in the election of 1885, the first after the passing of the Reform Bill. Among his building projects were St Alban's church and St John's church, both in 1877, the replacement of the old Assembly Rooms by a new store in 1878, and the Methodist chapel in High Street the same year. In 1881 he laid the first tramlines for the Warwick and Leamington Tramway Company at a cost of £14,300, and constructed most of the sewers in the south of the town, while in 1882 he was responsible for the new theatre in Regent Grove. His best known building is obviously the Town Hall, started in 1882 and opened in 1884, costing £14,000, and the following year he was first elected to the borough council.

Later in the 19th century two other architects left their mark on the town, for many of their buildings are still to be seen: David Squirhill (1808-63) and John Cundall (1836-89). Squirhill was admitted into the Royal Academy Schools in 1829 and arrived in Leamington in the late 1830s, being responsible for a plan of the town printed by John Merridew in 1838. What work he did before 1846 is unknown, but in that year he designed the lodges to the Jephson Gardens, followed in 1848 by the pavilion in the gardens. This building underwent several alterations and additions before being demolished in the late 1960s. His other works include the tennis court building in Bedford Street in 1846; part of the old Leamington College in Binswood Avenue in 1848-9; the original Congregational chapel in Holly Walk, 1849-50, no longer used as a chapel; and the original St Luke's church, Augusta Place, 1850, which was demolished in 1957. The Vicar's Grammar School in Priory Terrace, designed in 1848, still survives, but as a Gospel Hall rather than a school. In 1853 he also designed for the cemetery in the Whitnash Road the entrance lodges and chapel. The latter was demolished a few years ago like his public hall in Windsor Street, designed in 1857. According to an account in *The Builder* magazine in February 1869 the buildings in the cemetery were supervised by his assistant John Cundall.

While Squirhill's buildings have suffered alterations or demolition, those by John Cundall still dominate the skyline of the town. Cundall appears to have trained and may have practised in London before coming to Leamington some time in the early 1850s. In 1852 he designed Grafton House, in Warwick New Road, but it is not known if he did any earlier work in the town. He then lived in London. In 1856 he submitted designs for the completion of All Saints' church, but these were not carried out. In 1861 he made alterations to the Royal Pump Rooms and in 1868 designed the wings added to the original structure of the Warneford Hospital and a chapel for the Brunswick Street cemetery. In 1869, the year he designed the Hitchman Memorial Fountain in Jephson Gardens, he is thought to have lived in Birmingham.

Soon after this he began noticeably to make his mark, designing several of the new churches being built as the nuclei of the new parishes formed in the late 19th century. St Paul's, Leicester Street, came first, in 1873-4; St Alban's, Portland Street, in 1877 (demolished in 1968); and St John's, Tachbrook Street, also in 1877. In 1881 there were alterations and extensions to All Saints' church and Holy Trinity church, and he also built chapels for the Royal Midland Counties Home in Tachbrook Street and a Methodist chapel in Radford Road. His last and most dominant building is the Town Hall, designed in 1881, and begun in 1882. His son continued in practice as an architect in Leamington until the start of the last war.

Chapter Seven

Two Building Projects: *The Upper Assembly Rooms and* The Regent Hotel

To Architects, Leamington Spa, Warwickshire. A Premium of Twenty Guineas will be paid for the most approved ground plan and elevation for erecting public rooms at this much admired Watering Place. . . . Application to be made to the office of Messrs Tomes and Heydon, Warwick. Plans to be sent before the First Day of March next.

The quotation is from *The Warwick Advertiser* for 9 February 1811. The first public announcement of a proposal to build assembly-rooms in the New Town north of the Leam was made in *The Advertiser* in November 1810 when a subscription was opened for shares in the project. This chapter is concerned with the creation and fate of this building and the nearby *Regent Hotel* rather than with their place in the social life of the spa.

The more influential members of the Leamington Building Society, on whose land the rooms were to be erected, had always intended to use the important site on the corner of the Parade and Regent Street for a new pump-room. For this reason it was left vacant when the first houses were built. Mr. Greatheed spent much time and money trying to find saline water there in 1810 before looking at the site near the river where the Pump Rooms were actually built, so for him it was a disappointment when it became apparent that the best alternative use for the site was an assembly-room.

Greatheed, not himself a member of the Building Society, did not wish to become financially involved in a project which might well prove to be a financial disaster, for the success of an assembly-room not associated with a saline well was very uncertain. He would benefit much more surely by just selling land for building at £1,200 an acre than spending money which might return no profit. It has been suggested that his journal shows he was also reluctant partly because of the lower social status of some of the other shareholders, who included a grocer, an undertaker, a publican and a printer as well as his friends Tomes and Parkes. The other shareholders would not join the project without his financial participation, however, initially insisting Greatheed took five shares in it but compromising on three. Greatheed resentfully acceded: 'To this most unhandsome compulsion I have no alternative but to submit or to see my property deeply injured. . . . I will if possible turn my thoughts from this dirty business'.

Greatheed was greatly worried about the expense. The building and furnishings were expected to cost £6,000, so as holder of three shares of the total of 18 he would have to pay £1,200 'even supposing the cost should not exceed the valuation, (as is ever the case)'. The final cost proved to be £7,500. He cannot have been so financially embarrassed as he imagined, however, as on 21 May he had signed conveyances for the sale to members of the Building Society of the sites of 19 houses they had built on the Parade and six adjacent plots. For these he had received £3,371 10s. Most of this sum had been paid by men who also had shares in the proposed new assembly-room, and who perhaps rightly felt that the landowner himself should bear some of the risk of a project that should enhance the value of his other property if it proved popular. Fortunately for all, the project was successful although not very profitable.

Only three weeks had been allowed for submission of plans, so perhaps it was not surprising that the designs chosen were those of a local architect, C. S. Smith. Work started at once and the rooms were opened on 24 September 1812 with a grand ball. Sir Gray

Skipwith officiated as Steward, and patrons present included the Earl of Aylesford, Lord Chetwynd, Lord Clonmell and the Hon. Mr. Verney.

29. The Upper Assembly Rooms. A view published in 1822 by John Merridew of Warwick.

The Assembly Rooms were built of brick and their exterior was stuccoed. In the centre of the principal façade was a range of seven windows, each supported by Ionic pilasters. The main entrance was from Regent Street into a large hall; a second entrance from the Parade was through a porch supported by four Ionic columns. It had a Refectory and a large billiard room; a second, smaller billiard room was upstairs. Its Ball Room was 82 ft. long, 36 ft. wide and 26 ft. high, through which was a Card Room and beyond that a Reading Room. On ball nights the Reading Room was used as a tea room. The Ball Room was decorated with an ornamental plaster ceiling, there were crimson curtains with black fringes at the windows, cut-glass chandeliers, and the two fireplaces were of Kilkenny marble. Under the building were vaults occupied separately. In 1818 Oliver Mills established wine and spirit vaults there, and they were used for this purpose until almost the end of the 19th century. By 1900 they housed *The Imperial* public house.

The Assembly Rooms were soon leased out. Until 1819 when he became tenant of a new hotel in Clemens Street, *The Blenheim Hotel*, Thomas Rackstrow was lessee. Messrs. Sharpe and Baly took it over from him. Perhaps the most important of the later directors of the Assembly Rooms was H. T. Elliston, the son of the actor who had built The Parthenon in Bath Street a few years earlier. Under his direction the building was redecorated and refurnished. The programme of concerts, balls and dramatic performances that he arranged in 1831 was so successful that a complimentary dinner was given for him in November.

In their early years the Assembly Rooms were very successful and the balls held in the season attracted increasing numbers of visitors. In 1816 a ball drew 500 people, the largest number ever known. But, lacking a saline well, decline set in. Elliston took a 14-year lease of the building in 1830. The inventory made in February 1831 when he took it over can be compared with a valuation made in 1845 to give some idea of the decay. In 1831 The Reading Room had eight tables, four of mahogany and four of deal, 18 chairs and scarlet drapes. The Card Room had 25 chairs, valued at £1 17s. 6d., and various games including backgammon. Both the Card Room and the Ball Room had single chandeliers, fitted for gas. The Ball Room still had its crimson curtains and also 24 chairs valued at £54. The contents were valued down to the last teaspoon, £4 for 50 silver ones and 5s. for 50 plate ones, the total being £590 10s. 10d. By 1845 the upper billiard room had lost its table, and fittings to the value of £44 14s. 5d. were missing or written off. A few years later the Atlas Insurance Company insured the building for £3,500 – £3,250 for the structure and £250 for the contents.

As the Rooms declined more troubles developed for the proprietors. During the early successful years some of the first shareholders tried to regain their initial outlay by dividing their individual shares and selling them. Before long no-one knew how many shareholders there were and as the years went on no-one really cared who they were; the building was let on a full repairing lease and as its attraction declined no dividends were likely to be paid.

The crisis came in the early 1870s. By then it had long ceased to be used for stylish balls or concerts; part sheltered a library-cum-shop and in its later years it was used for the new craze of American roller skating and a rent of £4 a week paid. In 1873 the few interested shareholders tried to sell it. An offer of £4,500 was rejected and it was advertised unsuccessfully at £5,250. The Duke of Northumberland, who had inherited Mr. Greatheed's three shares, now decided to get rid of the building come what may. He found that this could not be done without the approval of all the other shareholders, many of whom could not be traced with any certainty. The original 18 shares had been subdivided into 108 by this date; moreover those shareholders who were consulted disagreed with the Duke over how the proceeds were to be divided. William Edwards-Wood claimed to be entitled to an eighth share in the property. Eventually the matter ended in Chancery. The case of the Duke of Northumberland *vs* Edwards-Wood was heard in Birmingham in July 1873 and the building was finally sold by auction in 1878, fetching £5,600.

The purchasers were Messrs. Collier and Plucknett, and John Fell converted the building into shops for them. It was later bought by Mr. Gamage who pulled down most of the original building and erected the present one on the site. This is currently occupied by Messrs. Woodwards. The rear of the original building, the entrance to the vaults and the cottage at the back, fronting on to Bedford Street, were left standing, the cottage being converted into three shops and the wine vaults used as a public house. Some years ago this part of the site was bought by Woodwards and taken into their shop. Even today the surviving part of Smith's building can be seen over the modern shop-front at the corner of Regent Street and Bedford Street, contrasting obviously with the late-Victorian building next to it.

The Regent Hotel has occupied the same prominent site in the town centre since its opening on 19 August 1819. It was built on a triangular plot, bounded on two sides by the Parade and Regent Street, and on the third by land then belonging to the Rev. Edward Willes on which Denby Villa and later the Town Hall were built. The site had been bought from Mr. Greatheed some ten years earlier by Tomes and Sanders for just under £1,000. C. S. Smith drew up a design. Amid great celebrations the foundation stone was laid on 18 July 1818 by Miss Greatheed, Greatheed's granddaughter, in the presence of a number of distinguished guests including Sarah Siddons, the actress. *The Warwick Advertiser* commented:

> From the well-known liberality of the projector and the ability of the architect employed we may anticipate a fabric which will add greatly to the ornament and advantage of this rapidly increasing place of fashionable resort.

When built the hotel was one of the largest in Europe and it is still the largest in the town.

Its proprietors were John Williams and his wife Sarah. They had once been Greatheed's butler and housekeeper, but seven years before had left his service to become the first tenants of *The Bedford Hotel* on the other side of the Parade. This hotel had proved very successful. It opened in 1811 with a dinner held on 4 December attended by gentlemen from the best families in the county. Tickets were one guinea each, the stewards being Sir Charles Mordaunt, Lord Middleton, Sir Gray Skipwith, Sir James Lake, Bertie Greatheed and Eardley Wilmot. According to Greatheed 128 persons sat down to dinner; they consumed 109 bottles of port and 49 bottles of sherry.

Seven years later the Williams and their backers judged the time had come to expand. In June 1818 Williams and his wife obtained for the purpose a mortgage of £10,000 from Samuel Galton of Birmingham, banker. It took a brief 11 months to complete this second and larger hotel, and on 19 August 1819 the opening banquet was attended by nearly 200 gentlemen. Once again ladies were excluded, according to the custom of the times. Attending were Lords Glenberrie, Hood and Dunsmore, the Lord Chief Justice of England, Sir Thomas Shepherd, and Sir John Sylvester, the Recorder of the City of London. Mr. Greatheed was in the chair – John Tomes 'a most zealous friend of the establishment was at home afflicted

30. *The Regent Hotel*, 1905.

by gout'. The dinner began at 5 p.m. and the party broke up convivially at a late hour. Tickets cost £1 11s. 6d., the menu including turtle and venison.

Dr. Granville, in 1841, hardly mentions the hotel, considering it too expensive, but in its defence Hopper, in his *History of Leamington Priors* published the same year, points out that the house was reputed to have cost £70,000 including the furnishing, and in spite of this the charge for bed and board with the use of the public rooms was only £3 3s. a week. The hotel was said to have had 100 bedrooms, just one bathroom, a large dining-room 58 ft. long, with leading off it through folding doors a drawing-room 'furnished in costly and elegant style' so that when the doors were thrown open 200 people could dine together in comfort. There were also numerous private suites and a coffee room. At the rear was stabling for 100 horses and space for 100 carriages, all now gone. To run all this originally required a staff of 60. On the north side was a small square of land laid out as a garden; recently this has been built on.

At first the hotel was known as *Williams' Hotel*, but in September 1819 the Prince Regent stayed at Warwick Castle and on the 10th he drove through Leamington in an open carriage with the Countess of Warwick and the Marchioness of Conyngham. As Moncrieff describes:

> He was received opposite Copps' Royal Hotel by the whole population who hailed his presence with loud cheers, which he most gracefully acknowledged by repeated bows; the band played 'God Save the King', the colours flying and everyone was on the tip-toe of hilarity. After visiting the libraries, the Pump and Assembly Rooms and expressing the highest gratifications intimating at the same time his gracious intention of making a stay here at some future period, the visitors returned to Warwick Castle leaving permission for 'William's Hotel' [*sic*] to be named after him 'The Regent'.

The following day an Address of Loyalty was passed at a public meeting at the Pump Room and on Monday the 13th Captain Stevenson, on behalf of the residents, took the Address to the castle for presentation. The same evening it was announced that the Prince had given permission for his coat of arms to be placed on the front of the new hotel. It can still be seen above what was the original entrance at the south side of the building. In the late 1840s another entrance from the Parade was made at the request of the Warwickshire Hunt Club to give access to their suite of rooms. Regrettably the portico facing the Parade bearing a similar coat of arms was removed some years ago and the inappropriate modern canopy erected.

In 1834 John Williams retired to live at Denby Villa and died there at the age of 78 in 1843. His wife Sarah died in 1830, living just long enough to witness the visit of the Princess Victoria on 3 August that year. From 1834 to 1874 the hotel was run by licensees appointed first by Mr. Williams and then by his executors. It was sold to the licensee, Mr. Lyas Bishop, in the latter year. When, in turn, Bishop sold the hotel by auction in 1904 it was bought by John Cridlan, whose descendants still own it. *The Regent* has been a hotel from 1819 to the present day without a break except during the Second World War when it was requisitioned for the use of services camouflage experts. It was reopened in 1948. Considerable modernisation of the interior has taken place since then so that it remains the spa's senior first-class hotel.

Chapter Eight

Taking the Waters

The primary *raison d'être* of Leamington was, of course, its mineral water. Dr. Amos Middleton of Warwick's *General Rules for Taking the Waters*, of 1806, were the first real rules for drinking saline waters. He reflected that mineral waters were appropriate only to certain diseases and that medical advice should be sought on the spot how best the water should be used in the individual case and to avoid the potentially bad effects of improper use. He pointed out, however, that Leamington waters could be used without danger 'for in all cases they invariably act as a mild and gentle purgative'. The season for drinking them was from March to September. He recommended for an adult half a pint of water to be taken first thing in the morning when the stomach was empty and another half an hour afterwards. Gentle exercise such as riding or a walk should be taken after drinking to prevent nausea or drowsiness. 'Should this be found insufficient to keep the bowels open' then a teaspoonful of the salts could be added to each half pint. A month or six weeks was the period usually allowed for a trial, but this was 'much too short for any constitutional change to be effected'. The longer taking the Leamington waters was continued the more relief they were likely to afford, especially in the cases of scrofula or 'cutaneous eruptions' for which they were famous. Dr. Middleton also suggests that children should be given the waters at mealtimes 'for they will take it at those times when you cannot persuade them at others; and it is wonderful how soon they acquire a taste for it . . .'.

Regular warm baths in Leamington spa water Middleton thought were of particular value for people suffering from stiffness of joints, gout and rheumatism. A combination of warm baths and drinking the water was 'an almost sovereign remedy for all diseases of the skin'. Cold baths he appears to have disapproved of, regarding them as dangerous in certain circumstances, particularly when 'proper caution' was neglected. Although large cold baths, usually filled only once a day, were still in use, by 1815 doctors were more commonly of the opinion that tepid or warm baths were far more beneficial than cold ones. The Rev. Field wrote that since immersion in cold baths was

> usually momentary and the moisture remaining on the skin is immediately wiped off, it is inconceivable that salt water, in this case, can be more beneficial than common water. But where the person continues immersed for some length of time, as is the case in warm bathing, the saline ingredients may then be imbibed by the pores.

The times chosen for bathing were normally either before breakfast or between breakfast and dinner. Bathing in the evening before retiring later became popular. The cost in 1815 was 2s. 6d. to 3s. for a warm bath and 1s. to 1s. 6d. for a cold, not a small sum for the period. Even just to drink the water was expensive: in 1800 the charge was a shilling a pint for water from the original spring collected in a person's mug or jug, and in 1806 at the baths charges were around 7s. 6d. per person for the season or 2s. for the week, the charge for a family being 4s. 6d. a week.

Dr. Granville said that he always recommended his patients to drink the water from the old well when he sent them to Leamington. It had 'more glauber salt in it than the Water at the Royal Pump Room and hardly a trace of iron'. He also recommended Abbotts' well, where the water was much the same. Other wells supplied sulphureous water which even Dr. Granville admitted was unpleasant to take, smelling strongly of rotten eggs. In

66

IMPERIAL FOUNT

CHALYBEATE, SALINE APERIENT, AND SULPHUREOUS OR HARROWGATE SPRINGS,

𝕸𝖆𝖗𝖇𝖑𝖊 𝕭𝖆𝖙𝖍𝖘,
CLEMENS STREET, LEAMINGTON SPA,
WARWICKSHIRE.

31. Advertisement for the Imperial Fount.

particular the waters at the Royal Pump Room had a nauseating taste and repellent appearance. Granville wrote that since the water came from a well close to the river,

> which was of a deep, dirty and muddy appearance, thickish and scummy on the surface and receiving the drainage of the town – the sulphuretted hydrogen gas may, by the infiltration of such river water through the bank, be derived, to some extent, from its decomposing ingredients. I merely throw out this hint, as of a possible case, not without the authority of experience derived from former and analogous cases.

He concluded that Leamington water 'as drinking water has I readily admit the several moderate virtues which belong to such a class of saline waters; but, as a water to bathe in, I consider it as very little better than common sea water'.

Granville clearly thought the spa was still very expensive and exclusive:

> . . . at Leamington, unquestionably, no dross of society or even ambiguous characters, will be found among those who assemble at the Pump Rooms for their health and waters. The place is yet too choice and too costly to admit of any but the very tip-top of Society and that not one tithe of the people who come to Leamington take, or are desired to take, the water . . .

The lists of visitors given in the local newspapers and in *Beck's Weekly List* reveal that almost all the nobility of the country visited Leamington at one time or other. But because it was so expensive not all visitors regularly drank the waters or took baths, and many were attracted by the social round rather than the treatment. Taking the waters was an opportunity to visit a popular watering place where old friends could be met or new acquaintances made in less formal surroundings than at home, where young ladies or wealthy widows could find husbands and fortune hunters could find wives, in a way not possible elsewhere during the last century.

Early visitors to the spa included the Duke and Duchess of Bedford, who came first in 1808, and the Duchess of Gordon and the Duke of Manchester's daughter who came two years later. In 1811 several members of the nobility including Lord Middleton and his family took up residence, and within ten years Leamington's reputation was so well established that the Duke and Duchess of Gloucester came for a moderately long stay. From the early years efforts were made to attract such high-class visitors: when in 1788 Satchwell advertised in a Coventry newspaper the merits of the baths recently opened by Mr. Abbotts he announced that the Hon. Mrs. Leigh of Stoneleigh was a regular patron.

In the following years the spa attracted not only members of the aristocracy but also people of many other social groups. These included business and professional men and their families from Birmingham and the Black Country, clergymen from all over the country, and even writers. Among these were Nathaniel Hawthorne, Charles Dickens, who came twice, and in 1841, John Ruskin. He later wrote:

> . . . they desired me, on my way, to stop at Leamington, and show myself to its dominant physician, Dr. Jephson – called a quack by the Faculty. . . . Jephson was no quack; but a man of the highest general powers, and keenest medical instincts. He had risen by stubborn industry, and acute observation, from an apothecary's boy to be first physician in Leamington. . . . He examined me for ten minutes; then said 'stay here, and I'll put you right in six weeks'. Here I was, in a small square lodging house, looking out on a bit of suburban paddock, and broken paling, mean litter everywhere about; the muddy lingering Leam, about three yards broad, at the other side of a paddock; a ragged brambly bank on the other side of it. Down the row, a beginning of poor people's shops, then an aristocratic grocer or mercer or two, the circulating library, and the pump room. . . . Jephson was as good as his word, and let me out in six weeks, with my health, as he told me – I doubt not truly – in my own hands.

Many wealthy people were among Jephson's patients: Viscount and Viscountess Sidmouth, the Countess of Farnham, the Earl of Shaftesbury, Earl Brownlow, the Duke of Argyll and Sir Gray Skipwith, for example. Dr. Jephson counselled moderation, which was what his patients liked to hear; unlike some of his colleagues he did not rely completely on the water in his treatment. He always prescribed a tepid shower bath every morning, an hour's walk before each meal – in other words a course of regular exercise, something often lacking at that time, and a diet which might include plain meat, poultry, game, potatoes, stale bread, plain puddings, lightly boiled eggs, sherry, black tea and butter. Baths or showers were to be taken either at noon or four o'clock, with the head covered and the feet in water. Patients were expected to rise between seven and eight a.m., walk to the pump-room, drink half a pint of water, and after another walk could return to their hotel or rooms for breakfast. Baths were taken at least twice weekly, sometimes four times a week, as Jephson particularly valued bathing. Patients stayed in Leamington for about six weeks.

Perhaps Leamington's rise in popularity was partly due to the moderate treatments prescribed there, for soon other practitioners were recommending similar courses of treatment to Jephson's. Some doctors relied on the waters alone, but no accounts survive suggesting that patients in Leamington were subjected to the horrific cold water treatments applied in other places. In Malvern, for example, patients were directed to go out riding wrapped in wet clothes soaked in extremely cold spring-water. Such treatment was discredited after Sir Francis Burdett of Bramcote, Warwickshire, died in 1844 while following it. Diet as well as taking the waters became the popular treatment at Leamington. William Lambe, practising first in Warwick and then in London, advised a vegetarian diet, no alcohol and suggested drinking distilled water instead of 'impure' natural water. This system was followed also in Cheltenham and became increasingly popular elsewhere during the last half of the 19th century.

Other treatments, some more extreme or bizarre, were also offered. In 1852 Francis M. Herring of 33 Bath Street advertised himself as a medical galvanist who could supply galvanic and electro-magnetic apparatus for treating asthma, sciatica, rheumatism, many diseases of the eye, deficiency of nervous energy, liver complaints of all kinds and glandular ailments. His treatments were recommended by Dr. W. Middleton and Dr. Henry Homer, both on the staff of the Warneford Hospital, and were widely used at that time even though there was little evidence of them doing any lasting good to the patient. Other establishments provided douche baths, vapour baths and eventually Turkish baths. In 1834 the Bazaar Marble Baths, on the west side of Clemens Street, could offer four saline baths, plus fumigating baths, warm-air, shampooing, vapour, sulphur, chlorine, camphor and iodine baths, drawing-rooms, a bazaar and arcade, library and an urn giving four different kinds of saline water to drink. The Turkish Baths, however, failed a few years after opening.

In 1825, before Dr. Jephson set up practice in the town, the waters were claimed to be beneficial for indigestion and other digestive disorders, jaundice, consumption, scrofula, kidney diseases, ulcers, gout and rheumatism, and as late as 1855 doctors at the Warneford Hospital extended the list to include dyspepsia, almost all diseases of the liver, paralysis and some forms of epilepsy, cholera, hysteria, eczema, herpes and many more afflictions. Such extravagant claims naturally excited conflicting opinions on the effectiveness of the waters and treatment based on them. One result was a steady flow of books on the value of taking the waters. Dr. Middleton's work was frequently reprinted, in 1810 appeared Dr. Saunders' *The Medical Powers of Mineral Waters* and in 1816 Dr. Loudon's *Practical Dissertation on the Waters of Leamington Spa*, the last edition of which was printed in 1831. Loudon lived in the town. Other writers included Dr. Weatherhead, published in 1820, and Dr. Granville, in 1841. Finally Dr. Smith of Milverton published *The Saline Waters of Leamington, Chemically, Therapeutically and Clinically considered with Observations on the Climate of Leamington*, in 1884. This work compared the composition of the Leamington mineral waters with those of the waters at other spas, including 15 of the most popular French and German spas. Being a local doctor he concluded that, as far as salts go, 'Leamington will be seen to compare favourably with them all'. Smith's claims for the curative powers of the waters would today be considered unfounded, but he also suggested that the mild climate of the spa and its pleasant surroundings might also benefit the patient and hasten the cure. In this he echoed the earlier comments of Dr. Saunders.

By the turn of the century claims for the efficacy of the saline wells were less extravagant; before the First World War the waters were said to be an effective treatment only for ailments like arthritis, gout, high blood pressure, dyspepsia and some skin diseases. The waters then were to be taken an hour before breakfast and not less than two hours after breakfast, followed by massage, radiant heat or diathermy high frequency treatment. The guides of the 1920s and 1930s stressed that three to four weeks stay was usually considered sufficient, and the worried or overworked businessman could expect great benefits from a sojourn in the spa under medical supervision, particularly if suffering from high blood pressure. Here was a change in style from the early efforts to attract wealthy aristocrats; they now preferred to visit overseas spas. Although some medical treatments at the Pump Rooms and Baths are still available under the National Health Service, sampling the mineral water is now almost entirely a visitor's pastime, though some older local people still drink the water regularly.

Chapter Nine

The Social Round

Naturally no facilities existed for entertaining visitors to Leamington before it began to develop as a spa. In 1807 the only place for assemblies, for example, was a small room attached to *The Bowling Green Inn*. But within a few years of the start of the building of the New Town, a number of social amenities were provided, among them proper assembly-rooms.

The first of these was the Assembly Rooms (later known as the Upper Assembly Rooms) in Union Parade, described in Chapter Seven. They opened on 24 September 1812 with a grand ball. The annual subscription was set at 10s. 6d. for ladies and one guinea for gentlemen; non-subscribers paid 5s. for a single admission. The rule book ordered that the balls were to begin at 8 o'clock and to end precisely at midnight, even if in the middle of a dance. By 1833 the regulations had become less strict, as the ball held on 16 January ended at 2 a.m. At first balls were conducted by stewards elected from among the nobility and gentry visiting the town, but in 1814 events were supervised by Mr. Jack Rackstrow and later a regular Master of Ceremonies was appointed, Mr. James Heaviside, who was responsible for the Assembly Rooms from 1814 until 1818 when he left to become M.C. at Bath. His successor, Captain Stevenson, took the spa's Loyal Address to Warwick Castle on the occasion of the Prince Regent's visit in 1819.

At first balls were monthly events. The season ran from April to the end of December, but as the visitors came mostly from May to November the first ball was usually not held until June. They arrived in force in July or August; the ball on 15 August 1816 was attended by nearly 500 people. Another busy period was the first week of September, the time of Warwick races. As Leamington grew in size and popularity the season extended well into December. By 1818 balls were weekly events on Thursday evenings during the season and there were also occasional card assemblies. The seats at the top of the ballroom were reserved for peeresses, and couples were to take precedence in the dances according to the rank of the lady. Gentlemen wearing boots were not admitted, unless they were army officers in uniform.

In 1819 R. W. Elliston rented the Assembly Rooms. The following year Mrs. and the Misses Elliston gave their first spring ball on the premises; subsequent balls were often given for the pupils of the Ellistons' dancing academy, for Mrs. Elliston was a successful teacher of dancing in Bath and London before visiting Leamington each season from 1818 until her death in 1821. One of her daughters then continued the academy. Elliston himself was one of the most popular actors of his day, who had been actor-manager in theatres in London, Manchester, Birmingham and Coventry. He first came to Leamington in 1815, when he played Hamlet, and the next year he made frequent appearances in the town's theatre.

In 1821 Elliston opened the Lower Assembly Rooms in Bath Street, later known as The Parthenon. These had, besides the ballroom, a library containing 12,000 volumes, reading room, card room and, most importantly since the drink was taken particularly in the intervals of theatrical performances, concerts and assemblies, a tea room. The Parthenon rapidly eclipsed the third important ballroom in the town, the Apollo Rooms in Clemens Street. Admission to The Parthenon balls was 5s. 6d. which included tea and coffee, subscriptions were 15s. a season for ladies and a guinea for gentlemen, subscribers paying

1s. for tea and coffee. For a time summer balls took place weekly in both the Upper and Lower Assembly Rooms on Tuesdays and Thursdays, and during the winter of 1826-7 there were nine balls in the former and ten in the latter. The competition bankrupted both proprietors.

The Parthenon was then used for a variety of purposes. Mr. Samuel Lee ran a 'Select Academy' there for teaching the latest dances, including 'Mazurkas, Royal Gallopades, Waltzing . . .' and later also the very popular 'correct ballroom polka'. By 1835 the building was in the hands of Henry Twistleton Elliston, the eldest son of the actor and formerly in charge of the library there. He removed the top of the portico in the face of local opposition in 1835 on the grounds that it obstructed the light inside the building and was used by undesirable people who lowered the tone of the building. It has been suggested that the columns were reused on the front of the chapel built in Spencer Street, but it cannot be established for certain whether this was the case. Elliston turned The Parthenon into The Leamington Music Hall. During its time as a music hall Mr. Frederick Marshall, the organist of Christchurch, ran his singing classes there; a few years later it was used for amateur dramatics; and in 1873 it housed the public library for a time. Fire destroyed the building in the early 1960s and the present structure is a replica.

Earlier, from 1831, H. T. Elliston had leased the Upper Assembly Rooms. Business there had been ailing for years; when Mr. Francis Stenton, the M.C. and lessee, died in 1829 he left his family penniless and a ball was given there for the benefit of his widow and eight children. Not long after, Elliston was appealing for support through the columns of *The Courier*, and in 1833 the first ball of the season was held as late as 17 July. By 1835 he no longer gave balls in the Upper Assembly Rooms, preferring the Royal Pump Rooms, although the move brought no greater success. In November of that year he organised a meeting of subscribers in order to fix the date of future balls and avoid interference from other events, and six months later a local 'amusements committee' was formed to agree regulations for the holding of future balls and assemblies in the town and fix the dates of the winter balls 'to avoid clashes with other private and public amusements'. From then the Upper Assembly Rooms became a theatre and concert hall.

In the 1820s, besides gossiping, match-making, drinking the waters, going on excursions or attending balls, visitors could spend several evenings a week at the theatre. The first theatre had opened in a small building behind *The Crown Hotel*, but it was a temporary affair succeeded in 1813 by a purpose-built theatre in Bath Street, near the spot now occupied by *The Chair and Rocket*. This new theatre was erected by Mr. Sims. It was unfinished on the opening night, the walls not being plastered and no ornamental painting had been done in case of damage from damp, but Sims promised that all would be completed by next season. The walls were later described as being decorated with views of places of interest in the locality, in Leamington as well as Warwick and Kenilworth.

The opening night, 26 October, began with an address written by Mr. Bisset and read by Miss Sims, the owner's daughter, followed by a play entitled *The Earl of Warwick*, written by a local resident, and a farce, *Fortune's Frolic*. The interval between the two plays was filled by vocal items ranging from *Lilla of Leamington*, a ballad written by Mr. Bisset and sung by Mr. Povey, to comic songs by Messrs. Swendal and Smollett. The receipts for a full house realised about £30, boxes on the first tier costing 4s., on the second 3s., the pit being 2s. and the gallery 1s. Performances took place three times a week during the season. Elliston made the first of his appearances in Leamington in September 1815 and in 1817 took over the lease of the theatre.

Although some of the well-known actors of the day appeared, including Kean, Macready, Munden and the popular comedian Charles Matthews, performances in these early years often fell short of the standards visitors demanded later on. A letter written by Matthews in 1815 reveals a chaotic state of affairs:

> I arrived safe and well in Leamington, and when I saw the handful of houses that compose the town I felt that Mr Ling had hoaxed me, and much did I repent that I was advertised, the arrangements were hurried; and no musician could I get far or near till seven o'clock when one wretched country-dance fiddler arrived from a distance of five miles. I soon found that he could not play a note and began my performance with an apology, stating that I had written forward to request that all the musicians in the town might be engaged; and that request be complied with. Ladies and Gentlemen, said I, strictly All that are to be found are now in the orchestra. HE is all. I hope, however, that all the defects of the singing may be compensated by the ability of the musician, and vice versa, and if the kindness of the audience will keep pace with our anxiety to please my friend and I cannot fail of success. This produced a great laugh and when we came to the first song, he in vain attempted to scratch a note or two, and he literally was not heard during the whole evening; except between the two acts, when to rescue his fame he boldly struck up a country dance, which he rasped away to no small amusement of the audience. I had all the visitors I believe in the place; and to my amazement they produced me £27.

On the night Edmund Kean first performed in Leamington so many wished to see the famous actor that the takings reached a peak of £97, three times the normal amount.

Mr. Sims sold the freehold in 1824 and the building survived as a theatre until 1833 when it was converted into a wine vault. For nearly 15 years the town had no theatre, although there were occasional performances in The Parthenon from 1835; these were mostly by the Leamington Amateur Dramatic Club, later known as The Garrick Amateur Dramatic Club. Then in 1848 a group of local people bought the vacant Independent chapel in Clemens Street, had the interior remodelled, and opened it as a theatre; it later became known as The New Elliston Rooms and Theatre Royal. Charles Kean and his wife were engaged for the opening performance, planned for the autumn of 1848, but the renovations were unfinished when they arrived in town so this had to wait until 6 February the following year. The Keans and company opened with Mrs. Centure's comedy *The Wonder or a Woman Keeps a Secret*, after a prologue written by Mrs. Nicholas Torre, and completed the evening's entertainment with Planchi's comedy *Who's Your Friend or the Queensbury Fete*.

Beck's *Guide* of that time describes this theatre as 'remarkable, neat and compact'. It had a portico with four square pillars supporting a well-proportioned entablature which gave a sheltered approach for carriages. Inside, instead of the usual boxes, pit and gallery, it had a

> drawing room, cabinet, stalls, parterre and the upper circle. The drawing room circle consists of a series of raised floors entirely carpetted and fitted up with chairs. A handsome crimson paper adorns the walls, while fireplaces, pier glasses, pedestal lamps, give an air of comfort and elegance to this portion of the building, hitherto unknown in theatres of this size and class.

The upper and lower cabinets were 'snug retreats for those who prefer privacy'. The proscenium was decorated with fluted Ionic columns and entablature, all picked out in white and gold. The manager and proprietor was Mr. W. Simpson of the Theatre Royal, Birmingham.

During the next 17 years many famous actors and actresses played the theatre. They included Edmund and Charles Kean, R. W. Elliston, Booth, Miss Foote and Mrs. Waglett. When Macready gave his farewell performance there, playing Hamlet, the building was crowded and the street outside crammed with people unable to gain admittance. But again financial problems forced the theatre to close, and the following year, 1866, it reverted to use as a chapel.

A company was formed to build a new Theatre Royal in Regent Grove on part of the land behind Denby Villa. It was built by John Fell at a cost of £10,000, and opened in

October 1882 with a performance of *The Lily of Killarney* under the direction of Sir Julius Barnet. In six months, however, the lessee, Mr. Tempany, was bankrupt, and though the building changed hands several times no-one succeeded in making it pay as a theatre. In 1886 the theatre company went into voluntary liquidation and the building was bought by Mr. Fell for £5,100. He leased it to a succession of people, none with great success, until Mr. Charles Watson took over the lease in 1916. He disposed of it to Mr. Watson Mill in 1921, who ran it until his death in 1933. The theatre then became a cinema and in the 1950s it became a warehouse for the neighbouring garage. It was demolished in 1985.

Originally most of the music in the spa was supplied by military-style bands playing at the various pump-rooms and during the evenings in the gardens open for promenading – the Pump Room Gardens and the Newbold Pleasure Gardens, renamed the Jephson Gardens. The band of the Royal Pump Rooms, for example, which played from 8 a.m. to 9 a.m. while the visitors were taking the waters, also played during the summer in the gardens. The repertoire was a mixture of popular marches, ballads, waltzes and selections from favourite operettas. Once the Upper Assembly Rooms opened in 1812, musical events could be arranged on a more regular basis, alternating with the balls. At the same time teachers of music were attracted to the spa. One of the first, Owen Owen, arrived in 1810 to teach the harp, like the piano an instrument considered particularly suitable for young ladies. As Leamington accommodated more permanent residents, musicians like Mr. Marshall set up music academies. Marshall himself gave a series of concerts in the Lower Assembly Rooms in 1819.

A meeting of professional and amateur musicians held at Elliston's Rooms in Bath Street in 1826 led to the formation of the Leamington and Warwick Philharmonic Society. Among the first members were H. T. Elliston, John Estom, S. Flavel and John Merridew. Their inaugural concert, on 25 January 1827, included music by Mozart, Haydn, King, Arne, Bishop, Winter and Spagnoletti. According to the local press the audience numbered about sixty. Dudley describes some of the society's rules: 'a fine of 1s. was imposed on every member absent from rehearsals at seven o'clock, the time for commencement', 2s. 6d. for missing rehearsal altogether, and 5s. for not returning the music in time. One concert was given in Warwick, but the audience was only about twenty so they never paid a return visit. After a series of misfortunes the society gave its fourteenth and final concert on 9 April 1829.

Mr. Marshall's Choral Society, founded about the same time, was more successful. It held regular rehearsals in the parish church and gave performances of sacred music; a concert of Handel's choral music, including *Messiah*, at Christchurch in May 1829 attracted a large crowd. The players who provided the accompaniment at these concerts eventually formed a town band under Charles Elston, for many years bandmaster of the Warwickshire Militia. Their promenade concerts were highly successful and during the winter season the band often played in the Newbold Gardens or Ranelagh Gardens. Highly popular firework displays, advertised as 'Grand Gala and Pyrotechnical Exhibitions' with music from the best operas, were held at the latter.

Later, concerts by professionals engaged by the proprietors of the Upper and Lower Assembly Rooms were probably competing for the same audiences as the musicians described above, resulting in poorer attendances than the promoters hoped for. Nevertheless Leamington was popular enough in the 1830s and 1840s to draw artistes of international repute. Miss Clara Novello came to sing at the Lower Rooms in 1833, although the Upper Rooms were perhaps more attractive to performers. Paganini appeared twice in Leamington that same year, Johann Strauss the elder came in 1838, Thalberg in 1833 and 1840, and Liszt gave two concerts in the latter year. There were also many of the less well-known; Madame Catalini, then a very popular singer, visited several times in the 1820s, Mr.

Eulenstein on the Jew's Harp and Master Hughes, the infant Welsh harpist, were two more long-forgotten turns. Many of these concerts disappointed the promoters; the poor audiences at Charles Elston's series of *Grand Concerts d'Été* held in 1840 meant it ended in a considerable loss, for example. Concerts such as those of Jenny Lind in 1848 and 1856 were rare; she sang to a full house although on the second occasion tickets were a guinea each.

During this period stylish society began to find Leamington less attractive, and the numbers staying for the whole season dwindled. Instead more continentals and Americans came, paying shorter visits, and they were not necessarily interested in concerts or balls. Between 1840 and 1850 spasmodic efforts to extend the spa's musical entertainments resulted in some hopeless failures and a few successes which had no lasting effects. The Rev. John Craig, assisted by H. T. Elliston, then organist at the parish church, tried to introduce choral music to his congregation by starting a choir school in Grove Place. This lasted for about twelve years. *Copps' Royal Hotel* had the unique attraction of regular performances by Patrick Byrne, a blind Irish harper, and Mrs. Merridew, herself an accomplished singer, and her husband organised a series of concerts at which many fashionable artistes appeared. Apart from the Leamington Glee Association, founded in 1840, the most significant activity of the decade was the Town Improvement Association's efforts to form a town band to give regular open-air concerts in Jephson Gardens. The first band was assembled in the summer of 1848 with the help of Mr. Godfrey, the Queen's Bandmaster. Thirteen musicians from London, conducted by Mr. Irwin, came to the town for nine weeks. The cost was met by donations from the townspeople raised by a public appeal. A local band was engaged in 1849 and a visiting band from Cologne in 1850. These *ad hoc* arrangements continued for several years. The Leamington Philharmonic Society was re-established in 1854 with Mr. Ward as conductor. It continued to give performances until his death in 1890, whereupon the Leamington Orchestral Society gave its first concert in 1891. The tradition of entertaining visitors to the Pump Rooms with an orchestra during the summer was maintained until just before the last war, one of the last being that directed by Jan Berenska; although a small orchestra was engaged after the war, the custom has now lapsed.

Libraries and reading rooms were among the other permanent amenities first provided in the spa. Contemporary records give the impression of a town buzzing with literary activity, a hive of library proprietors vying for the approval of their patrons in a series of reading rooms which opened, prospered, enlarged, changed hands with great rapidity and closed down equally quickly, making it difficult if not impossible to record their history. Perhaps the first was that opened by Mr. Olorenshaw in Clemens Street in 1809; he claimed to have available a particularly ample supply of the latest novels suitable for young lady readers. Many other facilities were provided by most libraries; there was usually a 'repository' or shop selling stationery, artist's materials, scents, sea shells, quantities of fancy goods and souvenirs, and having musical instruments for sale or hire, providing various journals and London and provincial newspapers. In 1818, besides Mr. Olorenshaw's, there were Mr. Perry's Circulating and Music Library in High Street, Mrs. Gill's Library at 20 Union Parade and Mr. Reeve's Library and Reading Room opposite the old well.

None of these libraries made the same impression as the Reading Room and Art Gallery established by James Bisset. A Scotsman and proprietor of a 'Museum of Curiosities' in Birmingham, Bisset first came to Leamington in 1811 and returned the following year with his ailing wife and sickly daughter, who both took a course of the waters. Realising the opportunities for an energetic businessman in the rapidly growing spa, Bisset took 'a large room which had been built for assemblies' and opened a library, reading room and picture gallery in Clemens Street.

The contents of the museum in Birmingham, 'consisting of upwards of three hundred valuable paintings, curios, British and foreign birds, etc.' were transferred to Leamington and the family settled in a newly-built house in Union Parade. Here Mrs. Bisset looked after the curios in the museum while Bisset ran the reading room and art gallery south of the river, because he could not find anywhere in 'the infant town' big enough to display the whole collection. Under this gallery was a billiard room. The museum was soon transferred to a house in Gloucester Street, near the original spring. In 1814 Bisset produced the first edition of his own guide to the spa, which became very popular and sold well for many years. According to Bisset's own *Memoir*, the guide was finished 'in one month from its first contemplation. The place only wanted to be known and I had the felicity of having my book much read, and most extensively circulated'.

In 1818 Bisset disposed of his museum and library to Mr. Perry and the building became known as the Apollo Rooms. Bisset took over the nearby business owned by Mr. Olorenshaw and enlarged the premises by constructing a gallery behind. He reopened the building with much ceremony on 1 May 1820, calling it the Paragon Picture Gallery. The lower part of the building was occupied by Mr. George Carter, the spa's first auctioneer, who described himself as 'auctioneer, appraiser, house, land and commission agent, china and picture dealer'. The new gallery was a great success and Bisset said in his *Memoir*:

> I had added considerably both to the splendour of my gallery and my collection of natural history and was honoured at my reading room by the principal visitors of rank and fashion as subscribers for the Season, or for months or weeks.

Among them were the Countess of Craven, the Earls of Warwick, Aylesford, Dartmouth, Thanet, Guildford, and Melville and Leven, the Duke of Grafton and the Duchess of Rutland.

Bisset was able to turn his hand to many things to make a living. He wrote guides and poetry, promoting the town and its saline springs and his own reading room and art gallery. He seems also to have been a competent artist, for many of his drawings of the original old cottages in Leamington, published as prints soon after he arrived in the spa, are very good aquatints. He was not above restoring or altering paintings by other artists to suit the fashion of the day or to please the fancies of his patrons. In 1825 he disposed of his gallery, at the same time extending Belle Vue Place, the house he had built on the corner of Clemens Street and Ranelagh Terrace in 1817, by constructing 'an art gallery to display the best of his pictures'. He died in 1832 aged 72, the gallery then containing 100 pictures.

The Upper Assembly Rooms from their opening in 1812 also had a reading room. About 1830 the end of the building containing this reading room was isolated from the rest of it and operated as a separate business. The new proprietor of the library was Mr. Hewitt, who had run a similar business a little lower down the Parade. Hewitt's Library, as it became known, sold not only books and music, but also jewellery, fancy goods and watercolours, and Hewitt eventually displayed a 'Royal Warrant appointment as Dealer in watercolours to Queen Victoria'. The Fairfax *Guide* described the library and reading room as occupying 'fine spacious rooms' and as 'the first in the town', i.e. north of the river. It was used for musical promenades in the summer, when cards and other games were played and dances took place.

Other libraries included that opened by the Ellistons at the Lower Assembly Rooms in Bath Street. When these assembly-rooms became The Royal Music Hall, the library became a separate business. It passed through several hands, including back into those of one of the members of the Elliston family. Behind it is an interesting building, still surviving although under threat. This is the Waterloo Gallery, a rare example of a purpose-built billiard room, constructed in 1825 by W. G. and H. T. Elliston. Billiards was growing in popularity as it gradually evolved into something resembling the modern game. The Ellistons' room, designed in the classical style, had an elegant curved staircase leading up to a balustraded gallery supported on the east and west sides by brackets and at one end, where it was much wider, by posts of classical design. From the gallery it was possible to watch the players on the table. The roof was supported by six slender iron pillars. There were long, glazed roof-lights above the table and at night the room was lit by gas lamps. About 1837 it became a bazaar and later part of Mr. Wackrill's drapery store.

The early lending libraries were so popular that by the middle of the 19th century the less wealthy residents of the spa had begun to demand access to libraries without the payment of the large subscriptions required by private proprietors. In December 1855 Henry Mulliner, a local carriage builder, called a public meeting to discuss the idea, but little was done until the following year when the town's improvement commissioners met to consider adopting the Free Libraries Act. The Rev. John Craig moved the adoption of the act; 94 voted in favour and 20 against. The first free library was opened on 16 March 1857 in the Board Room of the Town Hall in High Street. Mr. Saunders was the first librarian, in charge of a stock of 1,000 books. Being intended for working people it opened mostly in the evenings from 6 to 10 p.m., but it was open in the mornings on Monday, Tuesday and Wednesday and in the afternoon on Thursday, Friday and Saturday. Attendance on the opening day was four in the morning, ten at midday and 60 in the evening. A Free Reading Room had been opened earlier in Covent Garden, just off Warwick Street in the New Town,

32. The building on the corner of Bath Street and Church Walk used as the public library, 1858-73. For a time the ground floor was occupied by *The Courier* press. The building, erected about 1814-15, survives although much altered.

financed by Captain Dunscombe. He suggested that the new free library should be more centrally placed but, this proving impossible, his Reading Room was eventually merged with the library.

In November 1858 the library moved to its own premises at the corner of Church Walk and Bath Street. After another 1,000 books were purchased a lending department was opened in September 1859, and a ladies' reading room added in April 1863. By 1864 the library had outgrown these premises, so it leased part of The Parthenon, which had by then become furniture showrooms. The first Reference Library was opened in 1873. Further moves took it into the new Town Hall. The modern library, on the site of Perkins' Gardens in Avenue Road, designed by Mr. J. Mitchell Bottomley of Leeds and built by Mr. Richard Bowen of Tavistock Street, Leamington, at a cost of £16,000, was opened in December 1902 and the Art Gallery extension was added in 1927.

The early reading rooms owed much of their success to providing their subscribers with London and provincial newspapers, but equally as important were local newspapers giving information about activities in the spa and details of the arrival and departure of visitors. The only paper published throughout the early days of the spa was *The Warwick Advertiser*, founded in 1806, a principal source of information about the first years of the town. Other papers appeared in Leamington for short periods. One of these was *The Warwickshire Chronicle, Leamington, Warwick and Stratford Journal and General Advertiser for the Midland Counties*, published by Mr. Merridew in Warwick, the first issue of which appeared on 19 April 1826 and the last about ten years later. *The Leamington Herald* was advertised as also due to appear in July 1826, but there is no evidence that even the first issue was printed. *The Leamington Free Press*, a Leamington edition of a Northampton newspaper, *The Northampton Free Press*, was available every Saturday from July 1833 at Mr. Hughes' Bazaar in Clemens Street; it was later published by Mr. Crick at 1 Gloucester Street as the *Leamington Press and Warwickshire Journal of Fashion, Literature, Politics, Agriculture and Commerce*. In 1835 the title was changed again, to *The Leamington Chronicle, Warwickshire Reporter and General Advertiser for the Counties of Warwick, Worcestershire, Leicestershire, Staffordshire, Gloucestershire, Oxfordshire and Northamptonshire*, and it was printed and published by John Fairfax in Bath Street. The paper, ponderous title and all, disappeared after a few years. It was succeeded by *The Leamington Advertiser*, started in October 1848. Other papers included a revival of *The Leamington Chronicle* (1865), the *Warwick, Leamington and District Circular* (1896) and *The Leamington Daily Advertiser* (1897), all of which died young.

The only survivors are *The Morning News*, devoted to news of Leamington and local advertisements, and the *Leamington Courier*, a weekly newspaper which has appeared regularly since its first issue on 9 August 1828 under the title of the *Leamington Spa Courier, and Alcester, Atherstone, Coleshill, Henley-in-Arden, Kineton, Kenilworth, Knowle, Nuneaton, Rugby, Solihull, Southam, Stratford-upon-Avon and Warwick Borough and County Gazette*. This name was dropped in favour of *The Royal Leamington Spa Courier* in 1838, and the current name adopted in the late 19th century. The paper was printed on the north-west corner of Wise Street and High Street, in what was originally a Baptist chapel. James Sharp, the editor, and John Fairfax, the printer, started it, although Fairfax soon returned to his original printing business in Clemens Street. In 1841 he emigrated to Australia and eventually became the proprietor of the *Sydney Morning Herald*. In 1835 Sharp also published a Warwick edition called *The Warwick Standard*.

The winter of 1836-7 brought unusual difficulties for the publishers. At that time there was a newspaper stamp duty of 1s. 6d. per issue (which remained in force until late in the century) and the paper needed for printing had to be stamped in London before being used by provincial printers. In December 1836 severe and persistent frosts put the canal system out of action and the inevitable delays in transport meant that no 'stamped' paper was available at the end of 1836 for the weekly edition to be printed.

Ownership of *The Courier* passed from Sharp to Mr. Edward Howe and Mr. John Russell, and in April 1837 the paper was acquired by Mr. George Liebenrood. He sold it to Mr. Joseph Glover in 1855, who died in 1890. A private limited company was formed in 1909 with Glover's son as managing director and E. Hicks as director and editor. Mr. H. G. Clarke joined the firm as printing manager in 1913 and later became chairman of the company. It has remained with his family until the present day. James Sharp, junior, edited the paper until 1861 and on his retirement was succeeded first by Mr. Baxter and then by Tom Burgess, well-known for his many books on Warwickshire history and customs. The longest serving editor of *The Courier* has been Mr. Hicks, who was in charge from 1909 to 1944. The paper cost 7d. in 1828, very expensive for the time, and the price dropped to 4½d. in 1836, 3d. in 1866, 2d. in 1882 and 1d. in 1884.

The advertisement columns of *The Courier*, as well as the news items, reveal the life of the spa and the activities of its visitors and residents: as was usual in the early 19th century gentlemen and ladies filled their days in walking, taking excursions, riding, shopping, in conversation or gossip, dancing, visiting neighbours, libraries or art galleries, or with music and drawing lessons, and those who sought their custom advertised for it. To further their accomplishments, the number of music teachers in 1839 had increased from a single original harp-teacher to three teachers of the flute, four of the harp, two of the violin, three of the cello, four of the piano and one of the french horn. The teaching of singing was not, it would seem, in great demand. There were also eight teachers of art. Thirty or so years later there were twice as many. A number of them became well-known as local artists, examples of their work now being displayed in the Leamington Art Gallery. By the 1880s teachers were available for singing, the organ and the trombone, for languages, embroidery, sewing, and even modelling flowers and fruit in wax. Painting and sketching continued very popular and photography was becoming a more common hobby. The first photographers were at the Upper Assembly Rooms, where as early as February 1843 Mr. H. J. Whitlock of Birmingham attended to produce pictures by the daguerreotype process. For the next 20 years or so a series of photographers used these premises, usually coming from other towns for the season. By 1877 Bullock Brothers, photographers at 138 Parade, were advertising themselves as having been established in the spa for 20 years.

Chapter Ten

'Winding paths and boskiness'

(Hawthorne)

In the earliest days of the spa all the larger pump rooms and baths had gardens where visitors could promenade before or after taking the waters, or meet friends to pass the time of day. There was a small garden behind the pump room established in Bath Street in 1786, another behind Mr. Elliston's Lower Assembly Rooms and the Victoria Baths opened in 1806 had extensive gardens with a promenade along the south bank of the river extending almost to the present Adelaide Road bridge. The Royal Pump Rooms also had a promenade and gardens from their opening in 1814, they covered the existing Pump Room Gardens as far as the present central path leading to the York Road footbridge. The public were admitted to them free of charge after the Local Board of Health acquired the building and saline spring in 1861; before then they were the prerogative of the subscribers. The earliest pleasure grounds opened as an independent venture were The Leamington Nursery and Pleasure Grounds, later called the Ranelagh Gardens, south of the Leam. They were very popular when owned by Mr. John Cullis, but their popularity declined with the opening of the Jephson Gardens and they finally closed soon after Cullis' death.

The area now comprising the Jephson Gardens, covering about 10½ acres on the north bank of the Leam, was originally owned by Mr. Edward Willes of Newbold Comyn. In the early 19th century it was farmland. About 1834 J. G. Jackson, Willes' agent, laid it out as pleasure gardens, as a commercial enterprise. Some early views of the spa show part of the land still being farmed – originally the gardens ran only as far as the right of way from Whitnash to Lillington. When the gardens were enlarged this right of way was sunk below their level and part taken through a tunnel, so that users of the gardens could cross it but passers-by could not gain unauthorised access to the park. These Newbold Pleasure Gardens, as they were then named, were free to all between 7 a.m. and 10 a.m., after which entry was restricted to subscribers and patrons of Smith's Baths in Bath Street.

When the gardens were first opened Newbold Terrace was not complete. Even in 1839 it consisted only of a few houses at each end, the intervening space being unoccupied and still for sale; the gap was eventually filled in with detached villas. Mr. Willes, owning also this building land, entered into covenants with the purchasers that the gardens would never be built upon and that the occupier of each villa should have the right in perpetuity of free admission to the pleasure grounds. There were to be four villas, and after Mr. Willes enclosed the gardens with a railing each villa had a gate opposite.

In 1834 part of the area was set aside for the sport of archery and called The Newbold Archery Grounds, 'where laughing maidens practise at the butts, generally missing this ostensible mark, but, by the mere grace of their action, sending an unseen shaft into some young man's heart'. As the sport became more popular national meetings took place in the spa, the first being in June 1851. It was held on the cricket ground near the 'new river walk', the archers using eight acres close to the present Victoria Park.

On 24 May 1837 Princess Victoria attained her legal majority. Great festivities were held in Leamington: 250 people enjoyed in the gardens an open-air dinner of roast beef and plum pudding, with a pint of ale for each woman and a quart for each man. In the afternoon 1,200 children were given tea and a Montgolfier balloon rose from a field behind Victoria

Terrace and floated across the town. A loyal address to the Princess was presented by Lord Eastnor, the Hon. Captain Somerville and Dr. Jephson.

In April 1836 the Hon. Charles Bertie Percy, John Tomes, H. C. Wise and J. V. Barber leased the gardens from Mr. Willes for 2,000 years at an annual rent of £30. It was agreed that this rent would be reduced to a nominal sum if the leaseholders at any time repaid the £600 which Willes had spent in fencing the gardens. The gardens were not then very well planted. Dudley in his *History of Royal Leamington Spa* quoted a writer in *The Gardener's Magazine* who in 1840 described the gardens of the spa in some detail: Dr. Jephson had some beautiful specimens of Turkey and Luccombe oaks at his house Beech Lawn, Holly Walk was bordered with old oaks, elms and hollies, while Mr. Cullis' nursery, which extended over many acres in different parts of the town, had the largest stock of *Cupressus Tolurosa* in England. All that was said about the Newbold Gardens was 'that there is a piece of ground containing about 14 acres, which it is intended to be laid out as a public garden and for which we have made a plan'. The first major improvement to them came after 1840 when a Poor Relief Fund had been set up, followed in 1843 by a Labourers' Employment Fund started by Dr. Hitchman to create work for the poor who had no regular employment. The funds provided labour to lay out the walks, level the ground and excavate the lake.

Early in 1846 a movement was promoted for presenting to Dr. Jephson a testimonial in recognition of his services to the town, and on 7 May the proposal was discussed at a meeting held in the Upper Assembly Rooms. Sir Robert Cave-Browne-Cave of Kenilworth Hall put forward the resolution which was accepted with great acclaim, and a committee was appointed to approve the details. At a second meeting on 12 May the character of the testimonial was made public. The committee, having raised £1,850, had agreed to acquire the lease of the Newbold Gardens and, renaming them the Jephson Gardens, to dedicate them to the use of visitors to and residents of the town. A statue of the Doctor would be erected in the gardens and trustees appointed to maintain them. Later that day over 7,000 people assembled in the gardens, speeches were made, the national anthem sung and the gardens formally received their new name. Many of those there were wearing a commemorative medal struck for the occasion by Messrs. Bright and Sons, from a design by Mr. Ottley of Birmingham, a remarkable feat of production achieved in less than a week. The proceedings were followed by great jollifications and the customary banquet for subscribers in honour of Dr. Jephson.

The statue cost £1,000, and was executed by Peter Hollins. Hollins was a Birmingham sculptor, born in 1800 and trained in his father's studio, who had worked in London until 1822 under the famous sculptor Chantrey. The figure of the Doctor, in Carrara marble standing seven feet high on a pedestal of Sicilian marble, is in a Corinthian-style 'temple'. The foundation stone was laid by Lady Somerville on 13 May 1848, and the temple was completed and opened on 29 May 1849, by when the Doctor was almost blind. When the statue was erected it was considered to be an excellent likeness and the general expression faultless. Nathaniel Hawthorne, writing some time later, was of the opinion that it was

> very well executed, and representing him with a face of fussy activity and benevolence; just the kind
> of man, if luck favoured him, to build up the fortunes of those about him, or, quite as probably to
> blight his whole neighbourhood by some disastrous speculation.

The Labourers' Fund provided much money in the following two years to employ men supervised by Mr. Cullis to continue laying out the gardens. In 1848 to celebrate the completion of the first part of the improvements, two rows of evergreen oaks were planted, one on either side of the central path nearest the Parade entrance. Each tree commemorated someone who had achieved fame in the earliest days of the spa and they were named in a 'Festival of Oaks' which began on the morning of Monday 1 May and ended on the Thursday evening. All these trees have now been removed, replaced by the ornamental trees flourishing

33. The Jephson Memorial, erected in the Jephson Gardens in 1848-9 as a tribute to the Doctor in recognition of his work for the town. The statue of Dr. Jephson inside the building was carved by Peter Hollins. The doctor did not die until 1878.

34. The lodges at the entrance to the Jephson Gardens from the Parade, designed by David Squirhill in 1846.

today, but some of the shrubs and trees in the gardens now were planted by the first gardener, Mr. Aylott, in charge from 1848 to 1878.

Two lodges, still standing, were erected opposite the Pump Rooms to the designs of Mr. Squirhill. Their height was restricted to 30 ft. lest they should interfere too much with the surroundings of the Pump Rooms. Another entrance was made afterwards in Willes Road, where a lodge was built in Old English style to the design of J. G. Jackson; more recently a third entrance has been made facing Newbold Terrace. When the grounds were first opened, however, access was restricted to the gate on the Parade. The private gates of the Newbold terrace villas were closed although their occupants were still admitted free of charge. Miss Dawson, who lived at no. 6, objected and decided to test the legality of the trustees' action by having the gate opposite her house broken open. A suit brought against her for wilful damage and trespass was heard at Warwick assizes in September 1848. The court decided that, since Mr. Willes had not specified in the convenants any places for entrance, as long as the residents of Newbold Terrace had free access to the gardens that was sufficient. Miss Dawson appealed but lost, and for many years the Parade entrance remained the only one. Until quite recently one of the old gates could be seen in the hedge alongside Newbold Terrace. As the humbler people of the town had contributed to the Jephson Memorial Fund in gratitude for the Doctor's kindness to many of them, the gardens were open free every Sunday afternoon to allow them access. Until after the last war 1d. was charged for admission on weekdays, but now the gardens are open daily free of charge. In November 1854 the Trustees paid the £600 mentioned in the Trust Deed, reducing the rent payable to the Willes family to a peppercorn.

Under the Trustees the pleasure grounds were transformed from what were in places little more than an open field to the gardens that exist today. The plan is Cullis' original one, but many changes have been made. Some of the original arbours have been removed or adapted to other uses, for example. In 1909 Alderman Holt and Mr. Naylor of Harrington House in Newbold Terrace gave the town a glass auditorium and shelter. After the First World War the shelter was enclosed to form a covered hall for concerts. The new Spa Centre made it superfluous, and it was demolished in 1973 and replaced by a refreshment room. The clock tower, an anonymous gift, was unveiled in 1926 by Mrs. Davis as a memorial to her late husband, Alderman W. Davis. The lake's two spectacular fountains were modelled on those at Hampton Court. The first was the gift of Alderman Holt and was installed in 1925-6, the second the following year. The gardens were originally planted as an arboretum rather than as a flower garden, and many of the trees planted then are now mature, a fine collection containing unusual species not normally grown in this country.

Other changes included the demolition of Newbold Lodge, standing in the corner where the Parade and Newbold Terrace meet. The site was added to the gardens and the Hitchman Memorial Fountain built on it in 1869. In 1873 William Willes complained that renaming the gardens the Jephson Gardens was unfair to the memory of his father, who gave the land to the town. The Trustees then erected a memorial obelisk acknowledging the gift, with a simple inscription: 'Erected in honour of Edward Willes, Esq., of Newbold Comyn, to whom Leamington is indebted for the site of these gardens'.

Until 1896 the Jephson Gardens remained the responsibility of the original trustees, and was managed by a committee independent of the Corporation. While the Leamington Corporation Bill was under consideration it was suggested that one of its objects should be the acquisition of the gardens. The Trustees accepted this proposal subject to a guarantee that the name Jephson should never be changed, and when the Act received the royal assent that year, the gardens passed into the control of the Corporation.

From the beginning the gardens accommodated many public events attracting visitors to the town. Flower shows offered large prizes to competitors, many of whom came from all

35. Strawberry Cottage, owned by Edward Willes, stood at the corner of the Parade and Newbold Terrace. It was demolished about 1836 when J. G. Jackson erected Newbold Lodge there. The lodge also was pulled down and the site added to the Jephson Gardens in 1869 to allow the Hitchman Memorial Fountain to be put up. A fine view by William Rider, lithographed by Charles Hullmandel, a pioneer of lithography.

36. The Hitchman Memorial Fountain. A photograph taken about 1900 of the fountain erected in the Jephson Gardens in 1869.

over the country. These shows were well attended until after the last war, when they were discontinued due to the expense of mounting the displays; in later years the shows were held in the Pump Room Gardens rather than in the Jephson Gardens. A popular event last century was to visit the gardens illuminated by fairy lights. There have always been band concerts, firework displays, and occasional balloon ascents to add to the excitement. One of these very popular events took place in June 1849, when 30,000 people are said to have been present, and a similar event the following year also attracted a vast crowd.

A number of ascents took place in the town. At the first balloon ascent, held in the Ranelagh Gardens in 1820, there were 'pyrotechnicks' accompanied by the ascent of a Montgolfier or hot-air balloon, and in 1824 Mr. Green 'the famous balloonist' took flight from the bowling green at the end of Bath Street to celebrate the coronation of George IV; his balloon bore the words 'Coronation Balloon' and festive decorations. Having arrived in Leamington, it was exhibited at The Parthenon for a week before the ascent, and inflated on the day with gas from the new Leamington Priors Gas Works. It was airborne for about 30 minutes and landed near Northampton. At Princess Victoria's coming of age in 1837 a similar ascent was made by S. Gore and J. Hordern of Clemens Street to enable them to obtain a bird's eye view of the celebrations taking place in the Jephson Gardens.

While archery and croquet were the only sports allowed in the Gardens, there were other facilities for sport in the town. Real or royal tennis was a popular sport in the mid-19th century which is still played in the town. A movement was started in 1844 to provide tennis and racquets courts for the use of the 'gentlemen of Leamington', and a meeting was held in the Upper Assembly Rooms to form a committee to carry out the project and raise funds by the issue of shares at £10 each. The original committee included five lords and an M.P. as well as Dr. Jephson. The land next to Belsay House in Bedford Street was bought for £500, construction started at once under the supervision of J. G. Jackson and it was finished in 1846 at a total cost of £4,211 including furnishings. Besides the tennis and racquets courts the building contained billiard rooms, a reading room, library, meeting, smoking and other rooms as well as refreshment facilities. There were originally about 200 members, elected by ballot. In 1851 improvements were made, a spacious hall, card rooms and a portico, now demolished, were added. The building is almost unchanged externally since then, and still serves its original purpose.

Lawn tennis also has close associations with the spa. The game was invented in 1859 by Major Thomas Henry Gem, a solicitor, and his friend Batista Pereira, a Spanish merchant, who both lived in Birmingham. They played it first on a lawn in the Edgbaston area, calling it 'pelota', after a Spanish ball-game. In 1872 both men moved to Leamington, and with two doctors from the Warneford Hospital, Frederick Haynes and Arthur Wellesley Tomkins, played pelota on the lawn behind *The Manor House Hotel*. The hotel bears a plaque erected during the centenary celebrations held on 11 June 1972, which reads: 'In 1872 Major Harry Gem with his friend Mr B. Pereira, joined with Dr Frederick Haynes and Dr A. Wellesley Tomkins to found the first lawn tennis club in the world and played the game on nearby lawns'. In 1874 they formed the Leamington Tennis Club, setting out the original rules of the game which form the basis of the modern ones. *The Courier* of 23 July 1884 recorded one of the first tennis tournaments, held in the grounds of Shrubland Hall.

Croquet also enjoyed great popularity at the same period and was no doubt played behind the hotel as well as in the Jephson Gardens, a local club being formed in the last century. The Leamington Croquet Club, together with the Milverton Tennis Club, used a ground behind St Mark's church, New Milverton, in the years before the First World War, and tournaments were held there in 1911, 1912 and 1913. When the club was revived after the war it moved to a site in Guy's Cliffe Avenue, becoming the Warwickshire Croquet and Tennis Club. Croquet is no longer so popular, but the tennis club has thrived and still continues on the same site, almost certainly the oldest in the town specially laid out for the purpose.

The first golf club was formed by the Rev. Percy Coatès in 1890. It was followed by the Leamington and County Golf Club at Whitnash in 1909, where the club still retains its original course. Bowls, played in the spa since its early days, remains very popular. The Royal Leamington Spa Bowling Club was formed in about 1909, its original green being at Victoria Park Lodge in Avenue Road. The club later moved to its present site in Archery Road, where it forms part of Victoria Park, and the greens are frequently chosen for the All England Finals of the English Women's Bowling Association.

Cricket has also been long established in the town. Cricket matches with crack clubs were a feature of the late 19th century, a marquee being used for a dinner after the match, followed by a dance. Among the first of these was that in 1845 when the North and South of England teams met on the ground, then leased by Messrs. Parr and Wisden, and decided a contest started a few weeks previously at Lords, then also leased by the same proprietors. In 1848 the All England team met the Leamington District team on the same ground, which by then had been improved to such a high standard that it acquired the name of The Provincial Lords. Matches were played on this ground until 1897 and, when Victoria Park was created incorporating it, a new ground was purchased near the Lillington Road where the local club still plays. Apart from cricket the Avenue Road ground was used for other events including horticultural shows and the regular training of the Warwickshire Militia. While Clapham Terrace was the site of their barracks, the militia, numbering 600-700, drilled on the cricket ground; later in the century it moved to new barracks at Budbrooke, near Warwick.

Besides the Jephson Gardens and the Pump Room Gardens there were, in the last half of the 19th century, a number of privately owned gardens and nurseries. Ranelagh Nurseries of Brunswick Street survived the closure of Ranelagh Gardens and there was also the Victoria Nursery, bordering the south bank of the Leam from near *The Manor House Hotel* to the Adelaide Road Bridge. These gardens occupied about eight acres of ground running parallel to the river and formed a promenade open to the public. The present public library was built in 1902 on them. The rest of them became York Gardens and York Road, laid out about 1890. The York Road Footbridge linking the new gardens with those adjacent to the Pump Room was constructed across the Leam in 1893. Elsewhere in the town were the Fern Nursery, on part of the site of Belsay House in Bedford Street and Mr. Willes' nursery in Portland Place. Later, new open spaces generally had an origin connected with the celebration of some national event which the town wished to commemorate.

The Adelaide Road Bridge, built by J. Heritage of Warwick, was first opened in 1850 so that traffic could travel between Warwick and Milverton without using the Victoria Bridge in the centre of the town. The present bridge dates from 1891. In 1850 the railway bridge was built over the Leam. A new river walk was first proposed in 1854, but it was delayed until improvements to prevent flooding were imperative. The promenade from Dale Street to the railway bridge, a distance of half a mile, was opened only on 1 July 1862. At the same time a weir costing £1,500 was constructed near the viaduct while improvements were made to the adjacent sewage works, now the site of the local authority incinerator plant. The original 'new river walk' was slightly shortened by the laying out of Prince's Drive in the 1930s.

The Queen's Diamond Jubilee was marked in great style by the opening of Victoria Park. The ground, originally the cricket field alongside the river walk, was purchased for £7,600 and £3,000 was spent laying out the park. A lodge was built at the end of Avenue Road so the keeper could 'see that proper order is maintained and the daily rules observed'. The strip of land between Archery Road and the river walk was laid out for tennis, bowls and croquet, the rest being used for cricket, or football in the winter.

Jubilee day was celebrated very enthusiastically all over the county, but nowhere more so than in Leamington, with its privileged title of 'Royal'. In spite of the inclement weather, after a church service of thanksgiving the mayor and council, militia, Fire Brigade and a great number of the townspeople processed from the Town Hall along Avenue Road to the new park, where they crowded into a marquee to take refreshments. Four thousand five hundred schoolchildren thronged the park, hopefully keeping quiet long enough to hear the speeches, sing the national anthem and give the customary hearty cheers. Alderman Dr. Thursfield, the mayor, named the park and declared it open, saying that it covered 21 acres, had cost a three farthing in the pound rate, or 13d. for a man rated at £20 p.a., and was a bargain at the price. The first sports were held in the park later the same day, but by then the procession had returned to the Pump Room Gardens where the festivities continued with a dinner in a marquee for those over sixty-five. There were street decorations, the band played in Jephson Gardens which were illuminated with fairy and chinese lamps, and the day ended with a gigantic bonfire.

In 1902 the statue of Queen Victoria was placed before the Town Hall and the small garden and paved area facing the Parade was set out. This was a more modest tribute than the scheme proposed to mark the coronation of George IV, when it was suggested that an obelisk 250 ft. high should be erected in High Street, near the present railway bridge. A staircase was to be constructed to the summit to allow people to view the surrounding countryside. The parish council of the time wisely decided that the town 'could well do without it and apply the money to a much better purpose'.

Victoria Park was followed by the creation of other open spaces in the town. In November 1889 the mill site was bought from the Aylesford estate for £4,085, and the eight-and-a-half acres laid out as a playing field. In 1898 the Eagle Recreation Ground, five acres in extent, cost £1,300 to buy and £500 to lay out. The most recently created open space has been on the lower slopes of the Newbold Comyn hills, east of the town centre, near the place where some of the most exciting sporting events in Leamington's history took place in the 1820s and 1830s – the Leamington Grand Steeplechases.

Because the Warwickshire Hunt regularly met near Leamington many sporting gentlemen moved to the town for several weeks during the hunting season. A large kennels was provided about 1829 on Mr. T. Robbins' farm at Milverton, and that year the pack turned out three or four days a week. This stimulated interest in steeplechasing in the area. The first of the races, in March 1826, proved so successful that they became an annual event until 1840, and were revived briefly in March 1884. After several temporary courses had been tried the first of the Leamington races properly supervised by the Jockey Club took place on Easter Monday 1834 over two fields close to the Campion Hills near Newbold Comyn, land belonging to Mr. James Gill, saddler, of Lower Union Parade. Entries were made to the stewards at *The Half Moon* public house, in Satchwell Street. Also in 1834 a steeplechase was run on 14 November over a course set out at Ashorne. On this occasion the Marquis of Waterford's Jerry beat the local favourite, Captain Lamb's Vivian, which led to another contest in which Cock Robin, also owned by the Marquis, was backed against Vivian for £1,000. Vivian, with Captain Beecher up, was an easy winner, and after the victory of the local horse the church bells were rung and *The Bedford Hotel* celebrated by keeping open house. A coloured print showing 'Captain Beecher on Vivian', published soon afterwards, sold very well in the locality, and today a local pub, *The Fox and Vivian* still preserves the horse's name.

In 1836 a site near Southam was chosen for the course of the Leamington Grand Steeplechase, held on 21 March, but four years later the races were back on the Campion

Hills. The start of the four-mile course, which had 30 fences, was at the base of the hills and went northwards to finish beyond Red House Farm. For the first race the Marquis of Waterford riding Lottery backed himself for £500 to be first over the first seven fences and won his bet; Lottery was the first winner of the Grand National Steeplechase when it was inaugurated in 1839. On this occasion the company was more decorous than those sportsmen who had gathered at *The Bedford Hotel* some 20 years earlier. When John Mytton stayed there in 1826 he won an historic wager that he would ride his mare upstairs into the dining-room on the first floor, jump over the table and the heads of his fellow sportsmen who were at dinner, then leap to the street below clearing the balcony outside the window. He survived – and married a year later, another test of courage!

By the later 1830s the spa would not tolerate such reckless sportsmen. The town wished to remain respectable, to encourage wealthy families to come for the season and take the waters – drinking, gambling and racing gave the wrong image.

Chapter Eleven

Hotels and Hoteliers

At the time the second saline well was discovered in 1784 there was hardly any accommodation in the village for visitors apart from the two inns, *The Black Dog* and *The Bowling Green*, and varying kinds of apartments in private houses. Things had little improved by 1807 when an unknown visitor to the spa wrote in her diary:

> There are three houses of entertainment for board and lodging namely Sinkers' Hotel where you are found breakfast, lunch, dinner, tea and supper for five shillings a day, exclusive of what you drink, and your bed. Secondly Smith's Bath Hotel and Mrs Shaw at The Bowling Green Inn. The last two are more humble in their charge, their fare and their houses, you can mix at either of them although in private lodgings.

Once the other saline wells were found, however, improvements went ahead quickly. New hotels were opened both in the old village and the New Town, while more and more houses were built to provide furnished accommodation for families staying for the season. Many of these provided 'lodgings that were fashionable enough and dear enough, but rather limited in point of space and convenience' according to Charles Dickens in *Dombey and Son*. He may have been drawing on his own observations as a visitor to the spa when he described the room in which the 'Honourable Mrs Skewton being in bed, had her feet in the window and her head in the fireplace . . .'.

The first of the new hotels, *The Bedford Hotel*, was built in the centre of Union Parade and opened under the directions of Mr. and Mrs. Williams in 1811. Its 50 bedrooms were rarely unoccupied even if its popularity later declined because of competition from *The Regent Hotel* opposite. *The Bedford Hotel*, like all other hotels in the town had extensive mews for horses and carriages, especially horses, for while wives and daughters were engaged in the round of social activities which convention demanded, husbands and brothers could go hunting.

Local newspapers, first *The Warwick Advertiser* and from August 1828 *The Leamington Spa Courier*, published lists of visitors arriving or departing, these lists later being called 'fashionable movements'. Those in *The Advertiser* appeared only in the summer season, while *The Courier* provided information throughout the year. These columns, published every Saturday, read like combined editions of *Debrett's Peerage* and *Burke's Landed Gentry*. They were later joined by a weekly list printed by John Beck, well known for his guides to the town, so we now have a record of many of the people who came to the spa during the last century. The lists unfortunately did not always appear regularly, some of the largest hotels often being omitted for a week or longer when the management did not provide the information required by the press. Departures are not always recorded either, so that it is not possible to discover with accuracy how long some people stayed. Also the arrivals at the smaller hotels, lodgings and apartment houses, as well as private houses, are not often given, so some important visitors' names were not recorded. It is clear, however, that during the middle of the last century the spa was very popular with many of the wealthiest people in the country.

The position in the social hierarchy of each visitor on the lists was defined by where they stayed. *The Regent Hotel* always headed the list. Noblemen and their families, and people of wealth, social and political influence stayed there; batchelors, sportsmen, the 'gentlemen of fortune', rakes and mere businessmen went to *Copps' Royal Hotel*, *The Bedford*, *The Clarendon*, *The Blenheim* or some of the other hotels, inns and public houses in the town's less fashionable streets. Others took apartments and still more took furnished houses for the season. All the hotels hoped to appear rather more prosperous and important than they really were. Bisset wrote in his *Descriptive Guide* published in 1816:

> Here hundreds vie with anxious emulation,
> To render strangers kind accommodation!
> Of single lodgings many may be found,
> At ten and sixpence, or, at most a pound;
> Or from THREE POUNDS TO TEN, they may command
> Whole HOUSES! furnish'd; most superbly grand!

In 1818 Moncrieff's *Guide* listed six hotels, only one of which, *The Bedford*, was north of the river, three boarding houses and six public houses. By the late 1820s the number had already doubled and between 1816 and 1836 there were 60 new inns in the town, so that eventually there were so many hotels and boarding houses that guidebooks mentioned only the most important. Not all this plentiful accommodation was fully used, however.

Almost twenty years earlier R. S. Surtees dared refer to this problem and caused a great stir. He reported in *The New Sporting Magazine* in the spring of 1824 that the Warwickshire Hounds had visited Leamington for a few days. Members of the hunt had stayed at *The Royal*, but having discovered that the port decanters held only three quarters of a bottle they moved to *The Bedford*. Surtees continued:

> Leamington though not over flowing with company boasts a fair sprinkling of sportsmen this year – more than perhaps any other quarter save Melton. Still the hotels are empty – or nearly so – in which state they are likely to continue. *The Regent*, which makes up about 150 beds, has about half-a-dozen single gentlemen in the house, and Copps' *Royal* – of equal size – not many more. As to *The Bedford* no-one should think of going there who has not a hardy constitution and a long purse, and the large hotels are too numerous and too empty to spare many guests for the small ones. Still we can hardly say we were sorry for the innkeepers, for there certainly never were a more rapacious set gathered together, as every person that has ever had any dealings with them can testify.

Most proprietors in the spa wisely ignored these remarks, but Mr. Gomm, landlord of *The Bedford Hotel*, claimed he had been libelled and sued for damages the unfortunate printer, Mr. Ackerman, since he could not sue Surtees himself. Originally he asked for £500 but later increased his claim to £1,000. Gomm denied making extravagant charges, rapacious dealings or misconduct, claiming good name and credit in the county. The jury eventually found in his favour, but feeling no real harm had come to his reputation assessed the damages at only a farthing.

There is no doubt that some charges were high. Francis Smith, writing in 1831, quotes furnished houses as costing five to ten guineas a week, while in 1842 Dr. Granville mentions still higher prices, stating that charges were two to three guineas for two rooms and eight to ten for a first floor in the best position, servants, table and bed linen often being an extra charge. 'Everything in fact is extravagantly dear in Leamington', he claimed. Other sources, however, at the same date, stated that two rooms in a decent area could be had for 12s. a week and cooking without extra charge, or for 20-30s. in the best parts. Competition, it was claimed, kept charges low.

In spite of these problems speculators were still willing to risk their capital in providing even more new hotels. A number of quite large hotels appeared both in the New Town and south of the river. Some never managed to attract enough custom to prevent their owners from losing money, having problems from the outset.

The chief of the large hotels after *The Bedford* and *The Regent* was *Copps' Royal Hotel* (which had no connection at all with the Royal Family). Thomas Michael Copps arrived from Cheltenham in 1814 and took over *The Dog Inn*, formerly *The Old Greyhound*, from Mr. Sinker. Soon afterwards he purchased the adjacent *Balcony Boarding House*, originally Mr. Palmer's house, built in 1810. Both stood at the High Street end of Clemens Street. The boarding house was renamed *Copps' Royal Hotel*.

Business flourished and in 1826 Copps decided to rebuild. The foundation stone of the new *Copps' Royal Hotel* was laid on 13 November 1826 by his daughter, Maria, 'supported by several of her young female friends, and many other persons of the highest respectability in the town and neighbourhood'. The new hotel was built on the corner of High Street and Clemens Street, providing a High Street frontage of 155 ft. including the portion of Sinker's hotel allowed to remain; the site is now covered by one end of the existing railway bridge. P. F. Robinson designed a building in the Greek Revival style, stuccoed, with an ornamented balcony running its length, two wings embellished with Corinthian pilasters and a portico supported by four Doric pillars. It had 100 beds, a dining-room capable of accommodating 150 persons 'with ease' and a public drawing-room of the same size. The decoration was lavish. Stabling was provided for 50 horses and 40 carriages. At the housewarming dinner on 21 June 1827, 250 patrons sat down, under the chairmanship of Mr. John Tomes.

Dr. Granville stayed at the hotel for a short time and praised it lavishly in his *Spas of England*. He was impressed by all its arrangements and compared it favourably to 'the tip-top emporiums of fashion – The Imperial, The Clarendon and Lansdowne hotels; or even The Regent', all of which were more expensive. *The Regent* was the only other hotel in the town to provide a *table d'hôte*.

> The principal part of the establishment is its large dining-room, in which nearly all the inmates assemble to a copious breakfast, with every morning luxury; and again at a table-d'hôte dinner presided over by one of the senior dwellers in the house. The company then retires to the withdrawing room for the evening where cards, music and conversation are introduced to enliven and cheat the duller hours of a Spa residence. I met with many select and agreeable persons at these convivial meetings; and were I to take up my abode for a time as a visitor to Leamington, rather than be bored with expensive lodgings and housekeeping, I should settle in this very house and enjoy its public dinners. The most amusing part of this is the mutual small-talk, and scandal, which every guest at the table brings, so situated, a newcomer at Leamington need not remain longer than three days a stranger to the 'low and high doings' of the place.

Perhaps Granville was not very observant, or was encouraged not to be, for when he visited *The Royal* the proprietor was on the verge of bankruptcy. On 13 February 1841 an advert in *The Leamington Spa Courier* announced that the trustees of the late Thomas Tidmas were going to sell the hotel, so Copps had been forced to mortgage or sell the property, if, indeed, he had ever owned it. The hotel remained empty thereafter until its demolition in 1847. The following week it was announced that Copps' assets, which included a farm at Princethorpe as well as the contents of the hotel, were frozen subject to sale by trustees. He must have reached some arrangement with his creditors, for in August Copps opened *The Victoria Hotel*, in Lansdowne Crescent. This building is Victoria House, now used as the Masonic Rooms. Nevertheless Copps' problems continued. His farmstock was sold in September, and in February 1842 the contents of the new hotel were put up for sale. The hotelier seems to have left Leamington after this as he died in Guernsey in 1849, aged 70.

The Royal had a comparatively short life, a reflection of the difficulty in attracting wealthy custom as the town south of the river fell out of fashion. But as the hotel opened Leamington was feeling the effects of competition from other Midland spas, such as Malvern, and visitors sometimes wished to spend a little time in each place. In 1829 Copps was advertising a new coach running from his hotel direct to Worcester and Malvern three days a week.

Other hotels in the old village catered for a different class of customer. Also in 1827 J. H. Roby of *The Gloucester* hotel and commercial inn announced the enlargement of his premises by the addition of the adjoining house, and advertised to attract 'Commercial Gentlemen and their families'. The hotel had wine and coffee rooms, London and provincial

37. *The Manor House Hotel*, 1905.

38. *The Clarendon Hotel* and Christchurch, 1919.

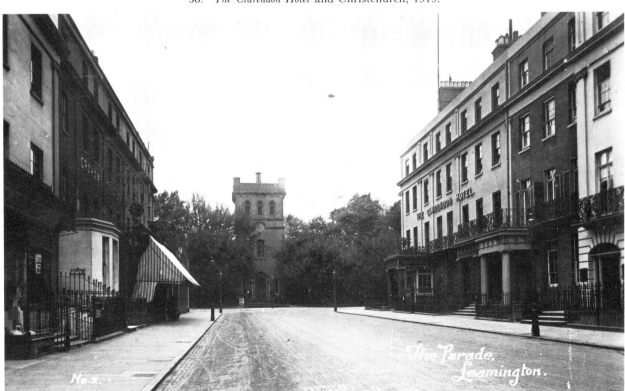

newspapers daily, and a coach left it each afternoon for Birmingham in time to catch coaches for Dudley, Stourbridge and Wolverhampton.

Leamington's oldest hotel, which finally succumbed to pressures for demolition and redevelopment about 1956, was *The Bath Hotel*. Built by William Abbotts in 1786, it passed to his daughter, Mrs. William Smith, after his death in 1805. It was enlarged and spacious mews were built at the rear. Mrs. Smith was widowed, married a man named Potterton, and finally disposed of the property to her son-in-law John Russell, then town surveyor, in 1820. A 'house warming dinner' to celebrate the new management was held on 4 May 1820 and the Russell family retained control of the hotel for many years, certainly until 1852. It remained in business long after the adjoining baths had disappeared, but before its demolition had become a public house.

Next in importance was probably *The Crown Hotel*, situated beside the turnpike road, later known as the High Street. Originally the building was the vicarage; built about 1808 for Rev. Wise, it replaced an earlier vicarage in Church Street. Joseph Stanley bought it and converted it into an inn in 1815. The building still survives, though its fortunes have somewhat declined since then. The front was remodelled in 1833 and has remained almost unaltered; it had two wings and a central portico to give importance.

Other hotels and inns in the neighbourhood included *The Blenheim Hotel* in Clemens Street. When this building opened as *The Oxford Hotel*, the street was one of the most fashionable in the spa. In 1822 the Duke of Marlborough stayed there, and Mr. Rackstrow, the proprietor, altered the premises and renamed them *The Blenheim*. He sold the business in 1830 to a Mr. Hughes, who renamed it *The Stoneleigh Arms*; the present *Stoneleigh Arms* was the taproom of the hotel, the rest being converted into houses and afterwards shops. Probett's *Orange Hotel* was also in Clemens Street and at a little distance in Brunswick Street was *The Castle Hotel*, both surviving towards the end of the last century.

The only old-established hotel in the old village is *The Manor House*, first used as a hotel in 1847 and opened by Isaac Curtis who had kept Wise's Baths. After a few years the hotel became a school, then it reopened as a hotel. Mrs. Wise disposed of it to Monsieur Duret and he to Mr. Percival, who sold it in 1855 to Mr. Lamplough. The hotel then had a succession of owners, including a local syndicate under Alderman K. R. England. Although named the *Manor House* the building was never the village's manor-house, but the Wise family home. Very little of the original building remains visible from outside the present one, and some years ago a block of flats, known as Manor Court, was built on part of the garden.

The original importance of these hotels near the turnpike road can be seen from the fact that at the height of the coaching era no fewer than 20 long-distance coaches left them every day. In addition there were coaches to all local towns either daily or several times a week, and much more frequently to Warwick or Coventry. In the early 1820s, for example, The Crown Prince set off daily for London from *Copps' Royal Hotel* at 7.15 in the morning, arriving at 9 p.m. the same day. At 6.30 a.m. a coach left the same hotel to allow businessmen to be in Birmingham at 9.30, and a second coach left for the same town at 3 p.m. A few years later Copps advertised a new coach leaving at 6.30 a.m. three times a week for Bath via Stratford-upon-Avon and Cheltenham. It made the return journey the following day. The Tally Ho left *The Bath Hotel* three times a week for Cambridge and another coach left there daily just after noon for London via Coventry, arriving at 7 a.m. next morning. Other coaches went from this hotel to Coventry, Leicester, Derby, Nottingham, Manchester, Liverpool, Shrewsbury, Chester and Holyhead. North of the river the Nimrod left daily for London and the Imperial for Cheltenham from *The Bedford Hotel* for some years after its opening in 1811.

In June 1837 Birmingham was linked to Liverpool and Manchester by railway, and in

"THE LANSDOWNE,"

31 THE PARADE & 61 WARWICK STREET.

31 THE PARADE & 61 WARWICK STREET.

LEAMINGTON SPA.

39. *The Lansdowne Hotel*, now demolished. A replica-fronted store occupies the spot.

40. Euston Place about 1900. This photograph by 'J. V.', entitled 'Euston Hotel and Place', shows the hotel at 3 Euston Place which in 1900 was run by Mr. and Miss Eggington. The terrace still stands although altered at ground-floor level. Many of the fine trees in both Euston Place and the Jephson Gardens, in the foreground, a feature of the town at this period, have now disappeared.

the following year to London via Coventry and Rugby. Coaches then ran from Leamington to connect with the railway system at convenient places; there were six coaches a day from *The Bath Hotel* to Birmingham and two to Weedon for this purpose. Coach services also continued to places such as Cheltenham, Bath, Oxford and Cambridge which were not then served by railways. The railway reached Milverton on the outskirts of Leamington in 1844 and this killed the coach trade. The decline of coaching was probably also an important factor in the decline of the inns and hotels of this part of town.

To maintain the numerous coaches, commercial and private, used in the locality the services of coachbuilders were needed. In the late 1820s there were four in the town: Mr. Reeves in Church Street, Mr. Mash in Regent Street, Mr. Taylor in Regent Grove and Mr. Deeley in Clarendon Street. In 1832 another competitor arrived; Francis Mulliner of Northampton bought Radford Cottage and set up in business. His firm later became famous for coach-built automobiles, such as the Rolls Royce, in the early years of this century. A few years later Michael Copps was also advertising as a coachbuilder, probably maintaining the coaches of the patrons of his hotel. By 1900 there were nine coachbuilders in the spa.

The Bedford and *The Regent* were not the only hotels north of the river. There were also *The Golden Lion*, open in 1810, and *The Angel*, open in 1814, both in Regent Street. The latter was said to have stabling for 100 horses, and hounds also. *The Warwick Arms*, also in Regent Street, was a long established family and commercial inn which retained its name until 1985.

As the town expanded north of Regent Street three other large hotels opened almost simultaneously, forming part of the terrace on the east side of Upper Union Parade. *The Clarendon* lasted longest, opening in 1830 and closing only in 1984. This hotel was purpose-built. Its façade has retained much of its original appearance, including its entrance portico. The winding oak staircase leading to the elegant first-floor rooms still survives, but the interior was greatly modified when a new wing was added behind the original hotel in the late 19th century. Charles Cox Hughes, who took over in 1850, extended the already ample mews accommodation for horses and coaches for the use of both visitors and residents of the town, and used his farm outside the town for training and grazing for 'gentlemen's hunters'.

The other two hotels opened in 1834. Halfway down the terrace was *The Imperial Hotel*. It was closed by 1850 and converted into shops. They, and almost all the rest of the terrace, were demolished and rebuilt in the 1970s. On the corner of the Upper Parade and Warwick Street, at the other end of the terrace to *The Clarendon*, was *The Lansdowne Hotel*. It was not very successful, and although in the early 1850s some of its rooms were being used by the newly formed Leamington Hunt Club, after a comparatively short time it was converted into private houses, and later these became shops. Replica buildings now stand on the site.

Competing with these large hotels and Copps' short-lived *Victoria Hotel* were numerous small family hotels, inns, of which there were as many as 90 in the 1890s, boarding-houses and apartments whose names abound in the advertisement columns of *The Courier* and local directories. Many were run by the wives of the town's professional and business men. A good number opened and closed rapidly because of financial problems, while of the hotels the only survivors from the early days of the spa are *The Regent Hotel* and *The Manor House Hotel*.

Chapter Twelve

Medical Men, Medical Matters

In a spa town where people came for the benefit of their health, doctors were naturally important people. Leamington had many doctors, but three were outstanding as its leading practitioners in the 19th century: Dr. Amos Middleton, Dr. Hitchman and Dr. Jephson. Middleton died in 1847, Hitchman in 1867 and Jephson in 1878, but during their lifetimes they worked together and were among the first medical staff at the Warneford Hospital when it opened.

From the spa's earliest days doctors valued the mineral waters for the treatment of diseases. Many of them analysed the waters as accurately as they could according to the scientific knowledge of the period, but few prescribed practical methods of treatment using them. Analyses ranging from simple leaflets to complicated scientific and medical tomes were published by the following, all doctors: Guidott (1691), Short (1740), Rutty (1757), Russell (1765), Allen (1788), Lambe (1794), Middleton (1806), Saunders (1810), Winthrop (1810) and Loudon (1816). Some of the later authors were local medical men, mainly from Warwick, with a vested interest in encouraging visitors to come to the spa; Dr. Middleton was one of these. The general rules he laid down for taking the waters, fully set out in the third edition of his *Analysis of the Mineral Waters* published after he had moved to the town from Warwick, was the first such guide. The type of treatment he specified remained standard until the arrival of Dr. Jephson.

Middleton was associated with the the earliest development of the New Town. He was among the Warwick businessmen who took shares to build the first terrace of houses in Union Parade in 1810, and he drew the second house in the ballot, now 100 Parade. Like the other houses in the terrace it was let to visitors for the season. With his other share in the Leamington Building Society he was involved in the building of *The Bedford Hotel*. Middleton also became one of the original shareholders of the Upper Assembly Rooms, opened in 1812, and was therefore partly responsible for financing the erection of the first public building north of the river. Later he bought other plots from Mr. Greatheed and Mr. Tomes in Bedford Street, on one part of which he built his home, Belsay House. He was the grandson of Sir John Middleton of Belsay Castle, Northumberland, which explains the choice of name. The description of this house when it was put up for sale in 1829 gives some idea of the scale on which a prosperous doctor might live. It had a large dining-room and drawing-room, a library, nine bedrooms, servants' hall, kitchen and brewhouse, stables, a double coach-house, hothouse with grapes, and almost an acre of garden planted with fruit trees. It was then rented out for £150 a year. A printing-works now stands on part of the site.

As a resident he practised medicine in the town until his death in 1847 and took a great interest in many of the town's activities. At the same time he became involved in the work of the 'Charitable Institution' founded in 1806 by Benjamin Satchwell to provide free baths for the poor. Up to 2,000 of such baths were provided before Satchwell died in 1815. In 1825 this institution was combined with the hospital and public dispensary in Regent Street, the president of the dispensary in 1829 being the Hon. Charles Bertie Percy of Guy's Cliffe House.

The general hospital and dispensary was a charity founded to give medical advice to those too poor to pay for it, and to provide home visits when the patient was unable to attend the dispensary. There was also a small hospital for in-patients, under the distinguished patronage of H.R.H. the Princess Augusta and H.R.H. the Duchess of Gloucester. Raising funds, however, was always a problem. In 1827, for example, average annual income was estimated at £150 while expenditure was £300-400 and expected to rise as more poor people needed help. The charity was dependent on contributions from the affluent who in return were allowed to nominate individuals for treatment, especially as in-patients. There were problems as a result in 1831 when the parish committee objected to poor persons from outside Leamington being admitted. The original premises of the free hospital stood near the south-west corner of Regent Street and Bedford Street, now nos. 62 and 64 Regent Street; the dispensary was at no. 62. They were next door to Dr. Middleton's house; the Doctor had built them, and rented them to the charity for £62 10s. a year.

When, in 1831, it was evident that the hospital was too small to cope with the increasing numbers of poor patients a committee was formed to consider building a larger one. One member of the committee, and a frequent visitor to the town, was the Rev. Samuel Warneford, a doctor of medicine who was then rector of Bourton-on-the-Hill in Gloucestershire. The new hospital fund was started with his donation of £1,500, £500 from his sister and £1,000 from residents in the spa. An acre was purchased from the Earl of Aylesford on the outskirts of the village beside the Radford road, still part of the hospital site. The foundation stone was laid ceremoniously by the Hon. Bertie Percy on 10 April 1832. The buildings, first named The Warwickshire General Bathing Institution and Leamington Hospital, had 50 beds. The final cost was £4,220, more than half of which was provided by the Rev. Warneford, since he and his sister gave another 1,000 guineas in June 1832 on condition that five beds remained in their family's gift forever. Warneford had married a wealthy woman who had died young. Being childless he gave nearly £200,000 to charities during his lifetime. When he died aged 92 in 1855 he bequeathed a further £10,000 for the work of the hospital, which was subsequently renamed The Warneford Hospital in recognition of his generosity.

In 1838 two upper wards of the original building were finally furnished and opened thanks to the generosity of Dr. Jephson who gave £1,000 for the purpose, and one is still known as the Jephson Ward. In 1862 a sanatorium was added, in 1866 a chapel paid for by a bequest from Mr. Oldham of Southam, and there have been extensions and improvements at intervals ever since, including the Victoria Wing, built to commemorate the Queen's Jubilee. Funds were also raised by collecting from visitors to the hotels, pump rooms, reading rooms and libraries, and by annual balls to provide money to support poor patients needing medical attention. Patients were not required to make weekly payments after 1837 except in the case of those brought in after accidents caused by their reckless or improper driving (of horse-drawn vehicles, naturally). By the mid 19th century the hospital was trying to cope with 600 or more in-patients every year and over 100 out-patients, while about 900 free baths were given.

Dr. Middleton was the first physician at the hospital until 1844 when he retired at the age of 65. The first surgeons were Mr. Franklin and Dr. Jephson. In 1832 Dr. Hitchman became a surgeon there and remained one until his death. The first house surgeon, Mr. Hulbert, was at the hospital from 1837-41.

Dr. John Hitchman was born in Chipping Norton in 1805, started his training as an assistant to a Banbury surgeon and came to Leamington in 1840. He set up practice in Clemens Street, where he lived until about 1843; he then moved to High Street and later to Upper Union Parade. He was both colleague and friend to Jephson and Middleton, and like Jephson was elected one of the members of the Local Board of Health set up in 1852. He started the Labourers' Fund in 1843 to give work to the unemployed in the spa. Workmen paid from it assisted in laying out the Jephson Gardens and planted many avenues of trees

41.   The Warneford Hospital, opened in 1832. The building forms the central block of the present hospital.

in a scheme, which he also initiated, to beautify the town. He was also a moving force behind the creation of the first of the two new cemeteries in the Whitnash road.

Hitchman was a firm believer in hydropathic treatment. In 1863, while he was a member, the Local Board spent £8,000 on improvements to the Royal Pump Rooms which they had recently purchased. He erected The Arboretum on the Tachbrook road for hydropathic medicine. The house, standing in 40 acres of grounds, provided 40 rooms for the use of patients. He ran this institution until his death, after which it was taken over by Dr. Mabberley and then by Dr. Owen. Some land was sold for building, but the rest was acquired by The Midland Counties Home for Incurables in 1955, and a new wing and chapel added.

In 1869, two years after his death, a committee presided over by Dr. Jephson decided to erect a memorial fountain. A design by Mr. Cundall was chosen and it was put up in the Jephson Gardens opposite the Pump Rooms on the site once occupied by Strawberry Cottage.

It was imperative for the town's prosperity that it should not become known as an unhealthy place to live. As the 1850 *Public Health Report* put it:

> Leamington is in a great degree supported by a class of persons who live upon their private fortunes and seek the place either for health, recreation or comfort. Health and cleanliness are the staple commodities which Leamington has to sell; and should a fatal epidemic break out in the inferior parts of the town, and be proved as it undoubtedly would, to be caused or aggravated by their filthy condition, the injury to the place would be considerable and lasting.

Parliament was concerned about the spread of cholera and in 1848 passed the Nuisances

Removal and Diseases Prevention Act. Action was taken under the act, for it was impossible for the richer residents and visitors to ignore the appalling slum conditions of parts of the town. A salaried Nuisances Officer was appointed, who reported in June 1849.

This action was too little, too late, for cholera appeared in the late summer of 1849. *The Times* reported that it had broken out earlier in the year, but this was hotly denied – the outbreak had been among canal boatmen at Offchurch, several miles away. The Warwick Poor Law Union nevertheless became the third worst centre of the disease during the epidemic of 1849-50, the worst being Coventry, where 202 of the total of 293 deaths occurred. In Leamington a deliberate effort was made to conceal the facts and the disease was only acknowledged if it proved fatal; many of the cases of epidemic diarrhoea which scourged the town at the same time – almost 1,000 cases were discovered in 15 days – must have been cholera. The Union records gave four deaths as being due to cholera and four due to diarrhoea.

At least one cholera death appears to have been concealed in Leamington before the epidemic became obvious, perhaps because the improvement commissioners and local doctors doubted it was cholera, or more likely because they wished to protect the town's reputation. Among them was Dr. Hitchman, one of the first in the town to demand a better water supply and sewage system and to press for the adoption of the Public Health Act of 1848. In August 1849 a case of cholera was reported in Radford Semele, midway between Offchurch and Leamington, followed on 8 September by another in Milverton. At this point the Poor Law Guardians recorded in their minute book that cholera had broken out in several places in the Union and they felt bound to enforce the Nuisances Removal Act vigorously. No public announcement was made and *The Courier* for 22 September assured its readers that cholera had not reached the town. A few days later the London *Daily News* reported it had and, although the following Saturday *The Courier* claimed this report had been fabricated by jealous rivals, by the following week it was useless to deny the presence of the disease in the town. But at no time did the paper admit that cholera deaths had occurred; instead it stressed the comparative healthiness of Leamington, which proved that 'there is no town in the kingdom which less requires extraordinary public sanitary reform than Leamington'. The paper ignored the posters which the Guardians had put up all over the town advising on measures which might halt the spread of cholera, although it did report Dr. Hitchman's complaint that the posters would induce alarm among the public.

The first recorded cholera death in Leamington actually occurred as early as 26 August. The victim, John Cullis, was a member of the improvement commission for the town and died soon after attending the town's horticultural fête. There were no other recorded cases of the disease until the middle of the next month, when a woman died at a public house, *The Greyhound*. Her death was first recorded by Dr. Watson, the medical officer, as diarrhoea although he later issued another death certificate changing the cause to cholera. Other deaths followed and by the end of the month the Poor Law Guardians ordered house-to-house visits to trace other cases, seven doctors were appointed to help Watson and a surgery was opened to dispense free medicine to the poor at any time of the day or night.

By the end of September 1849 the Guardians had discovered 'an unusual prevalence of disorders of the bowels, attended with diarrhoea, vomiting and cramps, and other symptoms regarded as premonitory of cholera' and in three days their doctors found 337 cases of this type. They extended the search by another week and urged the Leamington town improvement commissioners to take steps to stop the spread of the disease. Instead of co-operating, however, the commissioners insisted there was no cholera in Leamington. At a meeting in the Town Hall on 2 October Dr. Hitchman led a vociferous minority who criticised the activities of the Guardians as unsettling the residents of the town. Hitchman claimed 'that he had not seen a single case of cholera in Leamington and he did not, for a moment, believe that such a case existed'. It was pointed out, however, that there had already been four deaths where cholera had been certified as the cause. Faced with such evidence the commissioners had to set up a Sanitary Committee to deal as well as they could with nuisances. From the middle of October no new cases of cholera in Leamington were recorded in the Guardians' minute book, although new cases of diarrhoea continued to be treated.

The epidemic focussed attention on the bad housing conditions of parts of the spa, and the public inquiry conducted by the General Board of Health under the Public Health Act of 1848 took place within a few weeks. Opposition to the appointment of a Local Board of Health in Leamington was so strong that not until 1852 was one established. In the interim the improvement commissioners spent very little on the proposed new water supply and sewage system, but the worst nuisances received attention and, in 1850-1, 3,059 of 4,072 cases of nuisance were removed. But some bad places, like Hill's buildings and streets in the neighbourhood of Springfield Street, still caused trouble in the next year or two; in Hill's buildings 23 houses shared two privies, neither of which had a drain.

The third of Leamington's trio of outstanding doctors was Henry Jephson. All that can be done here is to give a brief account of the doctor and his influence on the development of the spa. A more detailed picture can be found in *Dr. Jephson of Leamington Spa*, a biography by the late Eric Baxter published in 1980, the first comprehensive study of the man to whom Leamington owed so much of its reputation. Thanks to Mr. Baxter's patient and time-consuming research it is possible to follow in detail the career of the strict but kindly doctor.

Jephson, born in 1798 at Sutton-in-Ashfield in Nottinghamshire, was apprenticed for five years to an apothecary in Mansfield and came to Leamington in 1818 as an assistant to Mr. Charles Chambers. Chambers was already well-known in the town as a surgeon, and was one of the 15 local people honoured at the planting of oaks in the Jephson Gardens in 1848. He was born in 1784, the grandson of the landowner and gentleman-architect Sanderson Miller, an early expert on the 'Gothick' style. Having trained as a surgeon in London, Chambers entered the navy in 1805. When he came to Leamington about 1817 he soon established a large, influential practice as one of the town's first three surgeons.

Jephson left him in 1822 in order to be admitted as a Licentiate of the Society of Apothecaries, which necessitated further study and six months in a hospital to get the experience to qualify. After six months at the Middlesex Hospital in London, under Dr. MacMichael, he undertook a further year's training under Mr. Brodie, a surgeon. In May 1823 Jephson was granted the Licentiate certificate and returned to Leamington licensed to practise medicine on his own account as a surgeon-apothecary. There he rejoined Mr. Chambers as a partner. He quickly established a great reputation: Bertie Greatheed wrote in his journal in December 1825 that a friend 'had returned from Leamington where, like all the world, she had been consulting Jephson'. He and Chambers were appointed parish surgeons, treating paupers unable to pay in the usual way. Chambers had also in 1823 become one of the surgeons serving the Leamington Charitable Institution, with its dispensary and free medical attention for the poor, and Jephson also became involved in the work. In 1826 he was one of the first surgeons to the enlarged hospital, later to become the Warneford Hospital. He then lived at 11 Union Parade, in the best part of town.

On 21 February 1824 Jephson married Ann Eliza Geldart, whom he had first met when she came to consult Mr. Chambers while visiting the spa. She was five years his senior. Her father, the Rev. James Geldart, was the fairly wealthy rector of a number of Yorkshire parishes. Their only child, a boy born at the end of 1828, died at the age of eight months.

In 1827 the partnership with Chambers was dissolved and the practice sold to Mr. Boulton and Mr. Pritchard. Chambers soon retired, probably due to ill health, while Jephson enrolled at the University of Glasgow to study for the degree of Doctor of Medicine. He was awarded it in 1828 and thus qualified to use the title physician. He then returned to Leamington, but after a short stay went to Cheltenham. Later in 1828 he came back, perhaps at the request of some of his former patients. By the end of that year he was established in a house in Upper Parade, rated at £40, among the highest in the town.

42.   Dr. Jephson. An engraving by C. L. Barber, 1839.

His practice flourished. While Mr. Greatheed suggested that many local people and visitors consulted him, little is known about his patients in these early years. The names of many famous patients whom he treated later, however, are known from diaries, memoirs, letters, occasional newspaper articles and from the list of patients and admirers who subscribed to his engraved portrait. Issued in 1842 as a mezzotint, the picture was copied from a portrait by Thomas Barber of Nottingham and sold in London, Nottingham and Hewett's Library in Leamington. The list included members of the nobility, politicians, clerics, business people and numerous Scotsmen, perhaps because of his connection with Glasgow University. Dr. Granville commented in 1842 that he seemed 'to have monopolized to himself the universal confidence of the patients, whether visiting temporarily or residing permanently in Leamington'. His rich patients came in increasing numbers, and although Jephson had settled in the spa at the right moment, when it was already growing in popularity, his presence did much to make the town well known.

Jephson was a firm believer in the value of the saline waters, allied to regular exercise and a strict diet. Proving his faith in the treatment, he subscribed £500 in 1861 in order to keep The Royal Pump Room open. When laying the foundation stone of the new double drinking fountain opened at the end of Bath Street in 1863 he said:

> I have witnessed in thousands of cases the good effects of the Leamington Saline Waters. It is a most wonderful natural medicine and I do hope that now we have the Pump Room restored the celebrity of the Spa waters will again be revived. It is the grandest medicine that can possibly be taken.

He allowed no deviation from the treatment and would often appear at unexpected times to see that his instructions were being followed. He was at the Pump Room every morning to make sure that his patients were taking the saline water, and would join them on their walks, often riding in his carriage while they walked alongside. Dr. Jephson possessed great tact in the management of patients, wrote Dr. Granville, continuing that he

> knows best when to assume the garb of severity, or even abruptness of manners, if their good requires it; for, at heart, there is not a kinder man; . . . In his attendance, when the case calls for such feelings, he is all kindness, softness and zeal. He will not waste time in repeating visits because desired to do so by some haughty aristocrat, or some whimsical lady of fashion, if he thinks it unnecessary. On the contrary, he will absent himself for a week from such patients. But where the case demands his vigilance and attention, he has been known to repeat his visits more than once daily, without the slightest reference to additional remuneration for his trouble.

Unlike many of his colleagues he could afford not to waste time with people not requiring essential medical treatment.

43. Beech Lawn, the residence of Dr. Jephson, about 1843.

As his prestige in the spa grew during the years 1828-48, so did his personal fortune. Jephson had already become a paving commissioner by 1826. This required him to own land of a yearly value of £60 or over, so by then his income was already substantial. By 1832 he was wealthy enough to build a grand new house, Beech Lawn, in Warwick Street; the architect was William Startin. His patient and friend, General Dyott, who was a frequent visitor, noted in his journal that he believed the doctor must have an income of £10,000 a year from his practice. According to Granville his income was over £20,000 in a 'good year'. Much of his money was invested in local businesses. He was one of the first directors of the Warwick and Leamington Banking Company, founded in 1834 and purchased by Lloyds Bank in 1866. At one time he owned 200 of the 10,000 shares representing the total capital of £250,000. In 1834 he helped to promote the Leamington Priors New Gas and Coke Company, to provide gas to the town, holding 30 shares at £20 each which he sold when he ceased to be a director in 1840. He also invested in the Warwick and Napton Canal in its early days, and in 1845 in the building of the Warwickshire and London Railway. After Jephson's death Beech Lawn was divided up. On two acres at one end the Victorian houses in Dale Street and Grove Street were built; the house became Beech Lawn School but was demolished before the last war. The County Fire Service Headquarters was built there in the 1960s.

These activities brought him personal gain, but he was equally active in charitable works. He provided coal for poor families, supported the Labourers' Fund to help the unemployed, was patron of concerts at the local Musical Festival and was President of the Mechanics' Institute. He was particularly concerned for poor clergy and governesses. He is reputed to have given any fee earned on a Sunday to his poorer patients. Jephson also realised the importance of improving the spa town to make it attractive to visitors and the wealthy people who came to it to consult him and other doctors. Thanks to his money an engineer was employed to examine the Leam in 1835 to try to remedy the inadequate sewage disposal system then in use. He also gave a substantial donation to improve the paving in Hamilton Terrace and Bath Street, and to enable the enlargement of the parish church to be continued.

In 1844 he was involved in the foundation of Leamington College, intended to rival Rugby School. When it opened in 1845 he was chairman of the Governors. Jephson's concern for the poor was shown by his association with Leamington's hospital from its earliest years until his death, subscribing considerable sums to it. He was also one of the first vice-presidents of the Leamington Provident Dispensary when it was formed in April 1869.

All his friends, and even his enemies, acknowledged that he was a hard worker. He rose at five, summer and winter, at seven o'clock opened his consulting-room at Beech Lawn to the poor, gratis, until nine, and then visited his patients in his phaeton.
By noon he was back home for two hours of consultations, during which a band sometimes played in the garden to entertain the patients waiting to see him. From two until six he was again visiting, and the evenings were free for entertaining and social life.

All this may have contributed to the ill health of later life, for he became blind in February 1848 and had to abandon his practice. His illness first became apparent during a long holiday in Scotland in 1847. After his retirement he went to Malvern for his health, but was back in Leamington before the end of the year. His investments allowed him to continue to live at Beech Lawn and to take an active part in the life of the town, contributing to good causes and remembering the poor. In 1852 when a Local Board of Health was at last set up to improve the sanitary conditions of the town, he was elected one of its first members and attended 23 meetings between September 1852 and June 1853. In 1854 his place was declared vacant due to non-attendance, however. Some years later he nominated four candidates for election to it, a surgeon, a chemist, grocer and a dealer in china, perhaps indicating his wide range of friendships in the town.

'The Father of Leamington' died on 14 May 1878 and was buried in the same grave as his wife at St James' church, Old Milverton. At his request it was a quiet private funeral, but though there was no public recognition then, two years later the church received two memorials to Jephson and his wife, a brass lectern given by his nephew James and a stained-glass window given by his nieces.

Chapter Thirteen

Rich Man, Poor Man

If the *Courier* reports are reliable, the rich and the poor, living side by side and yet widely separated by their differing lifestyles, almost ignored each other during the town's transformation into a fashionable spa. Such an impression is, of course, superficial, for the lives of both were intimately connected. From its earliest days, wealthier residents and visitors lived in the main streets, the squares and crescents of the New Town, occupying the Regency-style houses, while the developers saw nothing amiss in filling up any land left behind the large houses with sub-standard dwellings for those who crowded into the town looking for work.

The rich who came to take the waters were able to pursue health and entertainment thanks to inherited wealth, mostly land, and profits made in trade and industry from all kinds of investments and speculations – many had reaped notable benefits from the Napoleonic Wars. Business and leisure occupied them very agreeably, although the bank failure of 1837-8 caused irreparable financial damage to a good many well-off residents. Some of the town's most influential inhabitants were bankrupted and their comfortable lifestyle was lost forever.

A wide variety of pleasant occupations was available to affluent residents and visitors. Some have been mentioned in previous chapters – balls, the theatre, the libraries and reading-rooms, for example. Besides these there were riding-schools and stables where proprietors had gigs for hire 'on the usual terms at a minute's notice', and saddle horses for rent to ladies or gentlemen by the hour, day or month. Time could be filled with shopping, attending scientific or literary lectures, walking in the gardens or going to concerts. Some of these pleasures might be shared by the poor; they could walk in the Jephson Gardens on Sunday afternoons free of charge, for example, or they could go to the circus.

The circus was very popular from early days. Several companies stayed for long periods, some wintering in the spa. In 1833 the development of the Lower Parade was incomplete, especially on the west side facing Holly Walk, so for a season a tented circus occupied the site eventually taken by numbers 138-9, which was built on only in 1835. In 1835 Wombwell's Circus found a site on undeveloped land at the bottom of Milverton Hill and in 1836 the Victoria Circus enjoyed a successful season pitched at the Jephson Gardens end of Euston Place. Circuses were so popular that a permanent building, circular and with a distinctive domed roof, was put up at the end of the Victoria Colonnade, on the site of the present Loft Theatre. It opened in 1849 as Hegler's Equestrian Circus, afterwards being called The Circus, or Victoria Pavilion. By the 1880s, however, it had been turned to other purposes, including being used for Salvation Army meetings.

Permanent buildings were necessary for the animals, especially the elephants, and several buildings were erected for this purpose in the New Town. The elephant houses were situated in side streets at the northern end of the Parade. The only surviving example is now 38-40 Morrell Street. It was originally owned by a Mr. Lockhart, and the present owner still has the right, set out in his property deeds, to walk elephants down the Parade to the washing place on the south bank of the river near the present Priory Terrace. Access to the water is by a stone-paved slipway not far from Mill Street. The original washing place, also used for horses, was closer to the parish church in a spot now occupied by part of the post office, but in the 19th century it was resited at the request of the congregation because of disturbance during church services.

Ladies might have been amused or instructed by the curiosities and stuffed birds in Ogden's Museum at 30 Lower Parade, or found trifles of toys, jewellery, cutlery, glass, china and papier maché next door in Ellis' Bazaar. Gentlemen enjoyed dinners at the Oyster Club, founded in 1826 by Mr. Lubbock at *The Crown Hotel* in High Street, and they patronised other social clubs to be found in the town during the later 19th century. Pastimes for the sporting included real tennis at the indoor tennis club in Bedford Street, boating on the river or going to the races, occupations generally out of reach of the poor.

The 1841 census reveals something of the town's social structure. Out of the population of 12,812, 1,086 were persons of independent means, including army and navy officers on half pay, and 5,576 were persons engaged 'in trade'. There were 1,889 female servants, 553 male servants and 208 who were dressmakers, tailors, shoemakers, hairdressers, etc. The 311 in retail trade included 43 bakers and pastrycooks; there were 20 musicians and 12 booksellers, 185 coachmen and grooms, 67 publicans, 384 builders and 322 labourers.

The 1851 census provided a more detailed analysis of the town's population. That year there were 15,723 people living in 2,734 houses, an average of 5.75 persons per dwelling; at the time of the census a further 185 houses were unoccupied. By the 1850s the town had probably passed its peak as a popular spa, the number of visitors was decreasing and by 1861 the Royal Pump Rooms were no longer a source of profit to their owner. The 1851 census shows there were fewer people of independent means living in Leamington, but a growing number of professional and businessmen and their families. The two largest groups from the total of 329 of them were 70 teachers and tutors of both sexes and 54 clergymen. A number of the businessmen were probably engaged in 'the metal trade' in Birmingham and the Black Country, going to business by the new Great Western Railway line opened the previous year. These wealthier residents were served by the 43 per cent of the townsfolk who made a rather poor living by providing various services. The largest group were servants, as in 1841, of whom there were 3,029. There were also 1,320 dressmakers, tailors, shoemakers and laundry-workers, and 104 charladies.

Of the 995 engaged in retail trade, the largest group was 104 bakers. Miscellaneous services were provided by 693 persons, of whom 552 were labourers or railway workers. Building and allied trades accounted for 441, there were 150 coachbuilders, coachmen and grooms and 101 engaged in 'entertainment', including 32 Bath-chair attendants, 14 artists, six musicians, 30 teachers of riding, music and dancing, a tennis master and a cricketer. The most revealing figure is the 3,089 domestic workers. In this group there were 139 lodging-house or hotel-keepers, 570 male servants, 1,243 female servants, 469 maids of all work and 230 cooks; housekeepers and governesses accounted for 170, there were 104 nurses and 113 errand boys and girls. Almost all the servants lived-in at their place of employment. They earned £7.50 p.a., depending on their status. The census also shows that servants were not only from the immediate neighbourhood but came from all over the country.

In some cases wealthy families may have employed staff drawn from the area where they had once lived or owned property, so that large numbers of servants working for the occupants of some of the town's most impressive houses would have been far from their own birthplace. One of the larger terraced houses, 25 Clarendon Square, was occupied by Henry de Voeux, an Anglican clergyman born in Ireland, his wife Julia, who came from London, and their son and two daughters, all born in Binton in Staffordshire, where Henry had probably had a living. Their eight servants were a butler, born in Swinsford; a footman from Allesley, near Coventry; a cook from Norfolk; ladies' maids from Chalgrove in Oxfordshire and Belgium; a housemaid from Surrey; and two undermaids, one from Coventry and the other from Claverdon, near Warwick. Number 1 Newbold Terrace, facing the

44. Harrington House, Newbold Terrace. A house designed by Edward Welby Pugin, the son of
the more famous A. Welby Pugin. This house, built for Mr. Harrington, was one of the outstanding
Victorian buildings in the town. Demolished in 1970, the Royal Spa Centre, opened in 1972,
occupies the site.

Jephson Gardens, was occupied by five Scottish ladies, a baronet's widow, Agnes Murray
Carnagie, and her four unmarried daughters, all over 60, while Agnes was eighty-seven.
They had nine servants living in: a butler from Tewkesbury; a footman from Deddington
in Oxfordshire; a housekeeper from Northampton; ladies' maids from Warwick and
Westmorland; a cook from Staffordshire; a servant from Inchbrook; a kitchenmaid from
Herefordshire; and a maid from Cumberland.

There had always been some people with a sense of responsibility towards their poorer
neighbours. The first local 'friendly society' was set up in 1777 by Mr. Satchwell. Known
as The Fountain of Hospitality, it had 30 members paying regularly into its funds to provide
sickness benefit – there was, of course, no local hospital. Members received 3s. weekly during
illness after 12 months' membership, 5s. after two years and after 20 years' membership a
weekly allowance of 1s. for anyone over sixty.

During the 19th century charities were formed from time to time for specific purposes.
Dr. Hitchman's Labourers' Fund assisted unemployed men and provided some kind of work
for them; a charitable Lending Society, in Park Street, lent money to needy residents and
The Oddfellows established themselves in the town about 1836. Another friendly society,

the New Town Benefit Society, was established at *The Turf Inn* in Satchwell Street in 1823, and was followed by the United Tradesmen's Friendly Society in 1826. Similar societies were later set up in a number of inns, including *The Golden Lion*, *The Angel*, and *The Fox and Vivian*. Holy Trinity church had a coal club and a Benevolent Institution distributed food and clothing to the poor. The poorer inhabitants could not afford many new clothes; most of the back streets had old-clothes shops. Mrs. Lapworth ran one in Windsor Street, for example, which thrived and shortly after 1870 needed additional premises.

Many of the female servants were young, perhaps away from home for the first time, and at the mercy of employers who could dismiss them at a moment's notice. These girls were obviously in need of special attention, so in 1840 a servants' home was established in Park Street, with a management committee of 11 ladies intent on good works. According to a contemporary local guide:

> The varying state of the population of Leamington at times throws servants suddenly out of a place; young women, at such times, with, probably, no friends very near, or any asylum with its doors thrown open to give them protection against the various dangers to which they are exposed, stand in much need of a temporary home. In this establishment they find, not only employment of a light nature, such as needlework, but they are put into a condition, also, of having their characters improved by daily communication and conversation . . . It is also the intention to obtain such characters from the last place as shall guard the future mistress from the misrepresentation at times practised.

In 1840 the home dealt with 517 girls who registered there and provided 266 with places, while 119 girls found their own employment while living in the home for short periods.

Another charity ran the 'Penitentiary', in Wise Street, 'where females, to the number of 20, in a state of destitution are received and prepared to take once more a respectable station in society'. It was also stressed that

> for the most part, the poor find employment; and although want and distress will be found in every town which has a large population, yet the poor in Leamington are far better off, than in places dependent on manufactures, which one day give full employment, and shortly afterwards are unprosperous.

There were so many public houses and corner-shops selling beer in the town centre that supporters of the Temperance Movement took action to combat the menace. They held a meeting on 7 January 1836, in the Upper Assembly Rooms, to form a Temperance Society. There were weekly meetings in the former Baptist chapel in Guy Street, and in five years almost 700 members were recruited. In 1848 the society moved to premises south of the river, opening a Temperance Hall in the Apollo Rooms, but in 1860 they returned to the New Town, to Colley's Temperance Room in Warwick Street.

The two largest Temperance hotels in the town were *The Westminster* in Bath Street and *The Guernsey* in Church Street, where the first Band of Hope met in the late 1860s. For the rest of the century the Temperance Movement was active, but waxed and waned like the problem it was meant to counteract. At another level alternatives to alcohol were offered in tea and coffee rooms opened in Althorpe Street and Clemens Street, south of the river, and in Regent Street and South Parade in the New Town. One of the latter was The British Workman, opened in 1872. Its opening hours were from 5 a.m. to 10 p.m. Tea, coffee and cocoa were available at 1d. a cup; customers who brought jugs could be supplied by the pint at reduced prices: 1d. for coffee, 1½d. for cocoa and 2d. for tea. Milk, buns, sandwiches, ginger beer and lemonade could also be had, nothing costing more than 4d., and there were also rooms for reading and smoking. Payment could be made with special tokens 'good for one pennyworth of refreshments'. These Victorian tea and coffee rooms maintained their modest opposition to the public houses for many years. Even in the early 1900s, when the vicar of St Mark's was distressed at the tipsy inhabitants of his parish, he raised money to buy a coffee house near his church. It was called the Milverton Coffee House. Besides the usual refreshments there were recreational facilities and beds for homeless men. This coffee house survived until the 1930s, disappearing at the same time as the slum properties around it were demolished. The Stamford Gardens flats were built on the site.

The most intractable problem was bad housing, about which most charities could do nothing. The reports of the inspector of nuisances appointed by the Warwick Poor Law Union in 1849 and of the Public Health Inspector in 1850 revealed the shocking conditions of some of the streets and courts in both parts of the town and its general insanitary conditions. The northern part of Leamington, between Regent Street and Clarendon Square, built only 20 years previously, contained many of the town's best houses, but also many of its worst. The courts off Satchwell Street, for example, included in 1850 John's Court, built by John Toone, which had 16 one-bedroom houses and some stables. It was normally occupied by 85 people, three to seven a dwelling, but on occasion there were as many as 130 occupants. Another court nearby was described in 1847 by Dr. Watson, the medical officer for Leamington, in a report on nuisances which might cause contagious disease, as:

> a yard of twenty houses which are built in the smallest possible space, consisting of two rooms each eight foot square; and in the whole yard ninety-seven persons are living. In some of the houses there are as many as nine persons, including children, living in the same house, with one sleeping room only eight foot square. The centre of the yard is occupied by a large cesspit which constantly overflows and the water pumps are completely blocked up.

This report received wide publicity in the local newspapers, *The Courier* noting that the area had 'for many years been known as a sink-hole of crime and immorality'. Further inquiries undertaken by the local Police Committee revealed over a score of courts and yards which constituted a serious health risk. Little was done either by the improvement commissioners or the Local Board of Health to better the situation; the courts off Satchwell Street were not cleared away until the 1930s, for example.

Other parts of the town were in as bad condition. The Covent Garden Market was an interesting arrangement of shops and stalls around an open space. It was neglected, however; according to the Health Officer it was

> . . . a mere wooden shed, with an unpaved floor, no supply of water and very imperfect drainage. Opening from it, from Russell and Tavistock Streets, were certain long narrow alleys, unpaved and in a filthy state, without drainage and very damp.

There was a slaughterhouse and an open cesspit in the yard behind *The Prince of Wales* in Warwick Street, and other public houses were little better. Many properties in the town centre had pigsties behind them, usually in yards with privies or cesspits nearby, and often in close proximity to the pump supplying drinking water. Brook Street, built alongside the Bins Brook at the foot of Church Hill, was particularly unpleasant; in 1849 the stream ran at the foot of a steep incline behind the houses and received untreated sewage and all other kinds of waste from the ubiquitous pigsties and privies. In Priory Court, in the old village, 30 people living in seven houses shared a single privy. In Althorpe Street, now a modern factory estate, the disgusting state of the courts was directly attributable to the actions, or inactions, of the improvement commissioners themselves, who used one of the courts, lined by houses, to dump waste from cesspits waiting for disposal in the river or later on open land at Heathcote. Although the residents complained, it took a long time for the waste to be moved. Parts of Leamington in 1850 were the equal of the worst parts of the large industrial cities.

Whatever the poorer residents gained from the waters of Leamington Spa it was not efficient local government intent on cleaning-up the town's side streets and improving the housing conditions of the less wealthy. The main concern of most of the wealthier ratepayers, most of whom were also improvement commissioners, was to keep the rates down. Public health regulations were rarely enforced until an epidemic compelled action, and much of the food available, not only to the poor but to the wealthier residents and visitors, was prepared in premises so insanitary that it was more due to good luck than good management that more people did not suffer from fever and diarrhoea. Cholera lurked in the polluted mineral springs in which they bathed and the water that they drank, taken out of the Leam and untreated but for filtering out the larger particles.

Even the burial of the dead threatened the health of the living in 1850. The burial grounds were then almost all in the built-up area of the town and were very full. The cemetery adjoining All Saints' church received about 1,890 burials between May 1839 and December 1849. It was so crowded that at one point corpses were being placed four deep in each nine ft. deep grave, each burial receiving a temporary covering of earth until the grave was full. A new cemetery was laid out in Brunswick Street and consecrated on 10 March 1852, having two chapels designed by D. G. Squirhill, built by William Ballard and paid for by Matthew Wise. The entrance was between gate piers inscribed with texts specially chosen by the vicar, the Rev. Craig, and there was a 'quaint lodge near the gateway, which looks so picturesque from the highway'. Chapels and texts have long since disappeared and the cemetery has again been surrounded by residential buildings as Leamington steadily expanded between the wars.

Although the poorer people worked long hours for low pay to provide the services required by richer households, their lives were not all work and drudgery. There were sometimes holidays, for example, to celebrate special events such as the Queen's Jubilee. On such occasions they often saw important visitors. In 1886 the M.P. for Warwick and Leamington Spa was the Hon. W. A. Peel, Speaker of the House of Commons. He invited a group of distinguished Indian and Colonial personages to visit the town as they were in England preparing for the Jubilee celebrations to be held in 1887. His guests arrived by special train at the G.W.R. station on 28 July, carriages took them to their hotels, and those townsfolk lining the route saw the official representatives of Australia, Canada and New Zealand and also, according to Dudley, of '. . . other dependencies, together with dusky and turbanned potentates from Her Majesty's Asiatic dominions'.

The townspeople had a half-day's holiday and a special display of illuminations in the Jephson Gardens to celebrate the event. The Mayor gave a banquet for the visitors in the Town Hall, along with other entertainments which cost the ratepayers over £500 – at a time when most workers in the town would have considered a weekly wage of £1 to be real wealth. The guests saw Warwick, Kenilworth and Stratford-upon-Avon before returning to London, their visit being commemorated by the installation of a special stained-glass window in the Council Chamber of the Town Hall. But such red-letter days were infrequent relaxations for most of the townspeople.

Chapter Fourteen

Commercial Successes

In the early days of the spa the chief commercial ventures were hotels and boarding houses; there were few shops to serve the growing town. The majority of the 'working people' were employed as servants or in enterprises necessary to the maintenance of the houses of the richer residents and visitors, while others worked in Warwick where there were several cotton mills and a foundry.

The only cotton mill in Leamington, or more precisely near it in the adjacent parish of Milverton, was on the Warwick side of the River Avon near to Emscote. It opened in 1792 and closed at the end of the Napoleonic Wars, as did so many others. At one time it employed 50 hands plus a number of poor orphans from all over Warwickshire, and in its later years was owned by Benjamin Smart. In 1816, having found a mineral spring on his land in the centre of Leamington, Smart opened a bathhouse in Bath Street. The mill buildings, now known as Rock Mill, still stand at the end of Rock Mill Lane.

The Birmingham to Warwick canal finally opened in 1793, connecting the county town with the Stafford-Worcester canal, part of the canal system linking the Rivers Severn and Trent. Manufacturers in Warwick could now send their goods with ease all over the Midlands, while coal and iron goods could be brought from the Black Country more cheaply than ever before. Warwick's prosperity increased markedly and within a few years local industrialists were using their new wealth to invest in the new town of Leamington.

One of the earliest carriers on the canal was a certain Mr. Pickford. His boats worked from Birmingham to Leicester, using the Warwick and Napton canal, opened in 1800; the journey took five days. Although this seems a long way round, it was then the shortest route by canal between the two towns. From about 1814 goods could be sent by canal from Warwick and district to London, albeit by a roundabout route, as various independent canals joined to form the Grand Union. This process took many years; the Leamington section of the network was completed in 1799. The tonnage receipts show that large quantities of goods passed through Warwick and Leamington, necessitating the growth of wharfs along the canal banks, although there were few local factories in the early days to take advantage of the waterway. The peak year for the canal in Leamington was 1835, when the gross receipts were £198,000, much of the profit going to local shareholders.

During the period 1810-1835 there were few trades in the town apart from builders, furniture-makers, carriage-builders and those providing food, drink and clothing for both rich and poor. The workforce in 1833 included railway workers, navvies and at least six braziers and tinplate workers. There were five breweries, 36 builders and associated tradesmen, two ironfounders with showrooms on Upper Parade and South Parade, now Clarendon Avenue, and workshops in other parts of town, plus a few trunk-makers and some weavers in Clemens Street. Of course baths were made, generally the hip-bath type, both by Mr. Flavel and Thomas Oldham of the mill near the parish church. In South Parade the firm of Barwell & Co., Ironfounders and Brass Founders, ran a business in association with their foundry at Northampton, which produced kitchen stoves, grates, gates, railings, copper tanks, baths, and heating appliances with casings made to order.

Another important trade was clock and watchmaking. By 1833 there were several watchmakers spread around the town: John Eborall in Bedford Street; the Bright family, Edward and Henry, with premises in Charlotte Street and Lower Parade; and Edward

Court in Regent Street, not far from Mr. Covington who made artificial flowers. It is very likely that the watchmakers of Leamington also made parts for larger firms based in Coventry. Watchmakers were known in Clemens Street from the earliest days of the town's popularity as a spa, and in the Upper Parade and elsewhere for most of the 19th century.

Ironfounding was perhaps a more un-usual trade to find in a newly developing spa town. Apart from Barwell there were two others in 1833 living south of the river and probably working in foundries in the Clemens Street area, perhaps near the canal. William Carter had a shop in Upper Parade in 1833. He cast both iron and brass in his large foundry at Emscote on the Warwick side of the Avon. About 1849 he erected a steam-engine there and advertised that he made castings for rail-ways. Since the railway was then being extended from Milverton to Rugby he may have hoped to attract the trade of the railway company. Carter's business had been taken over by his son by 1852. Some of the street furniture made by Thomas Radclyffe in the Old Town Foundry in Clemens Street, started in the early 1850s, can still be seen in the older parts of town. He made all types of castings, including kitchen stoves. His foundry moved to the Old Warwick Road about 1884, being renamed The Imperial Foundry. It was subsequently taken over by Flavels.

William Flavel, oné of the first iron-founders in the town, would doubtless be proud to know that the firm he started has survived to the present day. He first advertised his Patent Kitchen Stove in 1829, although there is some doubt as to whether he actually took out a patent or not. Originally trading from Bath Street,

DEALER IN ARTIFICIAL FLOWERS AND OTHER
FANCY ARTICLES.

POTTER,

LATE

MRS. ALLAN,

LADIES'

STRAW, TUSCAN, AND CHIP HAT

MANUFACTURER,

TO THE

ROYAL FAMILY,

14, Clemens-street, Leamington.

The Ladies are most respectfully informed, that the usual display of Fashionable Tuscan, Whalebone, Dunstable, and Fancy Bonnets; also a good selection of real Brozzi Leghorns, Ostrich Feathers, Artificial Flowers, Ribbons, Trimmings, &c. are ready for inspection.

N. B. Leghorn and Straw Hats altered; also Ostrich Feathers, cleaned, dyed, and altered.

Entrance to the Show Rooms at the Side Door.

45.   An advertisement for a Leamington hatter.

by 1833 he was being described as a 'Kitchen Range Maker of Portland Terrace and Augusta Place'. The Flavel family originally came from Bilton, near Rugby, where William was born in 1777. His uncle, to whom he was later apprenticed, ran an 'iron warehouse and manufactory with supplies of gunpowder' in Coventry. As Leamington began to develop the family gave up both the Bilton and Coventry works and came to the spa, trading from premises opened in 1803 in Church Street.

About 1810 William Flavel opened new premises on the corner of Dormer Place. He was probably the first occupant of the building newly erected on the site by Isaac Wilkinson and now occupied by the National Westminster Bank. Wilkinson was almost certainly a member of the famous ironfounding family. He was a partner in a Birmingham bank and a treasurer of the Worcester Canal Company, from which he resigned in 1815 and came to live in Leamington. He had bought the largest block of building land sold by Mr. Greatheed in the Parade, at its southern end, paying £1,747 5s. for three plots totalling about 5,800 sq. yds.

Manning, in *Glimpses of Our Local Past*, described Flavel as 'a man of striking personality,' who possessed 'the happy combination of inventive genius and unusual mechanical capacity'. In 1815 he designed a Russian vapour bath for Major-General Sabloukoff, which the visitor declared was an improvement on the one in use in his own country. Not only did the Major-General, his family and suite stay the whole winter, but once it was fitted up for the use of visitors generally it attracted several other Russian families to the spa. In 1829 Flavel invented a revolutionary kitchen range. The original stoves were for solid fuel, the first gas stove being made by the company in the 1880s. A contemporary advertisement described it as

> the most ready means of performing in the best manner, either separately or at the same time, all the operations of cooking with only one fire, and that an open one, which may be of any size to suit the kitchen of the smallest cottage, or the largest mansion or hotel. . . . its arrangement is so simple, in every department of the culinary process, that servants cannot easily disorder or mismanage it.

Flavel's firm prospered and made good use of the canal to provide cheap transport for raw materials such as iron ore and coal and as a supply of water for steam-engines. In 1833 he built the Eagle Foundry on the south bank of the Napton canal. Part of the present Flavel works stands on the same site. The name of the foundry is preserved in nearby Eagle Street, the houses of which were built soon after the new works opened. An extensive range of castings was produced, much for domestic purposes. At the Great Exhibition of 1851 the firm won a medal, one of only 17 awarded among some 19,000 exhibitors, for its patent 'Kitchener Stove'. In 1857 it employed almost 100 people, and four years later the Eagle Foundry was described in the *Great Western Railway Illustrated Guide* as 'the largest manufactory of its kind in the world'. William Flavel died in 1844 and his son, Sidney, ran the firm until his death in 1892. Members of the family controlled it until the death of Percival, a great-grandson of William, in 1939. The company is now part of the Glynwed Group and manufactures gas cookers and other appliances.

The first gasworks in Leamington were erected in 1819 near the canal. They were a private venture, belonging to Mr. Thomas Roberts, a foundry owner in Warwick. Not everyone viewed the gasworks wholly favourably. '*Chemicus Junior*', of Gloucester Street, wrote to the *Warwick Advertiser* in June 1819 saying that he was worried in case the smell of the purification process discouraged visitors, although the proprietors had assured him that a new and less noisome process was to be used. In 1821 a prospectus was issued for lighting the streets of the old village from 'the south side of the canal bridge to the Old Well in one direction and from the west corner of Wise Street and Barford Buildings in the other'. A number of prominent businessmen agreed to pay from 5s. to £2 2s. a year to have the street outside their premises lit by a gas pillar.

In 1822 a new tariff was set out for the cost of supplying gas to the lamps. A single lamp burning all night for 313 days a year cost £4 4s., and larger burners cost as much as £10 10s. A charge of an extra sixth was made if gas was burnt on a Sunday. Payment was to be quarterly in advance, and if it were not received by 28 days after the date due the gas could be disconnected. Installation, both inside and outside the buildings, was to be done by Mr. Roberts' workmen at the customer's expense, and all fittings were to be supplied by him, presumably made at his iron foundry in Warwick.

To raise more capital, in April 1822 Roberts tried to sell ten £100 shares in the gasworks by auction at *The Crown Hotel*. The sale would appear not to have been a success, however, for on 9 June he advertised that he held all the shares in the Leamington Gas Company, and proposed to found a new gas company in which he would sell shares of £20 each. This company was obviously being formed to counter the Warwick Gas Company, which was supplying gas to the New Town. This firm set up 18 lamps along Union Parade in October 1823, supplied from its works in the Saltisford, Warwick, by a three-mile main along the Myton and Old Warwick roads, south of the Leam. It would seem Roberts was still short of money, for in February 1823 he announced that 'Books of Subscription are open for Shares . . .' in the 'Leamington Original Gas Works'. This establishment had 'no connection with any other concern' and he stressed the advantages of having the gasometer on the spot.

More land was acquired for the Leamington gasworks in 1823, but it slowly lost business to its more efficient rival. In August 1830, when 19 gas-lamps replaced the oil lamps in the parish church, the gas came from Warwick. Four years later the Leamington gasworks was reorganised as a new company called The Leamington Priors New Gas & Coke Company, the first meeting being held on 12 September 1834. This company was no more successful at first than its predecessor, however. For some reason the original six directors were disqualified and in March 1835 new directors replaced them. A Leamington Improvement and Lighting Act was then obtained. The new gas company in 1834 leased the gasworks to James, William and Henry Robinson. Their lease was renewed in 1848 and 1862, by when it had passed to the survivor of the lessees and his two sons. In 1838 a larger works was built on land in the Tachbrook Road area bought from Matthew Wise at a reputed cost of £40,000.

In 1864 the company and lessees decided to raise their charges. Protests from the townspeople followed and the local Board of Health considered the new price to be excessive. At a public meeting held at the town hall a plan was submitted by a gas engineer from London by which the Board could erect its own gasworks for an estimated cost of £30,000. In response the gas company asked Parliament for powers to improve their plant near the Tachbrook Road and to prevent any other company supplying gas to Leamington or any villages within a five mile radius of the town. The result was uproar. The inhabitants strongly opposed this plan, over 700 signing a petition against it. A Leamington ratepayers' association was formed to fight for 'cheap gas'. Legal action followed which cost the ratepayers nearly £3,000, but the Board lost the fight and an act was passed in March 1865. After the act was passed the company, feeling secure with its monopoly safe, reduced the price of gas.

The local Board of Health was dissatisfied, but did not use its power under the act to buy the existing street lamps. Moreover it discovered that the cost of erecting its own works as once planned would be closer to £60,000 than the original estimate. A sliding scale of charges was agreed with the company, and the following year the firm lowered the rate to those who had a meter installed. In 1877 a suggestion that the Board should build its own gasworks was considered but again set aside. The Town Council acquired powers to purchase the company under the 1895 Leamington Local Act, and made an unsuccessful attempt to do so in 1899. The firm operated until nationalised, along with the rest of the gas industry, after the last war. In the 1960s North Sea Gas reached the town and the town's gasworks were demolished and redeveloped. Only street names survive to show its location. A few old cast-iron lamps have been converted to electricity and fixed in the Pump Room Gardens and York Walk, beside the Leam, reminders of this Victorian enterprise.

A competitor of the gas company, the Midland Electric Light & Power Company which was the first electricity company, established their first works in Wise Street in 1887 and laid cables along the Parade at a reputed cost of £130,000. A considerable sum was spent in lighting the principal streets, but it was a commercial failure and the scheme was abandoned in 1893 in favour of gas lighting. By 1910, however, the *Abel Hayward Guide* could state that 'Leamington is one of the towns in England where electric light has been adopted with success as an indoor illuminant, a system of storage is in use at the works by means of which current is supplied for the whole of the twenty-four hours'. This storage was provided by a series of large batteries charged during the daytime working of the plant.

After the benefits gained through turnpike roads, the next real improvement in communications was the construction of the canal linking the spa by water to London, Birmingham and the rest of the Midlands. Visitors to Leamington still arrived either in their own carriages or by one of the many mail coaches, but the canal provided cheap goods transport. The new and rapidly developing railway system, however, largely replaced both road and water transport. The London to Birmingham railway opened in 1838, transporting passengers and goods between the two towns more quickly than by any other means; a mainline train leaving London at 8.45 a.m. could arrive at Coventry by 2.15 p.m. and reach Birmingham an hour later. The coach companies soon realised that their survival depended on co-operation with the railway operators, and began to run a regular service from Leamington to connect with the railway at Rugby. By 1840 only one coach ran daily from the town to London, although there were coaches running to other towns for some years.

In 1841 local businessmen proposed the construction of a branch line from Coventry to Leamington, and early in 1842 the plan was described at a public meeting in the Town Hall. The promoters pointed out that the scheme would produce good dividends for shareholders and the solicitor to the parish vestry, Mr. W. F. Patterson, supported it. Landowners affected by the proposed line, particularly those in the Kenilworth area, were concerned that it might injure their estates. A number of those opposed to the new railway formed a committee to fight it, which included Lord Aylesford and the Hon. Charles Bertie Percy. Their concerted action did not stop the railway, but it did secure payment of greater compensation than was usual for loss of land.

The necessary Act of Parliament was passed in July 1842. The line, with stations at Kenilworth and Milverton, was opened on 9 December 1844. It was single track, $8\frac{3}{4}$ miles long, and cost £175,000, rather more than the estimated £130,000. The track was doubled along part of the route in 1884 and along more in 1916. Contemporary accounts describe excited crowds arriving to see the first train, 'one of those grim green and yellow monsters', leave Coventry at 8.20 a.m. on its first 21-minute journey to Leamington over a route lined with sightseers. The successful event was celebrated that evening with banquets at *The Regent Hotel* in Leamington and *The King's Arms* in Kenilworth.

Newspapers recorded that about 2,500 passengers used the line during the first week. The first timetable listed six trains a day each way from Milverton to Coventry; only the first train from Milverton and the last from Coventry carried third-class passengers. On Sundays there were two trains. Fares were 2s. first class, 1s. 6d. second class and 9d. third, with reduced fares for day returns except for third-class passengers. Travellers could reach London in $4\frac{1}{2}$ hours from Milverton, via Coventry and Rugby.

The original terminus was almost mid-way between Warwick and Leamington; opposition from the principal landowners, including the Earl of Warwick, prevented it being sited nearer either town, although the inhabitants of Warwick had asked for a railway connection several years earlier. Prints published at the opening of the railway show a small building, with a booking office, water tower and a train shed to shelter waiting passengers. In 1846 the line was acquired by the London & North Western Railway to provide a quicker route to Rugby without taking passengers by way of their competitors' lines. The station at Milverton was enlarged and reopened in December 1850, and a branch line to Leamington and Rugby opened on 1 March 1851. Beck's *Guide* of 1852 said 'the waiting rooms are replete with every modern improvement that can increase the comfort of passengers and are elegantly furnished with ottomans, couches, etc.' The building was of brick with blue brick facings and Gloucestershire stone copings. It had an arrival shed so vehicles could pick up passengers in the dry, and extensive goods facilities. The station finally became little more than a halt on a branch-line with ever shrinking revenues; the line closed to passengers in January 1965 and the station buildings were demolished in 1968. Some of the buildings in the goods yard, however, have survived: one of the original goods sheds is hidden away behind a modern car-showroom and garage on the corner of Old Milverton Lane. Another surviving railway relic is a row of small terraced houses close to the station in Westgrove Terrace, built for railway workers. The line was reopened to passenger trains in 1977, first to Coventry and now it also provides a route from Paddington Station to the International Exhibition Centre near Birmingham.

Building the new line to Rugby involved extending the existing line from Milverton to Avenue Road, not far from the centre of Leamington. Here another station was built. A bridge was also needed over the junction of High Street and Clemens Street, and this required the demolition of two buildings both fairly recently built: Curtis' Original Baths, on the corner nearest the station, and *Copps' Royal Hotel*, opposite. The bridge, designed by R. B. Dockray, the resident engineer of the L.N.W.R., was a tube weighing 170 tons, composed of wooden members resembling an American lattice-bridge. It had the greatest span of any bridge of its kind in England when erected, and as such was of great interest to visitors after it was placed in position on Saturday 23 September 1850.

The basic construction was of two 150 ft. lattice girders running parallel to each other, clearing a span between buttresses of Derbyshire stone of 139 ft. 9 ins. The girders were composed of oak wallings at top, centre and bottom, running its length, linked by memel timbers crossing at an angle of 60 degrees. Transverse girders of wrought iron linked the two and carried the track. On top was a corrugated-iron roof. Straddling the tracks at each end were stone towers each decorated with a richly-carved scroll.

The bridge caused some trouble, however. Residents complained that the high iron roof threw a shadow on houses in the High Street, so it was removed. In 1861 the bridge had to be strengtened by placing iron pillars under it in the centre of the road, to reduce the unsupported span, and the next year it was replaced by a new iron bridge. Finally it was dismantled when the line to Rugby was closed in the late 1960s, leaving only the buttresses.

The Avenue Road Station was originally hardly more than a small hut standing to the east of the later station, not far from the existing subway under the track. From this small shelter Mr. Weston, the first stationmaster, issued tickets when the line to Rugby was opened in February 1851; there was little protection from the weather for passengers waiting for trains. In March 1860 a new station was opened, built to the designs of Mr. W. Baker, engineer to the railway company, in the Italianate style. The buildings were demolished in 1968 and the Regent Garage now stands on the site although part of the goods yard survives as a coal depot.

In 1852 a competitor appeared, the Oxford & Birmingham Junction Railway, linking the Great Western Railway at Oxford with Birmingham and forming an unbroken route to London by way of the G.W.R. through Oxford to Paddington. This line was later incorporated into the G.W.R. It was started in 1845, under the supervision of Isambard Kingdom Brunel, but financial problems delayed work for two years. One cause of the delay was difficulty in reaching an agreement with the L.N.W.R. to use part of their track which crossed the bridge over the High Street junction in Leamington. It proved impossible, so a second bridge was built alongside the first; although extensively altered and rebuilt, this is the bridge that survives today. Since the Birmingham to Oxford railway had to connect to the lines of rival companies using different gauges, it was laid to a dual gauge, to take trains of either the narrow gauge (4 ft. 8½ ins.) or the broad gauge (7 ft. 0¼ in.). On 1 May 1869 the G.W.R. ceased to run broad gauge trains from London to Birmingham, so the broad gauge rails were taken up north of Oxford.

The Leamington station on the Oxford to Birmingham Railway opened on 1 October

1852, having been built on the site of Eastnor Terrace. It was a typical Brunel design, with a glazed roof over the broad gauge track, the narrow gauge line having its narrower platforms to one side of the main station. The canopy roof was removed at the turn of the century and the platforms were demolished in September 1935 when the G.W.R. knocked down the old station and erected the present one. The new station took two years to build and opened in 1938.

By the early 1880s Leamington's population numbered 23,000 and Warwick's was nearly 12,000; for some years it had been obvious that an easy and cheap means of transport between the two towns was needed. As early as 1871 a committee had been formed to promote the laying of a tramway between them. The plan was approved by the Board of Health and the response of public meetings held in that year encouraged the promoters to issue a prospectus and a public appeal for local people to take up shares in the proposed tramway company. The public, however, hesitated over the scheme and it lapsed for five or six years.

In 1878 two local businessmen, Mr. James Richardson and Mr. Chadbourn, commissioned a survey of the proposed route and drafted a provisional order for the construction of the tramway, followed by an application to Parliament for approval. There was considerable local opposition, including objections from the Milverton Board of Health, which was responsible for the district between the two towns. Leamington Town Council met on 30 December 1878 'to consider the provisional order authorising the construction of tramways in Leamington, Milverton and Warwick', and after heated debate the tramway was accepted 'as it would bring people into Leamington and do good for the shopkeepers', but the plan to run down the Parade was unpopular and was passed by only ten votes to nine. The plan was approved in Warwick at about the same time although the route there lay along the High Street and Jury Street, one of the town's most important thoroughfares.

Some Leamington residents continued to oppose the scheme. On 26 February the Mayor called a public meeting in the Pump Rooms to protest about the route down the Parade. Two hundred people heard him express his fears of the disfigurement of the Parade and his views on the dangers posed to other road-users by the tramway. One local ratepayer, Mr. Robinson, complained, however, 'that some people held the Parade so sacred they would put it in a glass case if they could; he had even heard, he added, the opinion voiced that working men and their wives should not walk up it'. Despite the continued opposition of the Mayor the Council accepted the plan subject to some minor alterations and the Milverton Board withdrew its opposition when it was pointed out that it had agreed to the idea of the line in 1872. The company agreed that steam traction should not be used without the consent of the local councils and the House of Commons granted permission for construction.

Richardson and Chadbourn had no intention of building the line themselves, but had sought the order purely as a speculation. Accordingly in 1880 The Leamington & Warwick Tramway & Omnibus Co., Ltd. was formed and registered on 18 February. The directors intended to raise capital of £25,000 by the sale of £10 shares, purchase the provisional order from the two businessmen and construct the tramway. The public were slow to buy the shares, however, and by 18 May only 486 had been sold. The directors were forced to take up the rest. The provisional order was eventually purchased for £1,000 cash and £500 in shares, half the original price asked since there were no competitors for it.

Time was passing. The provisional order gave a 12-month time limit for starting work and as no work had begun within the year, opponents of the tramway threatened legal action, but did not pursue it. The directors had invited tenders for construction and 25 firms submitted quotes, but it was felt that all were too high and few firms would accept tramway shares in part payment. The contract was re-advertised in March 1881 but no acceptable tender was received until May, when John Fell offered to do the job for £14,800. Construction began at the end of June. The line began at the Leamington terminus opposite *The Manor House Hotel*, near the Avenue Road railway station. The last section of the three miles of line was laid in November 1881, but when Major-General Hutchinson of the Local Government Board inspected and approved the line he stipulated that no passengers should ride on the top deck within the parish of St Mary in Warwick because of the low archway where the tram passed under the East Gate. Permission was given for the company to take the tramway in a loop around the gate, however, and the loop was completed in January 1882. The Leamington & Warwick Tramway was opened for passengers on 21 November 1881. During the first seven months the revenue was £2,477 and working costs £1,812, so a five per cent dividend was declared on the 1,406 shares which had been issued to the public.

The timetable given in Beck's *Leamington Directory* of 1882-3 was typical of the service for several years. On weekdays there were eight trams each way, and one on Sundays. By 1892-3 there were seven tramcars, six in use and one in reserve or repair; 52 trips were made from Leamington daily and 16 on Sundays. The first car from Warwick left from Coten End, where the horses were stabled. The journey time was 34 minutes. The fares were originally 2d. from Warwick to Milverton Station and another 2d. from there to the Leamington Terminus, or 3d. all the way; any journey after 10 p.m. was 6d. Reduced fares were available for workmen at certain times and schoolchildren could have cheap season tickets. The fare stages were slightly extended in 1882. By 1884 special theatregoers' cars were operating, charging cheap return fares, but there were hitches when theatre performances ran late. The tramway directors often complained if the patrons were late catching the 10.15 p.m. car from Leamington.

There were few serious accidents. There was one fatal accident in 1889, when a three-year-old child was hit by a tram, but the usual incident was a collision with another vehicle and not always the tram-driver's fault. There were also the common snags when mischievous children altered the points or put stones in the grooved rails.

The days of the horse-drawn tram, however, were numbered. By the end of the century similar tramways were being converted to electric traction all over the country. The British Electric Traction Co., founded in 1895, acquired the Leamington & Warwick Tramway Co. in 1899, offering £10 a share to the existing shareholders. James Lycett of the B.E.T. Co. became a director of the Leamington and Warwick company to convert the horse-drawn trams to electric ones. The proposed use of overhead wires aroused great opposition locally, and to secure the consent of the two councils the company proposed, among other things, to sell the tramway to them at a price to be agreed by arbitration and in the meantime to pay them rent for the first 28 years of operation using electric traction. Warwick council accepted this in 1900 and Leamington the following year. Tramway orders were confirmed by Parliament, allowing three years to complete the work. It was calculated that running costs would be half those of horse-drawn trams.

Then there were delays. In 1902 the Leamington & Warwick Tramway & Omnibus Co. became the Leamington & Warwick Electrical Co., having obtained powers to supply electricity to other consumers in Warwick, and not until September 1903 did the new company begin to consider the design of the overhead system. The Leamington council demanded more ornate poles than the tramway company proposed, granite rather than wooden setts between all the rails and, vainly, an underground system of wiring. The company wanted a single line instead of the double track originally agreed upon. Through-out 1904 Leamington's council refused to accept this, feeling that no trams at all were preferable to a dangerous single track and suggesting that the tramway operators were trying to economise by making one track instead of two. Leamington ratepayers objected too, and within three days in March 1905 over 500 signed a petition against the whole

46.   The Parade in the early 1900s, showing the electric tram service in operation.

scheme. They said that trams were obsolescent and would interfere with ordinary traffic, that central poles would ruin the Parade and that motor buses would be quieter.

Their complaints were ignored, however; the last horse tram ran on 16 May, the old track was taken up and a new one quickly laid to the gauge of 3 ft. 6 ins. common in the Midlands. The overhead wires were hung from central poles with cast-iron brackets; two and a half miles of the three-mile track were double and wooden blocks were laid between the rails. Twelve cars were used for the electric service which began on 12 July 1906.

The power came from a station built specially near the Avon and the Grand Union canal. The river provided water for cooling the generators and the fuel came by canal. It was operated as a separate company, the Leicestershire & Warwickshire Electric Power Co., which became the Midlands Electric Supply Co. just after the First World War and was taken over first by Balfour Beatty & Co. and then by the local authority. The power station was nationalised after the Second World War and closed in the 1970s.

In its first years of operation the tramway beat off competition from motor buses. At the end of 1914, however, the Leamington council had to hold a meeting to discuss complaints about the running of the system, particularly inadequate repairs. After the war some new trams were provided, but it was obvious that the system was outdated and facing increasing competition from motor buses. The last tram ran in August 1929, leaving the route clear for the buses.

The tramway company itself began to run buses in 1907. Some of these they sold to the British Automobile Traction Co. in 1912 on the understanding that the two companies would not compete against each other. The rest were acquired in 1915 by the Birmingham & Midland Motor Omnibus Co. Ltd. An early rival to the electric trams was the Leamington

Williams's Directory Advertiser.

J. W. BAKER,

ALE & PORTER BREWER,

Castle Brewery, Leamington,

Continues to supply his much esteemed ALES and PORTER,
at the undermentioned prices:—viz.

ALE		PORTER	
X.	1 0 per Gallon.	XP.	1 0 per Gallon.
XX.	1 4 ,, ,,	XXP.	1 4 ,, ,,
XXX.	1 8 ,, ,,	XXXP.	1 8 ,, ,,

FINE OLD ALE

1s. 5d. and 1s. 9d. per Gallon.

EAST INDIA PALE ALE

One and Fourpence per Gallon.

In Casks, containing $4\frac{1}{2}$, 9, 18, or 36 Gallons each.

*Parties requiring TABLE BEER, are requested to order it
at least, ten days before required for use, as no Beer is kept in
store at a lower price than One Shilling per Gallon.*

BOTTLED ALE OR PORTER,

IN QUART BOTTLES.		IN PINT BOTTLES.	
s. d.		s. d.	
XX.	5 0 per dozen	XX.	3 9 per dozen.
XXX.	6 0 ,, ,,	XXX.	4 6 ,, ,,

In quantities not less than two dozen Quarts or four
dozen Pints.

The usual discount allowed to Hotel and Innkeepers.

47.   An advertisement for a Leamington brewer.

Motor Omnibus Co., which for a while ran buses between Leamington and Warwick. The company then concentrated on the route between Stratford and Kenilworth. In 1927 Stratford-upon-Avon Motor Services, the 'Stratford Blue', ran services between Leamington, Warwick and Stratford, and this proved so successful that the next year the tramway company started running a rival 'Green Bus Service'. In 1929 the Stratford concern sold out to the tramway. The rival companies operating between Leamington and Warwick were amalgamated eventually, in 1935, to form the Birmingham & Midland Motor Omnibus Co. Ltd., later known as the 'Midland Red'.

The motor industry made a marked impact on the town as local industries became more dependent on it. Among the first were Mulliners, the local coach-builders, who became famous as coach-builders and upholsterers for the early Rolls-Royce cars. In 1905 the fire brigade had a Leamington-built Crowden Fire Tender, carrying a crew of six, chemical firefighting apparatus, 300 yds. of hose and a 30 ft. ladder. In 1916 J. Warr, a local cabinetmaker, designed and made a motorcycle tricar. The real start of the growth in the local motor industry, however, was in 1928 when the Lockheed Hydraulic Brake Co. purchased the Zephyr Carburettor Co. and their works in Clemens Street, where the brakes were made for the first Wolseley cars. Beginning with 25 employees the firm, later named Automotive Products Co., Ltd., has become the largest employer in the town. It moved to its Tachbrook Road site in 1931. In 1937 the aircraft division produced the first retractable undercarriage for commercial aircraft. Also in 1937 Capt. G. E. T. Eyston's Thunderbolt, fitted with Lockheed hydraulic brakes made in Leamington, achieved the World Land Speed Record at 357 m.p.h. In 1947 John Cobb, in a car also fitted with Lockheed brakes, raised the speed record to 394.196 m.p.h.

Another important industry in the 19th century was brewing, which employed much labour. The Leamington Brewery was founded in 1839 when Stephen Lewis bought the Lillington Avenue site. In 1841 Lewis and his partner Sandeman were joined by John Haddon, under whom the business expanded from a small but well-established firm into a large thriving enterprise. When Haddon died in 1875 his estate was worth over £43,000, of which £24,702 was his share of the business and £5,812 a loan to William Ridley, a fellow partner in the firm. By this date the company owned seven local pubs. Stephen Lewis had died earlier, in 1871, and his son, James, joined Haddon and Ridley in a new partnership. In 1885 Ridley and Lewis sold the firm to Morton Lucas and his partners, who paid £75,000 for the brewery. It then controlled 35 'tied' houses, not only in Leamington and Warwick but also in Nuneaton and Rugby, and some as far away as Mickleton in Gloucestershire, Leicester and Oxford. They included *The Golden Lion*, Regent Street, then rented by Henry Goode for £100 a year.

Under Lucas & Co. the main brewery was rebuilt in 1896. In 1928 it was taken over by Ansells of Birmingham. The brewery was closed and the site and buildings sold in July 1934 on condition that the premises should not be again used for brewing. The Borough Council acquired it as a depot and used it until 1986. The original buildings have now been converted into houses and the rest of the site redeveloped for homes.

Chapter Fifteen

The Growth of Local Government

Leamington Priors was originally 'governed' by a manorial court under the lord of the manor, punishing wrong-doers, 'testing' the bread and beer on sale and controlling highways running through the parish. Then followed the appointment of Justices of the Peace, who from Tudor times to the early 19th century governed the county through the Quarter Sessions. They administered justice and, acting in a group in Quarter Sessions, were responsible for licensing alehouses, maintaining bridges and all public highways except turnpike roads. They also nominated the Overseers of the Poor in each parish, well-off individuals who, with the churchwardens, collected the poor rate from householders in the parish and made the necessary payments to the poor. The Quarter Sessions also authorised rates for such purposes as the repairing of roads, and the payment of the parish surveyor carrying them out.

There was also the parish vestry, a meeting of all the male parishioners to discuss the running of the parish. These meetings were held whenever necessary, although an annual meeting was required by law to ensure the maintenance of the church (except the chancel which was the responsibility of the rector), the churchyard and other church expenses. The vestry remained in being for these purposes until 1868. It was also responsible, with the Overseers of the Poor, for raising the poor rate until 1834 when Parliament passed the Poor Law Amendment Act. Under this act a number of neighbouring parishes were joined together and Boards of Guardians were elected who were responsible for building and maintaining the local workhouses.

Since it was impractical for all the parishioners to meet every time a decision was needed, a parish committee was normally elected which, with the churchwardens, ran the parish between annual meetings. The minutes of the Leamington parish vestry survive only after 1823. They reveal that although the parishioners were supposed to meet in the church vestry this was impossible since it was too small, so having met formally in the church they moved to the Apollo Rooms in Clemens Street. In later years they met in the Town Hall. Under the vestry in 1823 Mr. Carter was made collector of taxes and in 1824 Dr. Jephson and his partner Mr. Chambers were made parish surgeons at a fee of £10 10s. a year. The vestry also formed the first police force and provided a set of stocks in 1826; the previous year the inhabitants had been indicted for not having any stocks. In 1783 the stocks and the pound stood in what was later called Court Street. Leamington, growing in size, was made a petty sessional division in 1823.

By then the control that the Quarter Sessions exercised over the highways was proving inadequate to cope with the problems created by the building of the New Town on the north bank of the Leam, where streets needed to be made, improved, drained, paved and lit. There was also need of an organised refuse collection, sewage disposal and supply of water. As early as 1820 it was obviously becoming necessary for the townspeople to promote an Act of Parliament to provide the required powers. The vestry first met to discuss the matter in 1819, and two more meetings were held in 1820. Eventually, on 10 June 1825, a bill entitled 'An Act for Paving or Flagging, Lighting, Watching, Cleansing, Regulating and Improving the Town of Leamington Priors in the County of Warwick' received the royal assent.

The act provided for the appointment of commissioners to carry out the provisions of the legislation. They were to include all men who were owners of property in the parish worth £60 p.a., who at any meeting of the commissioners expressed a wish to act and took an oath of office before the chairman. In the early days of the spa this broad membership was not a problem as the number qualified was comparatively small, but as the town's population grew, so did the number of commissioners. While at the first meeting there were 28, there were 139 by 1839 and possibly 200 by 1850. Deciding the day-to-day business of the town became complicated.

The act did not allow a permanent chairman, so one had to be elected at each meeting. At the inaugural meeting on 28 June 1825, William Hunter was chosen. He served most often in the early years, but others included Dr. Middleton, John Russell (proprietor of *The Bath Hotel*), Richard Robbins (proprietor of Robbins' Baths) and John Cullis (owner of Ranelagh Gardens). Attendances varied depending on the business to be transacted. It was usually around a dozen, but at times was as many as 70 or more. Five was a quorum, a very small number in view of how many were eligible to attend. There were no provisions in the act to allow a permanent committee to be set up, but temporary committees were appointed for special purposes such as roads and bridges.

The powers conferred under the act occupied 70 large pages of legal text. Various officers could be appointed, including a clerk, treasurer, surveyor, scavenger, constables and watchmen. The commissioners could flag the pavements in front of houses, but not generally before undeveloped properties, particularly if extending more than 30 yds. between existing houses. They could provide cobbled street crossings, repair and maintain the streets, including the turnpike inside the town, plant and prune trees alongside the streets, number the houses, name streets, light them, collect rubbish, lay new drains, license and regulate hackney cabs, build a town hall and issue by-laws.

The act also provided authority to levy rates. This required the help of the Overseers of the Poor, and later the Board of Guardians of the Poor. These officers, the Poor Law authorities, controlled the assessment of rateable values and the compilation of the rating lists. Separate rates could be levied for the poor, the church or the improvement commissioners. The maximum rates the commissioners could demand were set out in the act: 3s. in the pound for houses in streets both lighted and paved, 2s. if one but not the other, and 1s. if neither.

Collecting the rates was certainly not easy. When the Audit Committee published the commissioners' accounts for the year 1 June 1828 to 31 May 1829 they suggested that their rate collector, Mr. George Carter, had not accounted for £2,875 18s. 10d. Carter took exception to this public statement implying that he had mislaid nearly £3,000 of public money. He asked them to retract it. They refused, so he set out a detailed account of his view of the affair in *The Courier* in August 1829. He declared that someone besides the three committeemen, Donald Harrow, Richard Robbins and John Allen, must have written a recent letter to the paper about the arrears since the letter was not in Harrow's style and 'the other two are incapable of writing a connected letter, either upon that or any other subject'. He accused them of 'endeavouring by every means in their power, to ruin my reputation'. He claimed to have horsewhipped Allen in his own house for propagating a report that Carter was £2,600 short in his accounts. Carter's own version of the accounts showed that there were a large number of defaulters, including Robbins, the committeeman, who had owed £20 on the day he ordered Carter to be sued. Defaulters owed at least £1,999 on the three rates levied by the commissioners between August 1826 and October 1828. He suggested that some of the rate assessments had been too high and were legally unenforceable, that money had been wasted by paving in front of new and empty houses and that the commissioners themselves had failed to authorise proceedings against defaulters and were now castigating him for not acting without authority.

Carter claimed he had worked hard and well. Rather than resorting to the law and distraining goods and chattels for non-payment, so causing distress to the families of hundreds of ratepayers, he and his two clerks had taken their rates 'by degrees as I could get them'. In two years and nine months he had raised 'the enormous sum of £9,611 7s. 6d.'. This was too short a time for the parishioners to find such a large amount. Understandably, when a general meeting of the commissioners approved the Audit Committee's accounts, he resigned.

Another area of the commissioners' activity was regulation of traffic and street-life. By-laws were issued many times in the early years of their authority: at least twice in 1825, three times in 1826, revisions in 1827 and 1828, and a comprehensive new set appeared in August 1829. These ordered that all hackney coaches, Bath chairs or hackney vehicles of any description, porters, basket men or women, and barrow men or women should be licensed by the commissioners. The name of the owner of each vehicle had to be displayed prominently and a metal licence plate carried. The number of passengers permitted to each vehicle was controlled, fares were fixed – not to be above 1s. a mile for a cab – and the places where vehicles could stand when waiting to be hired were defined. There were regulations against depositing coal or bricks on the highway during unloading, about collection of night soil, about the width of cart wheels and the size of cart teams, penalties for allowing cattle to stray on the town's roads. No-one was to write, paint or place immoral or offensive words or pictures anywhere that could be visible from the street. Signboards were not to project over the public way, no vehicles were to be washed in the streets, no-one was to sweep a public path without first sprinkling water to lay the dust, except during a hard frost. Chimney sweeps were not to walk on the pavement in their working dress, nor to carry a soot bag there. Carpets were not to be beaten against railings, lamp-posts or doors. No-one was to knock or ring at a door without business there. This was a fairly comprehensive set of restrictions, mainly aimed at servants and traders rather than the more genteel residents or visitors.

After some years it became clear that the 1825 act did not provide powers to deal with a number of problems, and by 1837 the commissioners were considering applying for a supplementary act. One problem was the small amount the commissioners could borrow for capital projects. Essential schemes had to be funded directly from the rates, often over a very short period. The reconstruction of the bridge linking the village and the New Town would have put a great financial burden on the ratepayers unless powers were obtained to extend the existing ceiling allowed of £10,000. The poorer ratepayers, who were not eligible to be commissioners, objected to anything which would increase the powers of the existing commissioners to levy rates. In March 1838 many of them attended a public meeting which strongly criticised the commissioners, passing resolutions that the town should either be incorporated as a borough or that the commissioners should be elected; they also suggested a much lower property qualification for being a commissioner. The following month the ratepayers tried to get an election procedure included in the proposed bill, but they met with such opposition from the commissioners that the proposal for a supplementary act was shelved.

One of the powers given in the 1825 act was the raising of a rate for 'watching', or policing, the town. The vestry employed two constables, plus a number of assistants and a town crier. In 1826 the county magistrates employed a separate force of four watchmen, who all received 10s. a week plus a uniform, belt, dark lantern, rattle and a staff. The improvement commissioners also exercised their powers and employed constables and a watchman, paying the constables 15s. a week and the head constable, John Palmer, £150 a year. By 1839 this police force was 16 strong.

That year the County Police Act, a national measure, came into force and empowered

48.   Mr. Bratt, the last town crier.

the county magistrates to raise a rate for policing. Leamington was included in the Knightlow Hundred section of the new county constabulary. The county authorities had no power to compel the improvement commissioners to disband their police force, but they agreed to do so providing William Roby, their head constable, became the county's new chief constable, and that Leamington's police station, then behind the Town Hall, became the headquarters of the Knightlow Hundred police. But when Captain George Baker, R.N., was appointed chief constable and the commissioners found that Leamington and the other seven parishes in the hundred would have only seven policemen between them, they decided to keep their own police force. They solved the legal problem by making Roby the town surveyor with the powers of parish constable conferred on him by the vestry. He had several 'street-keepers', all of whom happened to be former policemen. Baker objected and the two police forces disdained to co-operate. The county force was denied the use of the Town Hall as its headquarters and was expected to use a small house in Park Street. Baker refused to pay the rent asked by the improvement commissioners and was eventually ejected even from this.

A further motive, to acquire power to exclude the county police from the town and to exempt Leamington's ratepayers from paying the county police rate, was thus added to demands for a supplementary act. When one was passed in 1843 the town acquired the authority to appoint its own policemen – but only the county J.P.s were empowered to dismiss them. Roby was made chief constable of the new Leamington force, with ten constables under him. The borough force lasted until 1 April 1947 when, under the 1946 Police Act, control passed to the county.

After several public meetings in the autumn of 1842 a committee of ten commissioners and 11 ratepayers was instructed to draw up a new bill to be submitted to Parliament giving additional powers for the government of the town. The proposed bill included a reduction of the property qualification for a commissioner from £60 to £40 p.a. It also restricted the number of commissioners to 33, elected by all ratepayers. A third of them were to retire each year. The borrowing limit was to be extended by a further £30,000.

There was opposition to the latter from ratepayers. A letter to *The Courier* in March 1843 pointed out that the interest on such a sum would exhaust almost a quarter of the commissioners' current revenue, and that the rates were said already to be higher than in any other town in England. The writer blamed the number of streets laid out for building and kept in repair on the rates although not built up. In particular he objected to the powers allowing the commissioners to make roads in the parish of Milverton. Such actions would enable the development of New Milverton to be undertaken, allowing the Earl of Warwick to build on his land at Edmondscote and improve it at the expense of Leamington's ratepayers. In the meantime much of the three miles of frontage in the town was not built on and more than 200 houses were vacant; '. . . during the past ten years investments in land and buildings in Leamington had been unsafe to mortgagees and almost ruinous to owners'.

Ratepayers voted on the proposed bill later in the month in a poll lasting four days. Despite the opposition the bill was accepted by 960 votes to 921. It speedily passed through Parliament and received the royal assent on 27 June. The act, however, did not contain all the provisions approved in the public poll a few months before. Influential local people had managed to get the bill amended in favour of the existing commissioners during its passage through Parliament; they remained very much in control, as before, neither limited in number nor a third forced to retire for re-election. Borrowing powers were raised to £25,000. A general committee of 25 could be elected once a year to carry out business, and a chairman could be appointed, also for a year. The commissioners were also empowered to improve and culvert the Binsbrook, to inspect new houses to ensure party walls were 14 ins. thick, to prevent new houses being thatched, to build a gasworks, establish a market and enforce weights and measures.

During the 27 years the commissioners were in being they dealt with all sorts of problems created by a rapidly growing town. Streets were paved, trees planted, a police force set up, a town hall built in High Street, and bridges constructed. The powers of the commissioners, however, were limited. They could not acquire land for public parks, for example, which meant that the Pump Room Gardens and the Jephson Gardens were controlled by trustees and an independent management committee. Nor, importantly, could they take over the town's water supply, which for many years was operated for private profit rather than public benefit. The commissioners were also unable to improve the town's unsatisfactory sewage disposal system, the difficulty here being the expense and perhaps the indifference of many of the richer people to the living conditions of the poor. The result was that sanitary conditions in the town worsened and Leamington suffered in the epidemics of the mid-19th century. The pressure to adopt the 1848 Public Health Act became irresistible.

The act applied to all towns with a population of over 2,000, but it was not compulsory and could only be adopted if a tenth of the population of a place petitioned for its introduction or if the death rate exceeded 23 per thousand. The first step was for ratepayers to petition the General Board of Health for an inspector to visit the town, examine its sanitary condition and decide if the act should be applied to it. The inspectors' reports, which were published, exposed the appalling state of almost every town. This was no surprise in cities like Birmingham or Manchester, but lesser towns like Warwick or Stratford-upon-Avon proved to be no better. Leamington was equally as bad as others although it was a new town built largely since 1810. No thought had been taken for possible health problems. Small back-to-back houses were packed into the spaces behind the mansions of the rich.

The inspector's report, a *Preliminary Inquiry into the Sewerage, Drainage and Supply of Water, and the Sanitary Conditions of the inhabitants of the town of Leamington Priors*, was published in March 1850. It pointed to a variety of problems. The principal thoroughfares presented a well-ordered appearance, but this was misleading. The commissioners could carry out work and levy rates only in the parish of Leamington, although by 1848 about 145 houses of the town lay in the parish of Milverton. In 1848 £6,713 13s. 2d. was the assessed rate and, allowing for void houses, £6,167 5s. 1d. was collected. Sanitary conditions in parts of the town were appalling; there was overcrowding and no proper water supply or sewage disposal system.

Among the worst nuisances were the 34 slaughter houses behind shops in various parts of the spa. The inspector calculated that there were more than 800 pigsties behind houses. Should any of these cause a nuisance the commissioners would only convict where they could be seen from the street, ignoring far worse cases where the sties were surrounded by houses. One consequence of this was that several of the improvement commissioners had large piggeries attached to their houses or hotels. The inspector suggested that pigsties should be forbidden within the town. Owners of the large houses could afford to have their night soil removed, although it was often tipped into the Leam rather than taken a safe distance from the town. In the poorer parts of Leamington, particularly in the old village, it was just left piled up in the centre of the courts and only at intervals sold for spreading on farmland. The water supply was inadequate and available only to those rich enough to pay the cost of laying the supply pipes. Landlords often refused to lay on water to rented tenements, a problem not unique to Leamington.

Remedies the inspector suggested included:

> . . . the extension of the parish boundary to include the whole town; the constitution of a governing body elected directly by the ratepayer, whose funds they expend, and with a power vested in them compelling all house owners to provide their houses with a proper water supply, drainage, privy or water closet; to cause the yards to be paved and drained, to fill up cesspits, and to remove pigsties and heaps of manure and rubbish, and by the visits of an inspector of nuisances and the threat of certain summary penalties, to preserve in a state of cleanliness premises which there will then be no excuse for suffering to remain dirty.

The methods he suggested of implementing these recommendations were mostly not at all controversial. Many were carried out in subsequent years by the commissioners or the Local Board of Health. From this period dates the water supply laid on from a new reservoir at the top of Leicester Street, while a start was made in culverting the Milverton Brook from above the brewery on the parish boundary of Leamington to its junction with the main outfall into the Leam near Portland Place. The course of the Leam was straightened where it now runs through Victoria Park, weirs were built and sewers no longer allowed to discharge into the river. Steps were taken to remove most of the nuisances aggravating the sanitary condition of the poorer homes, a new cemetery was opened in Brunswick Street, and rates to carry out these improvements levied over the next twenty or so years. Almost all agreed with the inspector that 'The town should not only be clean, but preeminently clean; and such a reputation by attracting visitors to the place, would repay a much larger outlay than ought to be requisite to obtain the desired end'.

That it took nearly a year for the inquiry to be held and until 1852 for the results to be adopted indicates the opposition aroused. The commissioners in 1849 opposed it although they instructed their officers to co-operate with the inspector. In January 1851 the annual meeting of the improvement commissioners was due in order to elect the general committee for the coming year. These elections were contested by supporters of the Public Health Act who canvassed the town, naming the people they wished to be elected. All but three of them were chosen, so the improvement commissioners thereafter favoured adopting the act. There remained, however, opposition from powerful vested interests. Landlords of houses occupied by the poor argued that expense on improvements like a sewage disposal system would only increase rents or diminish their incomes. More important was the extension of the parish boundary into Milverton and Lillington. The Earl of Warwick and the Percy family living at Guy's Cliffe both objected to the inclusion of some of their land in Milverton in the area to be administered by the new Local Board of Health.

In July 1851 Dr. Hitchman held a public meeting to win the townspeople's support for a third special local Act of Parliament. Its aim was to give the commissioners more power rather than wait for the adoption of the Public Health Act. In November a special parish meeting, a vestry meeting in the legal sense, was held to urge the adoption of the act, already in force in 138 other towns, rather than press ahead with yet another local act. This meeting addressed a long 'Memorial' to the General Board of Health, calling for an inspector to be sent to hold another inquiry and confer with the landowners over the boundaries. Accordingly an inspector came in January 1852 and negotiated a compromise. By this only the part of Milverton immediately adjacent to Leamington was included in the area administered by the Leamington Board, and that only for sewerage. For the purposes of the Public Health Act this Milverton Main Sewerage District was defined as being 'so much of the parish of Milverton as is bounded on the north by the Warwick to Rugby road, on the west by the river Avon and on the south by the river Leam'. The Provisions of the Public Health Act in Leamington were at last confirmed by Parliament on 30 June 1852.

Under the act, where the town was not a borough the Board of Health had to be elected by the ratepayers. The first election was held early in August 1852 and a Board of 15 members elected for Leamington – five to retire annually in rotation – and one for the Milverton Drainage Board, first met on 18 August 1852. The first chairman was William Carpenter, lately the chairman of the improvement commissioners, and eight others were on the retiring general committee of the improvement commissioners. After the election the usual celebration dinner was held at *The Regent Hotel*.

The Leamington members were elected by the whole town, as it had not yet been divided into wards. The basic qualification of an elector was being either a ratepayer or the owner of a property in the parish. But this qualification was subject to other provisions which allowed extra votes, one for each £50 or part thereof of the rateable value of the property in respect of which the voter was qualified. This meant that the owner-occupier of a very large property could have up to 12 votes, the maximum allowed under the act. Dudley remarks in his history that 'under this system villa residents, nearly every one of whom had several votes, were possessed of the ruling power to the exclusion of the holders of single votes notwithstanding that the latter were in the vast majority'. In 1857, for example, 1,500 ratepayers had single votes but a further 430 had as many as 1,300 between them, and in the 1873 election every defeated candidate represented more ratepayers while polling fewer votes than those elected.

At the time of the first election a secret ballot did not exist. To be entitled to a vote a claim had to be submitted 14 days before the election to the chairman of the improvement commissioners. Voting papers were distributed by hand and completed papers, signed by the voter, were collected again on the day of election. To be a candidate it was necessary to be rated at £30 in the Board's district or to have real or personal estate worth £1,000 provided the candidate lived within seven miles of the district. As a candidate had to be nominated by only one elector to be eligible, it was possible for him to nominate himself, as Dr. Jephson did at the first election. There were 58 candidates for the 15 seats in Leamington and two for the one seat at Milverton.

The general powers in the Public Health Act were much like those in the improvement acts, but there were also extensive powers for dealing with the development of the town. The new powers enabled the Board of Health to appoint permanent officials: a clerk, medical officer of health, a surveyor and an inspector of nuisances to undertake work done today by Public Health Inspectors. For the first time they had a right of entry into premises such as butchers' shops, and there was compulsory paving of private streets and the cleaning of streets by the Board's employees, whereas before householders were expected to keep their own frontages clean. All new houses were to be connected to the town's drainage system, lodging houses had to be registered, no new cellars could be used as habitations and the occupation of existing cellars was regulated. Gas and water services could be provided where necessary, the widths of new streets laid out by private builders could be fixed and the Board could acquire by negotiation buildings or land to widen existing streets. For the first time public parks could be provided, burial grounds closed when full and new ones opened when a local Burial Board could not do so. Leamington had a Burial Board, however, after the Burial Act of 1851; it was abolished in 1890 and its powers vested in the Borough Council.

Perhaps the most important provision of the act was the removal of the limit on the sum which could be borrowed on mortgage against the rates. It was replaced by a limit equal to the rateable value of the town, which would increase as the town grew. This was very important to rapidly expanding Leamington. The Board took over from the commissioners a debt of £17,000, assets estimated as worth £12,000 and £1,200 cash.

While the Local Board's work mostly involved improvements to the town's sanitary condition, the inhabitants enjoyed other benefits, including the first public library, opened in 1855. There were improvements to the fire service, for the old brigade had been criticised for its occasional inefficiency. The first fire engine was kept behind the old Town Hall and the one fireman appointed by the improvement commissioners was assisted by local volunteers. Their failure to cope wih a serious fire at Dowler's premises in Regent Street in January 1850 led to an inquiry, but no-one was found to blame and the system carried on for another 13 years. In 1863 a new volunteer brigade was formed, maintained by voluntary contributions, and a Corporation Fire Brigade was created in the 1880s.

The Board began its career facing complaints from those who had to pay increased rates without the opportunity of influencing how they were spent. A ratepayers' association was formed in 1855, with the help of R. A. Wallington and T. Muddeman, themselves members of the Board. This rather ineffective group was replaced in 1864 by a far more active campaigning organisation which put pressure on the Board for more positive action in solving the town's sanitary problems. This was not easy, nor was it cheap. From 1856 to 1859 the Board negotiated with landowners on the Leam to straighten its course. The river was then widened and straightened from Victoria bridge to the confluence with the Avon at a cost of £20,000. £2,676 was paid to the Earl of Warwick during this work for the right to remove the mill and weir near the manor-house at Edmondscote.

The Board chose to deal with sewage by precipitation, discharging the effluent into the river. While straightening the river increased its flow, it could not prevent the level falling in summer, but the construction of a new weir at Prince's Drive and a better outfall beyond it achieved a speedier flow of sewage through the town. A second weir by the suspension bridge near the Jephson Gardens was erected many years later.

The untreated sewage in the Leam flowed quickly away from Leamington, but it polluted the Avon. The people of Warwick were, understandably, aggrieved and in 1868 a Warwick landowner, Thomas Heath, applied to the court of Chancery for an injunction to restrain the Leamington Board from discharging sewage into the Avon. Heath was successful and the finances of the Board were sequestered.

The Courier described the town in Chancery. 'The town is sequestrated. The parish brooms and wheelbarrows are to be seized by the myrmidons of the law. . . . and the very handcuffs of the Police Force sold to defray the fine of £5,000 ordered to be levied from the town.' The paper recognised Heath's complaint to have been justified. It had seen the situation coming and the failure of the Board to resolve it. It saw 'at all costs to comply with the law' as the only possible course, and said that 'A radical change must take place in the government of the town ere it can be said to have advanced one step in the direction of healthy progress'.

The Clerk of the Board resigned and was succeeded by H. C. Passman, who financed it with a loan from his own resources and managed to obtain a relaxation of the sequestration order provided that the sewage problem was remedied. A new policy of irrigation was adopted and sewage was pumped on to the Earl of Warwick's land at Heathcote. The cost of the land, buildings and equipment amounted to nearly £16,000. For the time being the problem was solved although occasional escapes of sewage into the river continued to cause friction between the towns until more efficient modern plants were built. The works at Heathcote remained in use until the new joint works was built at Longbridge, outside Warwick, in the 1970s.

The Board's last years were mostly concerned with improving Leamington's water supply. The supply of drinking water in the town during most of the 19th century was of poor quality. Much came from wells, the rest from the river and was certainly polluted. For many years water was distributed around the town from water carts owned by Mr. Oldham, who leased the mill near the parish church. Members of his family continued to supply the town with water until 1878. In 1832 the works at the mill were improved, the filter beds enlarged and the river water passed through them was pumped up to the Newbold Hills into a new reservoir. From there it was piped to the town by gravity.

In 1870 Dr. Frankland, a medical officer of the Local Government Board in London, declared the water unfit to drink and the Leamington Board was forced to make some improvement. The most popular suggestion was better filtration, but a prominent local resident, Henry Bright, led a group which favoured sinking boreholes to tap underground sources of water. They claimed that this would be safer than drinking river water no matter how carefully purified. Opponents of the scheme feared pollution of or damage to the saline water supplies, which would ruin the town as a spa. Bright was elected to the Local Board of Health in 1872, however, and persuaded it to adopt the plan.

A borehole was sunk near the sewage-pumping station at the end of New River Walk in December 1872, but the water was partly saline. A second borehole on the site of the works proved successful. In 1877 a new waterworks was begun at a cost of £20,000, and Bright, who was then Mayor, laid the foundation stone. They were opened in 1879. To commemorate the event and Bright's efforts a drinking fountain surmounted by a granite obelisk, standing at the Parade end of Holly Walk, was put up and inscribed 'Erected by public subscription to record the services of Alderman Henry Bright to whose untiring exertions this town is chiefly indebted for its supply of pure water. 1880'.

As early as 1855 tentative moves were made towards getting the town a charter and a new form of local government. In 1858 a petition to the Privy Council was approved by 'upwards of forty of the most influential inhabitants', but when Dr. Jephson withdrew his support the scheme was dropped. In October 1872, 56 ratepayers signed a petition to the Board requesting a charter at a meeting in the Town Hall presided over by the Rev. Craig, who as vicar was chairman of the parish vestry. A committee was elected to enquire into it; it was chaired by S. T. Wackrill, one of the originators of the idea, and J. T. Burgess, editor of *The Courier*, was secretary. The committee worked diligently, and by the time they reported to another public meeting in December they had written to every borough in the country to enquire about the advantages and disadvantages of incorporation and decided a charter should be sought. The meeting approved the idea and a petition to the Privy Council was prepared.

Opposition within Leamington was strong, however, and Milverton and Lillington were against the built-up portions of their parishes adjacent to Leamington being included in the proposed borough. The threat of the costs to be borne if the charter was not granted put off some supporters until Mr. Wackrill offered to pay the whole sum. The Privy Council ordered a public inquiry which took place in the public hall in Windsor Street in October 1874. Influential local people spoke on both sides: the chairman of the Leamington Local

Board of Health supported it but the clerks of the Milverton and Lillington boards spoke against it.

In February 1875 the Privy Council decided to grant a charter to Leamington, but excluding the area of the town in the other two parishes. Apparently a victory for both sides, the compromise was short-lived, for in 1890 a special Act of Parliament included New Milverton and Lillington within the boundaries of Royal Leamington Spa. The charter made Leamington a borough, with a corporation consisting of a Mayor, six Aldermen and 18 Councillors. The town was divided into three wards. West Ward lay, roughly, west of Kenilworth Road, the Parade, Clemens and Brunswick Streets; North-east Ward lay north of the line of Regent Grove and Holly Walk, South-east to the south of them.

The first election was held on 2 July 1875. Sixty-one candidates stood, 17 in South-east Ward, 19 in North-east and 25 in West. The number of votes cast was 5,528, 1,942 in West Ward, 1,793 in North-east and 1,793 in South-east. Not all the candidates wanted to stand, for it was not necessary to have a man's consent to nominate him, and not all were serious. The candidates were all 'independents' although there was an underground ratepayers' association which claimed afterwards to have a majority on the council. There were some irregularities, for example hired coaches were used to convey voters to the poll instead of private ones, and particular lists of candidates were displayed in the polling stations. The votes were counted single-handed the following day by the returning officer, John Watkins, closeted alone in the Town Hall. The poll was approximately 50 per cent.

The six candidates with the most votes were elected aldermen at the first meeting of the new corporation on 12 July. The vacancies thus created among the councillors were filled at a second election. T. Wackrill was unanimously elected Mayor and he was re-elected to the office at the first annual meeting of the Corporation, held on 9 November. He again served as Mayor in 1885-6 and 1886-7. Dudley describes him as having

> industry, intelligence and impartiality. His hospitality was dispensed on a scale of magnificence in every way worthy of the event and the festive annals of the spa. In October [1875] over a hundred of the leading burgesses were his guests at a sumptuous banquet at the Regent hotel, and while thus 'feasting the rich' he never forgot the poor for in March 1876 several thousands of the inhabitants were generously entertained in the Public Hall at most enjoyable concerts. Refreshments, of which there was no stint, were provided.

The Public Health Act had provided that borough councils should act as the Local Board of Health, so the new Council took over the functions of the existing Board. After the boundaries were extended in 1890 the number of aldermen and councillors were increased to eight and 24, at which they remained until 1974. The wards were re-arranged as Lillington, Milverton, Jephson and Brunswick wards in 1935. Alderman Wackrill presented the Corporation with a mayoral chain, robes, coat of arms and his chosen motto: '*Sola bona quae honesta*' (Those things alone are good which are honourable). H. C. Passman was chosen as first Town Clerk and the Board's surveyor became the Corporation's Surveyor.

In 1876 Leamington took another step forward as a local government unit when the Council successfully petitioned for a separate Commission of the Peace for the Borough. The jurisdiction of the county magistrates ceased and Borough magistrates were appointed. They first sat in October, in the old Town Hall. Many of them were aldermen or councillors. Encouraged by this success the Borough tried to obtain a separate parliamentary constituency for Leamington, Lillington and Milverton, but failed. The town is still linked with the Warwick constituency, although a few years ago the other outlying areas were formed into the new constituency of Kenilworth and Rugby.

From 1859 to 1890 Milverton and Lillington had their own Local Boards of Health. The Lillington Board room was next to the Police Station at the junction of Cubbington Road and Pound Lane, and survived as a library and, more recently, a community centre. The

Milverton Board room and Magistrates' Court, in Rugby road, has now become a County Council Music Centre for young people. In 1888 Milverton parish was divided into the parishes of Old and New Milverton, the latter being entirely in Leamington's built-up area. When the two boards were wound up in 1890 and parts of the two parishes amalgamated with the Borough of Leamington, the remnants of Milverton and Lillington were united to become the civil parish of Old Milverton and Blackdown. This in its turn was absorbed into the Warwick Rural District Council area, and until 1894 was entitled the Rural District of the Warwick Union, being controlled by a separate Board of Poor Law Guardians.

Warwickshire County Council was established in 1888 with varying powers covering the whole of the county. In the borough and other built-up areas in Warwickshire its powers were generally limited to holding parliamentary elections, granting licences for music, etc., management of asylums, and some police duties including responsibilities relating to Magistrates' courts and Quarter Sessions. The new council also had responsibility for some roads and bridges. Lillington and Milverton elected one member to it and Leamington elected four; this was increased to five in 1890.

The Borough had limited powers – it was essentially a Local Board of Health 'potholed with gaps'. These were filled in a variety of ways, mostly by independent boards elected for specific purposes. Thus there were School Boards, Burial Boards and a joint Hospital Board for the infectious diseases hospital at Heathcote. The Corporation administered the police and fire brigade, gradually improved the water and drainage system, laid out new public parks, acquired the Pump Rooms and their gardens in 1875 and in 1896 the Jephson Gardens, and built the public library, technical and art schools in Avenue Road. After the Great War it built the art gallery and began slum clearance schemes in Satchwell Street and the Court Street area. The right to build council houses was obtained in 1922 and the first of them were erected near the Tachbrook Road. One of its last projects was the Spa Centre built in Newbold Terrace on the site of Harrington House, and handed over to the new District Council free of all debt charges. It was designed by Sir Frederick Gibberd and was opened in June 1972 by the Earl of Avon, Anthony Eden, the borough's M.P. for many years.

In 1974 the administration of the town was taken over by the newly formed Warwick District Council, formed by amalgamating the Warwick Borough Council, the Kenilworth Urban District Council, the Warwick Rural District Council and the Borough of Leamington Spa. Warwick and Kenilworth now have town councils with status similar to parish councils, but Leamington lacks an independent local authority; requests to be allowed a town council have been refused on the grounds that the town is too large. The visible reminders of the old Borough are now the responsibility of Charter Trustees, who have no local government powers. All the councillors elected for the various divisions in Leamington automatically become Charter Trustees and the longest serving councillor becomes the Mayor, serving in rotation. The post is merely ceremonial and has no power. Those who created the original Corporation with so much optimism and vision might have found it a lamentable conclusion to a century of civic endeavour.

Chapter Sixteen

The Town Hall

Perhaps the most prominent building in the town centre, not only because of its contrast with its Regency neighbours but also because of its size, is the Town Hall. It was opened in 1884, having caused controversy over its style and its site. In 1875 Alderman Wackrill, the first Mayor, had suggested that a new town hall should replace the inadequate accommodation in the original 40-year-old Town Hall in the High Street. He moved a resolution at the first annual general meeting of the Corporation that a committee be appointed to consider the building of a new town hall. It was passed and there started a local 'Battle of Styles', one party favouring a Regency-style building, built on part of the gardens next to the Pump Rooms, while others wanted something more original elsewhere in the town.

The Corporation became involved in a wrangle about the choice of final plans and architect for the new building. Originally the Pump Room Gardens site was chosen, and interested architects from all over the country were invited to submit designs for a new town hall on it in accordance with a set of conditions drawn up by the Borough Surveyor. The designs were to be submitted under a *nom-de-plume*, the architects' names remaining secret until the successful plan was chosen. Forty-six sets of plans, consisting of 187 drawings, were submitted early in 1881, most complying with the conditions supplied although many failed in respect of essential requirements. Some, for example, according to the highway committee, destroyed 'the character of the Pump Rooms by dividing it into several offices, whilst not a few spoilt it by reducing its height to eighteen, sixteen or even fourteen feet, without producing sufficient new means of lighting'. Others would probably be more costly than the Council could afford. The committee decided that until they had made their report to the Corporation the public should not be allowed to view the plans. It was recommended that three of the architects, Mr. Vince Freeman of Bolton-Le-Moors, Mr. J. A. Cundall of Leamington and Messrs. Scrivenor and Sons of Hanley, should be invited to send in more detailed plans, as the conditions of the competiton had laid down. Alderman Wackrill proposed the committee's report be accepted, and here the wrangling began, *The Courier* reporting every detail.

The alternative site, the one the 'Goths' wanted, was a piece of land known as the Pingle, which lay south of *The Regent Hotel*. It had been acquired by the first proprietor of the hotel, John Williams, from Mr. Willes soon after the hotel was built, and he had built a Gothic-style villa on it. This house was called Denby Villa – spelled that way on the Ordnance Survey maps of the town and in official documents, but 'Denbigh' in *The Courier* and guide books. It stood in a large garden. After Williams' death the property passed with the hotel. Both were bought by Mr. Lyas Bishop, an improvement commissioner and one of the first aldermen to be appointed after incorporation, for £23,500 in 1874. The house accounted for £6,000 of this sum. In 1881 Bishop sold the villa to Mr. John Fell, a local builder, for £10,500. Fell built a theatre on the garden behind it, which opened in 1882. This he sold to a local syndicate, keeping the house and substantial front garden.

Some councillors suggested a postponement of a decision in the competition in case the Council could acquire the Denby Villa site instead of using part of the Pump Room Gardens. Alderman Magrath was satisfied that it would cost more money to alter the Pump Room than it would to erect entirely new premises on the Denbigh Villa site . . . Although not, perhaps, architecturally faultless the present Pump Room was a sightly building, and it would be a pity to pull it about and destroy it.

The Mayor wondered whether it was honest to ask the three architects 'to prepare plans for buildings at the Pump Rooms which it was intended to build on another site' and to change the plan would be to be unfair to the other competitors. Mr. Wamsley added that he would not be surprised at anything – the Council knew that the Denby Villa site was available when the Pump Room site had been chosen, so why had they not picked it then if they wanted it? Others pointed out that it was not necessary to pay for the Pump Room site. The Council finally decided to invite the three selected architects to submit completed designs by the next council meeting and the plans were to be placed on public exhibition for a week.

By the next meeting, in May 1881, Cundall's plans had been accepted by a sub-committee. He wrote expressing his thanks to the Council

> for the honour you have done me in adopting my plans for your proposed new municipal building and to state that I shall be happy to make what further sketch plans as may be required for altering or re-adapting any part of my designs as may be deemed advisable, free of charge.

Cundall was aware that a new site was likely to be chosen and had written to make sure that the councillors knew he would adapt his scheme to the Denby Villa site without further cost to the Corporation. The unsuccessful Mr. Freeman was dissatisfied and complained that an official letter sent on his behalf by the Mayor of Bolton had not been read by the Mayor of Leamington. Moreover, first, Cundall had submitted a perspective view in violation of the conditions of the competition and therefore he should have been disqualified, second, the decision to adopt Cundall's plan was largely influenced by criticisms of his, Freeman's, plan which were untrue, and that he should have the opportunity of replying to, and third, he would have been able to do so as he had arranged to be at the judging but was prevented by a telegram from Leamington's Mayor. He called for 'a disinterested professional referee, whose decision would be received with confidence by all'.

The Council ignored his protests and proceeded to discuss other business. One matter was a claim that the Mayor had obstructed the press by refusing to allow local reporters to see documents and minutes which were to be discussed at that council meeting. It was the first time for 20 years that this had happened. The members were largely in favour of allowing reporters access to documents discussed by the Council, and the Mayor, 'discerning the feeling of the Council, agreed to hand over the documents to the reporters, without any formal resolution being passed'.

Mr. Watt now introduced his motion that the Denby Villa site should be acquired. First he denied that he was bringing the matter forward at the instigation of several members of the Council who stood to benefit by the purchase of the site. He claimed it would be cheaper to build from scratch than to repair the Pump Rooms. He therefore proposed that the resolution passed on 20 December 1880 to build on the Pump Room site be rescinded, and that part of the Denby Villa site be bought instead at a price not exceeding two guineas a square yard. Mr. Whippell proposed an amendment that in view of the lawsuits in progress against the Council and the recent addition of a School Board rate to the 'already heavy local taxes of this Borough', the Council should postpone deciding to build the new municipal buildings for a year. Alderman Wackrill also proposed an amendment, that the question be deferred so that the Council's present legal situation could be discovered.

The votes were 11 for and 11 against Alderman Wackrill's amendment, 10 for and 11 against Mr. Whippell's amendment, and 11 for and 11 against Watt's proposal for buying part of the Denby Villa site. The Mayor gave his casting vote in favour of Mr. Watt, but after protests a ballot was held. The result was 12 for and 11 against Watt's motion. Mr.

Wamsley then handed in a written protest objecting to Alderman Bishop's vote on the grounds he was an interested party. Nevertheless it was decided to proceed with the purchase of the site on which the present Town Hall is built rather than erect the new town hall beside the Pump Rooms. Surprisingly it was found that the scheme prepared by Cundall for the competition actually fitted the new site, without any major changes.

When the Council met again in June, the arguments were just as bitter. The opposition still suspected that certain members of the Council were pressing for the purchase of the Denby Villa site for their own financial benefit, while other councillors wished to go ahead as soon as possible. The chairman of the finance committee pointed out that the Corporation was already in debt for at least £4,461 for work already authorised and the problem of unpaid rates was getting worse although the collector's commission had reached £400 p.a., making him one of the best-paid borough officials in the whole country. At the same time the owner's solicitors were pointing out that Mr. Fell could not keep the matter open indefinitely – no doubt they wished to prevent any further changes of mind. If the Council were not in a position to make a decision by the end of the month he might have to start building on the whole of the site as he originally intended. The Clerk said that he had replied stating that although the Council had approved building a new town hall on the site, such expenditure needed the approval of the Local Government Board before it could proceed. On 10 June 1881 the vendor's solicitors offered the Council as much land as they required at two guineas a square yard, the maximum price that had been approved.

Mr. Watt moved a resolution that 'the Clerk be instructed to obtain authority to borrow such sums as might be required for the erection of the new public buildings on the site selected by the Corporation' and negotiate with the vendors for 3,200 sq. yds. as shown on Cundall's plan. It was opposed on the grounds that the plan had not been examined by the councillors in detail; Mr. Wamsley spoke of rumours of scandal; and the cost and financial situation of the Corporation were reiterated, but the motion was passed by 11 votes to eight. Wamsley again gave in a written protest against Alderman Bishop's vote, alleging that the Alderman had not yet parted with possession of the villa to Mr. Fell.

A month later the matter was raised again. Fell refused to drop his price. The Clerk reported that he had applied to the Local Government Board for approval to borrow £30,000; the Board had replied they could not consider the application without plans and detailed estimates. The Surveyor had provided an estimate as follows: 2,800 yds. of land at £2 2s., £5,800; cost of building, £23,000; fees to the architect and clerk of the works, £1,500; furnishings, £2,500; 500 yds. of land to widen the street in front, £1,956; which according to the Clerk totalled £33,930, almost £4,000 more than he had applied to borrow. On completion of this report Mr. Wamsley was heard to remark 'I hope the Board will never give its consent'. A discussion followed which was 'rather lively while it lasted', and accusations were made that the scheme was being rushed through without proper thought. The Mayor said that anyone who objected to the scheme would have an opportunity to be heard by the Local Government Board Inspector when the inquiry was held. Eventually members agreed to proceed to the next business. This was equally controversial – fixing the general rate for the half year ending December 1881. It was set at 1s. 6d. in the pound to cover estimated expenditure of £8,027 15s. 4d., leaving a possible surplus of £35 for emergency expenditure!

The public inquiry was held, approval was given by the Local Government Board to borrow the money, Cundall's plans were finally accepted and the foundation stone was laid on 18 October 1882. Twelve tenders had been received from builders. The Council accepted that of John Fell, from whom they had bought the site. *The Courier* pointed out 'that the whole of the work was entrusted to Leamington men, a consideration which obviously influenced the Council in accepting Mr. Fell's tender [of £14,000] which was exactly £11 in excess of that submitted by Messrs Parnell and Son of Rugby'. Fell was eventually elected councillor and became Mayor in 1887-8. The new Town Hall was erected on the front garden of the villa, the house itself remained standing. Denby Buildings – shops and offices – now occupy its site.

49.   The Town Hall, opened in 1884. A photograph taken early this century.

The original design had had its critics, and when the building was finished some felt their misgivings had been justified. *The Courier* tried hard to be complimentary about it when it was due to be opened in December 1884.

It was originally decided that part of the present Pump Rooms should be utilized and that there, in one block, should be provided Corporation offices, a pump room and modern baths, a large assembly hall and a convenient library. Before work could commence the Pump Room site was abandoned . . . and singularly enough it was discovered and publicly declared that the plans which had been accepted would fit the Denbigh Villa site even better than the one for which they were ostensibly prepared. If this be the fact, awkward and ugly as the angles of the principal elevation and the elevation in Regent Grove undoubtedly are, the public should be grateful that the change was made. Anything more unsightly or inartistic than the bare structure facing the Regent Hotel which meets the view on passing down the Parade would at the Pump Rooms have been intolerable.

The original contract was subsequently judiciously supplemented by one for £2,000, for the additional stone work in the centre of the principal façade. Had not this been done it is painful even to contemplate what the building, as originally approved of by the then majority of the town council, would have looked like when completed. Happily the town has been delivered from such a misfortune, which would have made it extremely difficult to determine which of the three public buildings submitted in the competition was the ugliest, a method of adjudication never exactly complimentary.

The newspaper laid the blame for the defects in Cundall's building more on 'the attempt to build so large and pretentious structure for so small a sum as that to which the competing architects were by the conditions restricted' than on the Renaissance style adopted. Much of the building had had to be left 'bald and bare', inartistic ornamentation had been used and the materials limited to red brick and Campden stone. On the other hand the paper also observed that

> the architect is to be congratulated on the magnificent building, and in some of the more important parts the enrichments are so crowded it is really a marvel how the designs could have been executed for the money. Mr Fell's work is we believe, in every particular, unexceptionable!

So much controversy was aroused by the building of the Town Hall and the cost of fitting out its public rooms that in 1883 a local election was partly fought on the issue of the type of wood to be used for the panelling. Some ratepayers thought the cost was too extravagant while others wished to use the best materials available, so one sandwich-board man was seen trudging up and down the Parade bearing the slogan 'Vote for Stanley and mahogany'. His influence on the result of the election is not clear.

The official opening on 17 September 1884 was celebrated with much enthusiasm, the local shopkeepers decorating their premises and closing early, while some tradesmen, shop assistants and domestic servants had a holiday, depending on how their employers viewed the event. A special edition of *The Courier* gave a summary of the town's history as a spa as well as covering the day's events. Many people came to the town to witness the festivities. When the procession arrived at the Town Hall the crowd was so large that it was beyond the control of the handful of police. There was so much pushing and shoving that it was impossible to hear the Mayor's speech further off than two or three yards. One can guess that he said how good the building was and that all concerned, particularly the councillors, should feel proud of themselves. Probably not everybody in the crowd thought the same.

The Courier described the Town Hall and its furnishings in great detail. There were splendid stained-glass windows made by Mr. Holt of Warwick, presented by various aldermen wishing to be remembered as donors. They incorporated the names of past mayors and scenes from Shakespeare. The Council Chamber and Mayor's Parlour were furnished in the latest style by Messrs. Plucknett and Stevens of Warwick and Leamington, the survivors of the famous Warwick school of wood-carvers, which had been very popular earlier in the century. Details were given of the Town Clerk's office, desk, chair and cast-iron stove. His stove was decorated with Minton tiles, costly, it was implied, for a mere official. The Surveyor had to make do with a smaller and less well-furnished office, and without tiles on his stove. The rest of the staff were accommodated in the basement.

The size of the assembly-room was the cause of much adverse comment. *The Courier* complained that it was too small, especially since it was 'more likely to be of service to the town than any other part'. The most scathing remarks were reserved for the outside of the building, however, no doubt reflecting local opinion. The north elevation, facing *The Regent Hotel*, came in for most disapproval although the rest of the building was considered little better. The paper's critic thought this façade 'utterly destitute of anything approaching architectural beauty'. The principal features, five semi-circular headed windows, reminded him of a Methodist chapel and 'it has been suggested that the heavy unrelieved brick panels above these might be turned to profit as advertising spaces'.

The official opening of the building did not mark an end to the problems it caused. Hardly had the paint dried before legal arguments arose between the Corporation and Alderman Bishop, owner of *The Regent Hotel*, over the ownership of the 'private road' between the two buildings leading to the hotel stables. Windows on the north elevation of the Town Hall overlooked this 'right of way', and it was planned to provide a doorway leading from the central corridor on the ground floor of the new building to allow access from the road to the rooms to be used by the public library.

Bishop, as alderman, had been one of those councillors who promoted the scheme to build the Town Hall. Having sold the site to Fell he had always been aware of possible problems over the road, but waited until the building was in use before doing something. Failing to reach agreement with the rest of the Corporation over the problem and claiming the road exclusively for the hotel, he took direct action. One night in January 1885 his workmen erected a hoarding close against the wall of the Town Hall, blocking one of the windows, ostensibly to protect his 'rights of light'. It prevented the use of several offices.

The Town Clerk recommended that the hoarding be removed immediately and should Bishop object he could sue the Council for trespass and damages. These he thought would be small as both properties had belonged to one owner and the right to use the road for access was vested in the easement which was included in the site purchased by the Corporation. He also recalled that Bishop had been on the committee which approved the drawings showing windows on the north side of the building and the entrance to the rooms allocated as the library. The alderman had raised no objections then.

A resolution was put that the hoarding be removed by the Surveyor the following morning, but there were loud cries of 'Tonight!'. Very soon the posts supporting it were sawn through by the Town Hall porter in the presence of almost all the Council. 'The hoarding fell with a crash into the roadway, amid loud laughter and the cheers of the onlookers', according to the report in *The Courier*.

The Corporation was served with a writ by Alderman Bishop, claiming damages for entering the plaintiff's land on 25 January and taking down a hoarding. He also served an injunction to restrain the Corporation from opening a doorway on to his land. The defendants in the action were Mr. De Normanville, the Surveyor, and the Mayor, aldermen and councillors. The Clerk observed that Bishop was thus both plaintiff and defendant, while it was the first time he had had the honour of being solicitor for both parties in a case. Moreover, if Bishop won and obtained damages there might be a levy on his property as well as those of the other councillors to satisfy the court.

Bishop had never previously fenced off the land or prevented public access to it, which was the usual procedure where ground was claimed as private. The gateway to the hotel mews was the barrier to the private property behind the hotel and the land facing the Parade had by lapse of time become public property. The suit was eventually settled by a compromise, maintained to the present day. The windows of the Town Hall still overlook the disputed access, but the northern entrance was never made and the public library found a home elsewhere.

The Town Hall still functions today little changed from when it first opened, except that the Council Chamber was enlarged to seat a greater number of councillors after the formation of the Warwick District Council in 1974. Its future as a centre of local government is uncertain, however, unless its accommodation can be modernised and extended. A few years ago demolition was suggested to allow the site to be redeveloped. This threat had the townspeople fighting to keep a building they had come to admire. Time brings changes, and Victorian architecture has become fashionable and deemed worthy of preservation. Decades of grime have been removed from the building and Mr. Fell's brickwork now glows rosy and unabashed alongside its less prominent Regency neighbours, with their pastel-coloured stucco fronts.

Chapter Seventeen

School Benches, School Boards

In the early days of the spa educational opportunities were limited. Until the establishment of the first National Schools, private schools were available for the children of the wealthier residents or visitors, while the poor relied on the schooling provided by the local churches. Leamington's school system evolved gradually during the 19th century, however, until all children in the town received at least a basic education.

The first private schools in the new town offered tuition in subjects ranging from reading, writing and arithmetic to cookery, needlework, music and dancing. Young ladies had lessons in deportment – of considerable social importance. By 1818 Leamington had three academies for young ladies and three for young men, Mrs. Elliston and her daughters were giving dancing lessons and a dancing master, Mr. Newbold, could be found at 7 Upper Union Parade. Early guides to the town show that most of these private schools were held in the ground-floor rooms of dwelling houses in the main streets of the town centre. By 1830 the number of schools had increased. There were then at least nine schools for girls, including Miss Hawkin's boarding school for young ladies in Chandos Street, and Miss Walker's Academy, which had been in Upper Union Parade in 1818 but had now moved to Newbold Comyn House, rented from Mr. Willes who had left the town. These schools were probably of the type described by Jane Austen:

> . . . a real, honest, old-fashioned boarding school, where a reasonable quantity of accomplishments were sold at a reasonable price, and where girls might be sent to be out of the way, and scramble themselves into a little education, without any danger of coming back prodigies.

In addition there were many individual 'proprietors' giving instruction in music, singing and painting, essential accomplishments for young ladies moving in the 'polite society' frequenting the spa during the season. The demand for such facilities grew with the town.

Among the first of the schools for the upper classes was **The Warwickshire Proprietary College**, later known as **Leamington College**. A company was formed in 1844 to found a college to provide 'for the sons of the nobility, clergy, and gentry, a sound classical and mathematical education in accordance with the principles of the Established Church'. It was a fee-paying day-school, although the founders hoped to attract pupils from the many middle-class families in the district by keeping the fees low – £20 p.a. according to the first prospectus. Its promoters included Dr. Hitchman, Dr. Jephson and Dr. Middleton. Capital of £6,000 was soon raised by selling shares of £20, Dr. Jephson investing £1,000. The first formal meeting of the company took place in February 1845. The school's first premises were in Eastnor Terrace. In 1846 the company bought land in Binswood Avenue to build a college to accommodate the increasing numbers of pupils.

Dr. Jephson laid the foundation stone on 7 April 1847 and the new college was opened on 1 August of the following year. The building, designed by David Squirhill, was in the Tudor style, using red and grey brick with stone facings. It included a great hall and a chapel. In 1851 the new headmaster, the Rev. T. Burbidge, unsuccessfully urged that the college should be made a public school. He resigned in 1862 and was replaced by the Rev. E. St John Parry, from Winchester College.

In 1865 financial problems forced the college to close. The trustees considered auctioning the buildings in 1867, but thanks to S. T. Wackrill they decided against it. A scheme for reopening it was published and The Leamington College Co., Ltd., was incorporated in

50. Leamington College: the original building by David Squirhill built 1847-48 in Binswood Avenue. This view was published in 1851.

July 1867. The buildings were bought from the trustees for £3,000. Capital totalling £8,000 was raised by the issue of 100 shares of each of three classes, priced at £100, £50 and £10, the individual shareholders having rights to nominate pupils to the school. The college reopened in September 1867 under the headmastership of the Rev. J. W. Johnson, and within a year a scholarship fund of £400 was raised. In 1870 £4,000 was spent to buy and rebuild the house next to the college. The new structure was designed by John Cundall and was used as a boarding-house for 40 pupils.

In 1876 there were so many pupils that a new chapel was required. Also designed by Cundall, it cost £1,800. Two years later the building adjoining the college was bought for £1,100 and a similar amount was spent in 1880 to provide a sanatorium. The Rev. J. Beaumont paid £1,000 for a new organ for the chapel, given in memory of his son, a former scholar. He later also gave a large collection of books to the college for the library. In 1884 two more boarding-houses were established and in 1885 the school's first laboratory was built.

The college's great academic success could not prevent closure in 1902 because of further financial difficulties. There was by then a mortgage of £15,000 on the property, so the shareholders, reluctantly, decided to wind up the company. When the contents of the college were dispersed the Beaumont Library went to the local public library; many of the books are now housed on permanent loan in the library of the University of Birmingham. The organ was acquired by Holy Trinity church.

In 1886 a rival school had been established, **The Leamington Collegiate School**. It then occupied premises in Waterloo Place, in Warwick Street, described as 'a noble structure containing every requisite for education and home life', but this school also closed early in this century. In Somerset House, not far away in Clarendon Place, was a kindergarten school run 'on modern principles' for children of the wealthier residents, one of the earliest in the town.

In 1903 the buildings of Leamington College were purchased for £10,000 by the Society of the Sacred Heart and became a convent and a training school for young ladies. It was one of the Roman Catholic convent schools which found refuge in this country after such institutions were prohibited in France in 1901. It was attended by many foreign girls during its stay in Leamington, closing in September 1916. During their occupation the Society enlarged and improved the premises, chiefly by the addition of a new wing to the north-west of the original great hall. After the Society left in 1917, **Dover College**, compelled to evacuate its own school due to the bombardment of the channel ports, occupied the buildings. In 1920 they were bought by the Warwickshire County Council and from 1922 to 1977 they housed **Leamington College for Boys**, a local authority grammar school. In 1977 it became **Binswood Hall**, a co-educational sixth-form college, part of North Leamington Comprehensive School.

The original Leamington College refused to take boys whose parents were not 'gentry', so the Rev. John Craig, vicar of Leamington, opened **The Vicar's Grammar School** for the sons of the middle-class residents and tradesmen of the town. It aimed to provide 'a grammar school education based on christian principles'. The first headmaster was the Rev. John Montague, one of the vicar's curates. The buildings, designed by David Squirhill, were erected in Priory Terrace, the foundation stone being laid on 15 September 1847. It was intended that they should form an enclosed quadrangle, but the original scheme was never completed.

Although well patronised at the time, the school was short-lived and closed in 1853 because of financial difficulties. It was purchased by Signor Aspa who demolished some of the buildings in order to erect Priory House on the corner of Priory Terrace and Church Street. The school hall became a printing works, owned 1870-7 by John Vincent, publisher of the *English Labourer's Chronicle*, the journal of the newly-formed National Agricultural Labourers' Union. In 1907 it was purchased by the first of a series of religious groups; its present owners, the Christian Brethren, acquired the hall just after the last war.

Private schools continued to spring up like mushrooms to serve the educational needs of the wealthier families. Up to 1914 they were found in all parts of the town. Many were quite modest establishments and few were in purpose-built buildings. They included **Beech Lawn School**, a boys' preparatory school in Dr. Jephson's old home, which survived until the 1930s. One of the largest of these schools, supervised for years by Miss Wright, was in Oak House, Holly Walk, a day and boarding school for young ladies. Many clergymen offered accommodation for young men and tuition in a wide range of subjects, and in the town could be found tutors for classics, mathematics, music, painting and the army entrance exams, as well as for less popular subjects. In 1893 there were two schools for 'Indian children', presumably for those whose parents were in government service overseas.

Two of the private schools of the 19th century have survived and thrived: **The Kingsley School for Girls** and **Arnold Lodge School**, originally for boys but now co-educational. The Kingsley School, which moved to its present buildings in Beauchamp Avenue in the autumn of 1922, held its first classes in 1884 as the Leamington High School for Girls; its first premises were in a house in Upper Parade. One of its founders was Rose Kingsley, eldest daughter of the Rev. Charles Kingsley. The school changed its name just after the last war in her honour and to avoid confusion with a local authority school of the same name. The original school was intended for sisters of Leamington College boys.

Arnold Lodge School was founded in 1864 in 2 Lillington Place, then on the outskirts of the town, by Alfred Kirk, who had been a master at Leamington College. Numbers 1, 2 and 3 were houses built in 1859 by Mr. Squirhill, and the school still occupies 1 and 2; the road has been renamed Kenilworth Road. The school was named in honour of Dr. Arnold, then headmaster of Rugby School. In 1934 it was acquired by Mr. H. D. F. Hall and Mr. D. A. Hardy; Hardy retired in 1938 leaving the whole to Mr. Hall. The present proprietor, Mr. H. D. P. Hall, took over from his father in 1963.

The real battles were over the establishment of church and later local authority schools for the poorer children. The story has been told in Frances O'Shaughnessy's *A Spa and its Children*, a story of squalor and overcrowding, of teaching often poor but sometimes good, the work of dedicated teachers in bad conditions. As in other towns the forerunners were the Sunday schools, the first in Leamington being started about 1813 in the curate's own house where the Rev. Trotman was assisted by Miss Walker, the founder of Leamington's first private school for young ladies. Similar schools were then set up by Nonconformists, the first being in the Union Chapel in Clemens Street in 1816.

The first day school for the poorer children was a voluntary school established in 1822 with 30 boys and 30 girls by the vicar, the Rev. Wise, again helped by the Rev. Trotman. By 1836 it had twice as many pupils and even then could offer schooling to only a small number of the spa's children. The first master, Mr. George Liebenrood, was also churchwarden and the school pence of 2d.-4d., depending on age, had to be collected from all pupils every Monday to augment the master's salary – penniless pupils were sent home. In 1829 the overcrowded school was transferred to Kenilworth Street in the New Town, where it became the first National School. The pupils were segregated when Miss Oliver became the mistress for girls. In 1835 Liebenrood resigned after being in charge for 13 years; two years later he bought and became editor of *The Courier*.

When the Rev. Craig exchanged livings with Rev. Downes in 1839 he agreed to keep the National School going. He found the children still housed in the Kenilworth Street building, crowded into one room and badly taught. The school needed new premises to alleviate crowding, so he took a 99-year lease at a pepper-corn rent of the former workhouse in Court Street. (The inmates had been moved to the new union workhouse in Warwick that year.) Half the pupils were moved from Kenilworth Street and two new teachers were appointed. In 1843, when Robert Baker and Hannah Hall were appointed master and mistress of the 'workhouse school', they each had 100 pupils and clearly the premises had become inadequate. The situation was made worse because the improvement commissioners had retained the ground floor to house the town's fire engine and their horses and carts. The school occupied five rooms on the first floor and five in the attic, some of which housed the master and his family and the schoolmistress. The small space between the school and the Town Hall served as a playground, but could not be used when the magistrates were in session or other meetings were held.

In 1846 the lease of the Kenilworth Street premises expired and the vicar closed the school. Most of the 300 pupils had nowhere to go, although a few were accepted at the workhouse school. By 1850 that school had 160 boys and 140 infants and girls. That year massive arches and an embankment carrying the London and North Western Railway line to Rugby were constructed beside it and the following year the building of the Great Western Railway line brought its demolition. The L.N.W.R. gave £250 and the G.W.R. gave £1,500 compensation to the parish so the school could be rebuilt. The Rev. Craig closed the school at Christmas 1851 and passed the compensation and the responsibility of providing a new boys' school to the parish vestry. He moved the infants' and girls' schools into part of the vicar's grammar school; when this school closed just over a year later these schools had to move yet again.

The vestry transferred the unfortunate boys to 'temporary premises' in a building already scheduled by its owner for demolition, the old Apollo Rooms in Clemens Street. This building was very unsuitable, in bad condition, according to *The Courier*, and with shops underneath it. Nevertheless the school remained there for over three years. The owner became desperate to regain possession so he could rebuild on the site, so he said, but the building still stands. Financial problems dogged the school. The annual report for 1854-5 stated that funds had shrunk until there was only 10s. 6d. to pay the quarterly salaries of the master, mistress, two pupil teachers and the monitors as well as the running costs. *The Courier* protested:

> . . . in addition to the injury done to the health of the master by the impurity of the air he is compelled to breathe, there is added the distress of mind consequent upon the non-payment of his salary . . . Is it not a disgrace to us as a parish that he should be compelled to ask mercy of his creditors for his daily bread? The income of £70 a year is in itself too small a pittance for him to support, clothe and educate his seven children without any consideration for himself and his wife.

The trustees unhurriedly considered sites and eventually purchased part of a market-garden in Bath Place for £1,250. They applied for a government grant for the new school, but the imminent lawsuit between the vicar and the vestry over parish finances had an adverse effect on subscriptions towards the church school. The Charity Commissioners, looking into the school's finances and administration pending the award of a government grant, held an inquiry in February 1857. This inquiry caused more bitterness between the vicar and townspeople. Craig said that when he became vicar public subscription raised about £90 a year towards the school and there was another £9 p.a. from Miss Campion's legacy. The rent of the Kenilworth Street premises alone was £60 a year, and there were the salaries also, so he had had to subsidise it. Now he wished to have nothing else to do with it. The chairman of the trustees stated that after the new site had been bought £447 17s. 6d. remained. The government inspector for schools in the Midlands said that only one school in the town was eligible for a grant as the others were poorly run and poorly housed. If a new National School was built it would receive a grant towards its running costs.

Nothing was done until 1859, however. A government grant of £1,000 was received and construction began early in the year; the new school was opened in November. Mr. Baker, the former-master who had resigned earlier in the year, led the 513 children into the building for a celebration tea; the usual congratulatory speeches included one from the vicar who had done little to help. The tender for building the Gothic edifice was £1,494. It still stands, at present used as a community centre, but it is scheduled for demolition. The new master was paid £70 p.a., with a house and the school pence from every child over the first hundred; the mistress received £40 and a furnished house.

While the Church of England was struggling to run its first National School the Nonconformist chapels also began to set up their own schools. Several of them achieved marked popularity. The first of these schools was started soon after the Methodists opened their first chapel in the New Town, in Portland Street in 1825. It began as a Sunday School, but a day school was built behind the chapel in 1839, part of which still exists. The pupils at first numbered 85 boys and 30 girls, and they attended five days a week and Sundays, when up to 150 boys and 70 girls received instruction. The school premises were never really large enough because of the cramped site, but increasing numbers of pupils attended. After 20 years a school inspector condemned it as inadequate, especially as it had no playground, but no action was taken until 1870. Then, when a new chapel had been built, the original chapel became classrooms. The school remained in use until 1924.

The Methodist school was perhaps a little better than the school attached to the Spencer Street chapel. This boys' school opened in 1840 in a dark, damp basement beneath the chapel. New classrooms were built behind the chapel only in 1856. The first teacher, Thomas Coles, was paid £30 a year and all the school pence, but out of this very limited income he had to provide books and pay any pupil teachers he employed. Although the school had no playground and overlooked the graveyard, then still in use, the boys were luckier than many for besides the three Rs they had lessons in geography, history, scripture and singing.

Other Nonconformist chapels were not even as successful as this in starting day schools. The Baptists at Warwick Street had no room nor enough money to buy a separate site although some schooling was provided for girls and infants in the public hall in Windsor Street. After a split within the congregation, however, the breakaway portion was able to build a school behind their new chapel in Clarendon Street; it opened in 1863, the same year as government regulations for grant aid were revised. The regulations set new standards for buildings and curricula, which made grants more difficult to get. Each child was supposed to have eight sq. ft. of space, and the grant per child was dependent not only on attendance but also on his knowledge of reading, writing and arithmetic. As a result it was necessary to concentrate on these subjects and scripture, and others such as geography, history, laundry work and sewing were ignored. The surviving school log books from Leamington show that the local School Board exercised strict economy and teachers were paid 'by results'. Within a year the Baptist school had nearly 150 pupils, so, since regulations specified no more than 91 there, government aid was refused for several years. Lacking funds the school closed in 1881.

The first Catholic day school for boys was built in New Street, near the Roman Catholic chapel in George Street. The school, opened in 1848, had two classrooms, a playground and a house for the master, Mr. Jennings, who was paid £30 a year with extra payments for having a certificate and instructing a pupil teacher which brought his income to £81. The building still stands, a well-constructed edifice for its period and one of the best schools in the town. Because there were few Catholics in Leamington and because the congregation was wealthy it was probably the least crowded school in the spa. Its original pupils, 25-30 boys, paid only 1d.-1½d. a week; there was room for eighty. The playground, qualified teacher and ample space meant it received a government grant from the start, and for 12 years it was the only school in the town to do so.

Encouraged by the success of the boys' school, in 1850 the Sisters of the Charity of St Paul, then living in a house in Augusta Place, opened a school for girls and infants. Attendance was small, however, and it failed to qualify for government aid until 1877.

Most elementary schools were promoted by local clergymen, but one of the few innovations of the time was the establishment in 1834 of two undenominational infant schools, organised by Alfred Woodhouse, a local draper. Both took children as young as 18 months, to allow their mothers to continue working. **The Victoria School** in Ranelagh Terrace was in a villa once owned by James Bisset. The other school was in the New Town in the former Baptist chapel in Guy Street. The schools were well supported by wealthy people in the town, but the Guy Street school was taken over by the congregation of Christchurch in 1851 and later became a National School, and the other closed in 1878. Both school premises were criticised in the public health report of 1850: that at Guy Street had an undrained privy, one of 18 in the street, and under the other school was a basement containing nine ins. of contaminated water, while behind it was an open cesspit.

When the parish of All Saints was divided the new parishes started their own schools.

The first vicar of St Mary's parish on the east side of the town, the Rev. Marsh, promoted schemes for education with enthusiasm; in the 1860s, when Leamington had six Church of England schools, the largest number were in this parish. Once the new church had opened a fund was set up to build a school. A site was bought for £500 and a school built and opened in 1842 for £1,000, which left a mortgage of £500 to be paid off. It stood in Holly Walk, on the site of the later St Paul's School, and had one classroom, 76 ft. by 32 ft., divided by an oak partition into boys' and girls' halves. There were 78 boys, 80 girls and 50 infants on the roll at first; they paid 4d. a week, part of which was returned in clothing. The mortgage was not cleared until 1857, but when solvent the school became eligible for government grants.

Children at the far end of the parish found the school too distant and in any case it became overcrowded and the working-class population of the parish was growing, so with a legacy from Mrs. Perfect, a parishioner, Rev. Bromley built another school on the corner of Leam Terrace East and Radford Road. When it opened in 1858 it had 20 pupils in the charge of a single mistress and a pupil teacher, but it soon grew. The school was small, one room for boys, girls and infants, a smaller one for very young children, and a playroom; it, the schoolhouse and furniture all cost just £449, including the £80 15s. paid for the site.

Church schools were also attached to Holy Trinity and St Luke's churches. **St Luke's School** stood beside the church and opened only a few months after it. The Rev. Clay, St Luke's first minister, intended the school to strengthen '. . . its Protestant defences against the attacks of Popery' – St Luke's stood opposite the catholic school. Beside it there was also a school of industry to train 40 girls as servants.

Members of Holy Trinity church opened a school in John Street in 1860, the site of which is now occupied by the telephone exchange. There were up to 148 children on the register. The school was well-run and received government grants for most of its life. New premises were provided behind the church in 1868 although it took some years to raise the £500 needed. It was

> a very plain building, even when new, and the hard local brick and Welsh slate have not mellowed with time. The omission of ornament or indeed any architectural grace whatever shows how narrowly the collected money sufficed to build a school. There is no inscription, not even a foundation stone.

The L-shaped building had two rooms. The smaller one, for the infants, had windows facing the church garden but a high wall hid the view and blocked the sun; the larger had no windows in its south wall, facing the garden. The trustees announced when the school opened that their policy was not 'to educate the children unsuitably to their rank, but they wish to give them a sound religious, Church of England education'. A 24-year-old master, John Lamsdale, was appointed and he stayed for 40 years, teaching the Sunday school and also singing in the church choir. In 1895 master and pupils moved to the new Leicester Street Board School and the Trinity Street School closed; the church still uses the building for community activities.

In 1863 the Congregationalists built a new school alongside the graveyard behind the Spencer Street chapel. At last the boys could leave the small room over the rear of the chapel in which they had been taught since 1856. This new school cost £1,000 and for several years there was an outstanding debt of £600 which made the school ineligible for government help, but in any case the Congregationalists would not accept public money until the early 1870s. Although the school was short of money and the teacher badly paid, the trustees decided in 1872 to open a girls' department. The new classes used part of the boys' school. Another school was opened behind the Congregational chapel in Holly Walk in 1870; after six years it was amalgamated with the Spencer Street school, so that at least one should remain open with the limited funds available.

The Methodists opened a second school in Court Street in 1872, the building paid for by

Miss Harvey and her friend Miss Holly. It accommodated 178 pupils. Eventually it was taken over by the new Trinity Methodist church in Radford Road, and was converted into a boys' school. When it came under the control of the School Board, scholars and staff moved to the Shrubland Street Boys' School, which opened in 1891.

The Education Act of 1870 set up local School Boards who could enforce compulsory education for all children up to 13 years old. The cost of building any necessary new schools was to come from local rates, helped by government grants. A government school inspector visited Leamington in 1871. His report treated the town as a special case because a third of its population was middle class and their children would receive private education; there were about 500 children in private schools in the town at the time. Leamington's existing schools he thought could provide adequate accommodation for 3,298 children while the estimated total for the town was 2,800. As a result it was not necessary for the town to elect a School Board. The inspector considered both the Catholic schools in the town were 'inefficient', however, which annoyed the local Catholic community. New premises were built for the girls' school in 1879, but the infants' school in Augusta Place was not replaced until the 1980s and St Peter's Boys' School not until 1967.

The 1876 Education Act made education compulsory for all children between the ages of five and ten, and this created further problems in Leamington, especially in the rapidly growing parish of St Mary's, whose population exceeded 7,000 in 1871. In 1874 this parish was divided to form St Paul's parish, and the school in Holly Walk became **St Paul's Church of England School**. The small school run by St Mary's in Radford Road was enlarged in 1877, but it was still overcrowded so a new school for girls and infants was built in New Street. It cost £1,500 and shortage of money delayed its completion until 1881 although it was in use in 1877.

The new parish of St John's was created south of the river in 1878, but a boys' school had been opened there in makeshift premises in 1876. The girls and infants still used the old school in Ranelagh Terrace opened in 1834, but when this was closed moved to rented premises in Tachbrook Street. Shortly after, the boys were moved to an 'iron building' specially erected for them in East Grove. A school inspector in 1880

> would only recognise the building on the undertaking that steps would be taken to build a suitable boys' school without delay. . . . The building is a mere makeshift and is no better than an ordinary shed with tin roofing. The heat of the summer makes it completely unfit for use as a school.

The building was also extremely overcrowded. The managers, however, would seem to have had no plans to provide a new school since they had no funds to do so. The inspector pointed also to four other unsatisfactory schools in Leamington and stressed the need for appointing a School Board.

The Corporation objected to the proposal. It asserted that a School Board would only result in an increase in the rates which would be an unnecessary burden on local residents. The trustees of **St John's Boys' School** pointed out, however, that theirs was a working-class parish and the task of providing a new school was beyond it. A meeting was held in the Pump Rooms in December 1880 at which was proposed a public appeal for money for a new school in the parish. The obvious intention was to delay the appointment of a local School Board. The vicar of Leamington pointed out that many of the borough's wealthy residents contributed nothing to local school funds. St John's parish was typical. There were hundreds of houses in the parish inhabited by working class families, but only 143 occupied by people of means. Of these only 46 subscribed to school funds, paying about £40 in the previous year. Parents of the school's pupils had contributed £118 in school pence.

As required by law the Borough submitted returns to the Department of Education in January 1881. These showed that the 14 schools in the town provided 4,053 places, figures which excluded the Congregational school in Holly Walk which had closed through lack of pupils and the schools in St John's parish which were to be closed as unsatisfactory. The Corporation drew attention to four important facts: first, a large number of the residents of Leamington were ladies whose families were grown up and, where they were not, did not require to be educated at Board Schools, there being a large number of private schools in the town where education of the highest order could be obtained. Second, that the list of schools and places showed that there were more places than the average weekly attendance. Third, that the Catholics were to erect a new school and that three of the other schools could accommodate a further 460 children if required. Fourth, a large school in Holly Walk, capable of holding 300 children, had closed recently for lack of pupils. It concluded 'there is no necessity for a School Board. We are strongly opposed to change, as we believe that in no town in England is the education of the children looked after better than it is here.'

The Schools' Inspector replied that the figures were incorrect, most of the schools were unsatisfactory and too crowded to take extra children and the Congregational School in Holly Walk had closed due to lack of funds, not pupils. In his view a School Board should be formed immediately. The Corporation resisted doggedly, and at a meeting of all school managers a resolution was passed opposing the formation of a Board, alleging that there was already more than enough accommodation for children in local schools, although to his credit Henry Bright, the Mayor, opposed the resolution. Nevertheless, in March 1881 the Department of Education served an order on the Borough under the 1870 Act setting up a School Board.

The election for the nine members of the new Board was held in April. The new members were mostly school managers, five Church of England, two Congregationalists, one Methodist and a Baptist, representing one of each of the religious groups except the Catholics, who gained a seat later. The first chairman was the Hon. and Rev. J. W. Leigh, vicar of All Saints, whose parish's schools remained independent of the Board. Feelings about state-funded education in the town were mixed; the editor of *The Courier* wrote on 16 April:

> The education given at the cost of the ratepayers ought in reality to be elementary. It cannot be just that any person should be taxed to give the children of other people a better education than he is able to give his own. Furthermore, respectable and intelligent members of the working class will inevitably feel some repugnance at sending their children to sit side by side with the children of the idle and dissolute, brought in by compulsion from the gutter and whose associations are as pernicious as their clothing is dirty and objectionable. It is undesireable that the two classes of children should be brought up in close proximity, keeping them distinct would be anxiety served.

When the 1881 census figures were published they showed the population of the spa had risen to almost 23,000, of whom about 4,000 were children of school age. The new School Board's urgent task was to provide school buildings capable of accommodating this large number since the existing buildings could take no more than 3,590. Only seven of the town's schools, half of the total, wished to be taken over by the Board.

For the purpose of administration the Board divided the town into three school districts. The teachers were given notice and re-employed at new salaries, all but the few for whom no suitable posts existed. The buildings of the schools taken over were rented, while St John's boys' school, in the 'tin hut', was demolished. The boys were sent to the Spencer Street school and the infants to the school in Queen's Street. These arrangements were approved by the Schools' Inspector, but were temporary and rather unsatisfactory because the smaller children in the St John's area lived so far from their school. The Department of Education asked for new girls' and infants' schools to be built in the North and South Districts, but action was deferred for years. In the meantime the inspector condemned several of the existing buildings as inadequate and overcrowded. The department pressed for the new schools to be begun, and the inspector was once driven to comment that compulsory school attendance was almost unknown in Leamington. Nevertheless he praised **The Leamington School of Cookery**, the only recognised school of cookery in the district, attended for several months a year by senior girls from schools in both Leamington and Warwick. Pupils paid 1d. a lesson.

The first new girls' and infants' schools were not ready for three years. New sites were difficult to obtain: in the North District, the only land available was in Leicester Street and cost £1,699 10s.; in the South District the site in Shrubland Street cost £1,422 6s. Building the two schools cost £10,659 each, and both held 504 infants and 300 girls. The average cost per head was thus £6 12s. 7d., well below the national average of £12 3s., but even so a rate of 3d. in the pound was necessary. By exercising strict economy the Board was able to educate nearly 1,500 pupils at a cost of 19s. a head, again well below the national average. School pence were still charged and parents who could not or would not pay were allowed a week's credit and then their children were excluded from school.

The Board still endeavoured to avoid building any new schools until the Board of Education insisted on urgent action. Although the overcrowded St Mary's boys' school on the corner of Leam Terrace and Radford Road was condemned by 1884, it was not replaced until 1890. This school, and girls' and infants' schools in New Street, also condemned, were moved to new schools built in Clapham Terrace at a total cost of £9,552; the new schools accommodated 1,028 chidren. The 'new school embodied all the most recent improvements and methods in school construction, a due regard being given to economy', one of the new elements being cast-iron roof trusses over the assembly hall and classrooms. Another boys' school was built in Shrubland Street in 1891 to replace the Court Street School. **The Leicester Street School** was finished in 1895, together with **The Court Street School of Cookery**, so that by then the Board owned ten schools built since its formation.

A major advance took place in 1891. The Education Act of that year gave all local School Boards a grant of 10s. per child annually. It made 'free' education possible as all fees were reduced and very poor children were admitted free. Attendances soared and there was a real possibility of education for some children to the age of 16 years. Schools were jubilant, the Leicester Street Girls' School and other local schools making 1 September, when the act became law, a holiday.

Both Lillington and New Milverton had their own schools. The **Milverton school** was associated with the 'Pepper-box Chapel', whose congregation established it, as a National School, in Heath Terrace before 1879. This school and additional premises in Woodbine Street, for boys, provided for the children of both New and Old Milverton. In 1872 the Milverton School Board was formed and eventually a new boys' school was built in Rugby Road in 1888 and an infants' school a few years later. In 1890, when the Borough of Leamington's boundaries were extended to take in New Milverton, the Milverton School Board was absorbed into Leamington's. The **Lillington Church of England school** was built on the Cubbington Road in 1865 by the vicar, the Rev. John Wise. In 1897, Queen Victoria's Diamond Jubilee year, new classrooms and an infants' school were added because of overcrowding; these buildings still survive.

While the Leamington School Board was slowly building new schools the remaining six voluntary schools struggled along, educating many more pupils than the Board but receiving only half the government grant. The deficiency was made up from subscriptions from local people already paying rates for the provision of Board Schools. This situation was particularly damaging to church schools: the **Bath Place National School** in All Saints' parish, for example, had 468 pupils on the roll in 1881, and only 146 parishioners subscribed to the school funds, providing an inadequate annual income of only £176. When the new infants' school was opened, therefore, fees had to be increased; many older girls left when they were asked for 6d. a week school pence. St Paul's School in Holly Walk also suffered after Greenways Bank failed, causing the loss of most of the school funds. Severe economies were necessary, and again pupils left the school because of increased fees rather than stay on longer than they were compelled to.

The Education Act of 1902 swept away the seventh School Board and divided schooling between the County Council, responsible for secondary education, and the Borough, controlling elementary education. The situation remained much the same except that the new Education Committee took over not only the Board Schools but also the voluntary schools. These were fully incorporated into the state system after the Second World War.

An art school was first started about 1867 by G. T. Robinson, an architect, who held a free evening class for artisan youths in his office. (The office, in Orleans House, Warwick Street, is now used as a Conservative Club.) Robinson left Leamington shortly afterwards to work in London, but the school was continued. In 1885, during the year the Town Hall first opened, it moved into the top floor of the building; later it joined the **Municipal Technical School** organised by the Corporation in 1894. The Corporation opened a new building for the Free Library, Technical Institute and **School of Art** in 1902, and the two schools were later taken over by the County Council. Classes were usually in the evenings, and in 1903 a secondary day school was opened in the same building. The art school later withdrew to a separate house, 1 Beauchamp Hill, and finally became part of the Mid-Warwickshire College of Further Education, at Thornbank.

Adults had few opportunities to widen their education except through the Free Library. In the late 19th century several literary and scientific societies organised public lectures which were held in various places, but mostly in the Public Hall in Windsor Street. The first group to offer educational facilities was the Mechanics' Institute formed in 1836 at a public meeting held in the Royal Assembly Rooms in March. The 130 members could meet in the assembly rooms every evening from nine to ten o'clock. During this hour they could hear lectures or read the daily newspapers supplied in the library.

In 1848 Dr. Jephson and other local people formed **The Royal Leamington Literary and Scientific Institution**, and soon enrolled over 200 members. The Institution organised a reading room, library and classes on mathematics, French, drawing and music with lectures of scientific and other interest. Its temporary home was in The Parthenon; more permanent premises were found at 23 Upper Parade, on the corner of Warwick Street. Here, in limited accommodation, people eminent in the fields of science and literature gave lectures. The Institution moved to the Public Hall in Windsor Street when it opened in 1854.

This building, owned by a private limited company, was entered through a portico leading to a large entrance hall. There were three floors, the concert hall on the first floor being 80 ft. long and 33 ft. wide and having a good organ on which public concerts were given. There were soon financial problems, however, and the project failed. The hall was sold in 1857 to Mr. Goold. It was used by a variety of people in the succeeding years. Joseph Arch held one of the earliest meetings of the National Agricultural Labourers' Union there, and from its platform Leamington audiences heard H. M. Stanley, the explorer, Matthew Arnold, Charles Dickens, Fanny Davies, Paderewski and Professor Herschell, among others. The opening of the Town Hall made other and larger rooms available, so that in 1896 the building became a furniture warehouse; it was demolished in 1957. By then the Literary and Scientific Institution had been replaced by other schemes for adult education organised by the local education authority.

Chapter Eighteen

The Parish Church: Vicar versus Vestry

The Domesday survey of 1086 records a priest living in Leamington Priors, and perhaps the parish church of All Saints dates from before then. The church is first recorded in the 12th century, being then a chapel of the neighbouring parish of Leek Wootton, whose church has the same dedication, rather than a parish church in its own right. There is no record of the date the parish was founded.

Early records provide a few clues to the appearance of the building before the alterations and extensions of the 19th century. It was small, with a nave, chancel and west tower much like other small neighbouring churches. Its rather squat tower was in the style of the 15th century, with an embattled parapet and pinnacles at each corner; the nave was obviously of an earlier date. Some alterations and restoration took place in 1624 when Hy Clarke was vicar. In 1781 a faculty was granted allowing the erection of a small gallery containing three pews in the north side of the church. Before the 19th century the interior appears to have been rendered, the roof tiled and four bells installed in the tower. Towards the end of 1799 the church was 'greatly beautified', the internal arches altered, the walls wainscotted and the chancel rebuilt. There were sittings for 130 people in the 21 pews in the nave, 97 being allocated to local ratepayers.

In the early 19th century the patrons of the living were the Wise family. The vicar, the Rev. John Wise, was also vicar of Lillington, and lived there. He employed the Rev. Edward Trotman as curate from 1807 until 1822 when he died aged 61. Trotman had previously been been vicar of Radway and Ratley. He occupied as parsonage an old timber-framed house which stood on the west side of Church Street. A guide book of 1818 stated that Trotman was engaged only to give one service each Sunday, 'but for the accommodation of visitors he performs a second entire service in consequence of which subscription books are opened for his exclusive benefit at Mr. W. G. Elliston's Library and at the Royal Pump Room'. He seems also to have taken a new house in Upper Union Parade, and run it as a lodging-house for some years. His successor was the Rev. Robert Downes, who became vicar of the parish after John Wise died.

In April 1816 Wise made the first of the many 19th-century alterations to the church. He changed its character by adding a wing providing an additional 300 sittings, to accommodate a congregation growing with the expansion of the town and the increasing number of visitors. By 1825 the town had grown so much it was necessary to enlarge the church again. The tower was taken down, its base strengthened, and it was rebuilt to a greater height and topped with a small spire. The nave was also enlarged to provide room for 504 more people, while on either side extensions were made which in effect turned the original nave into a large transept of the church. Part of this old church, on the north-east side, was used as a vestry in 1874. The 1825 extensions differed from the style of the original nave, being in the Perpendicular style with embattled parapets and pinnacles.

As the church expanded it had to encroach on the churchyard, and so a catacomb capable of holding 184 bodies was made under it. In 1820 the first organ was installed and the church band became redundant, and in 1825 the four bells were recast and a peal of six provided. From dates found on the old bells it seems that the treble bell, at least, dated from 1621. Minor enlargements were also carried out in 1829 and 1832.

By 1834 the parish church again needed enlarging to hold its congregation, so the

51. All Saints' parish church. The church as it appeared between 1816 and 1825.

52. All Saints' church, about 1826. A view showing the new tower and spire built in 1825 when the church was enlarged.

churchwardens and vestry entered into an agreement with the vicar that he should bear the cost of the alterations on condition that he should have the right to let, for his own benefit, the pews that would be added to the church. The vicar, Downes, built additions to both sides of the chancel and to the north side of the nave. He removed the old small gallery on the north side and had a much larger one built with extra pews and sittings. These changes were the starting point of the building which forms part of the existing church, and considerably increased the vicar's income from pew rents. Three years later the parish was transferred to the Diocese of Worcester.

Downes exchanged livings with the Rev. John Craig, whose benefice was Fetcham in Surrey, in 1839. Craig paid Downes £1,000 for all his interest, title and income from these additional pews, which by then were a great financial asset. Most of the structure of the present church was built in Craig's incumbency.

In 1842 Craig required more accommodation in the chancel. Again money could not be found in the parish so the vestry approved a resolution authorising him to apply for a faculty to make improvements, providing no expense fell on the parish, and granting him the right of letting the additional pews to recoup his expenditure. All the improvements carried out before were dwarfed by the scheme which he proposed on 15 September 1842 when he revealed to the vestry his intention of erecting a new nave with a lantern and bell tower over the crossing between the nave and transepts. The sum needed for the first stage was £3,500, which Craig raised at no cost to the town. As a preliminary step several of the old cottages encroaching on the churchyard were acquired and demolished.

The laying of the foundation stone of the lantern tower took place on 9 September 1843 with great ceremony, attended by 40 clergymen from all parts of the country. After the service ended the clergymen 'retired for refreshments to the Regent Hotel; while the humbler participators in the processional arrangements went to the Town Hall where they were all hospitably entertained'. The masons held their banquet at *The Bath Hotel* where Mrs. Russell 'furnished a repast in the good old style'. The opening service for the nave at ten o'clock on 9 May 1844 was attended by all the local clergy, 40 priests and three deacons, who processed 'in full canonicals' from the vicar's house, The Priory, to enter the church through the west door. In the evening a reception was held for the clergy and their friends at the Royal Assembly Rooms, and more than 200 were present. Perhaps some of the company perceived that Mr. Craig might have even grander plans for the church.

53. The Rev. John Craig. A silhouette made during a visit to Brighton in 1833.

The new nave, then generally admired, was 50 ft. long, 32 ft. wide and 50 ft. high, while the apex of the roof was 23 ft. higher. The aisles were 14 ft. wide and 30 ft. high, and were lit by four-light windows. Clustered shafts supported the clerestory, some of which were continued upwards to support the roof trusses. The clerestory windows had five lights and were surmounted by tracery forming moulded panels with trefoil heads. Under the clerestory were pierced openings over the arches, corresponding with the windows above and close beneath the roofs of the aisles. The nave roof was open, all the timbers being exposed to view. There was a moulded arch between each pair of piers, springing from the moulded stone capitals 12 ft. below the wallplate. On each side were three moulded purlins, while on the rafters was boarding. The space between this and the slates was filled with 'powdered coke, to prevent excesses of heat and cold'. The aisle roofs were similar in design but the pitch was flatter. Much of this work has remained unaltered.

The Evangelist piers which were to support the lantern tower were to be 37 ft. high and 4 ft. 6 ins. square. By 1844 the two on the south side had been built up to the old roof-level with an arch between them rising to 62 ft. above the floor of the church. These and the pair on the opposite side of the church are clearly visible in the present building. They were never completed to the original design, finishing just above roof level. Prints exist which purport to show the church in 1845 complete with its tower, lit by lancet windows, rising to a considerable height above the nave and topped with a spire, but this was the projected design, not the reality. The tower was never completed as some years later experts thought the four pillars incapable of sustaining the weight of the tower and bells. The Evangelist piers, according to Dudley's *History*, marked the centre of the old church, but it is not clear if this is correct. Old prints of the building show the nave to have been short and stumpy-looking for its height, perhaps because the design was altered as work proceeded. It was later extended to its present length.

The west end of the nave as first built had a large seven-light stained-glass window. The apex of the gable above was 74 ft. high, over which was an 11 ft. cross. The canopy and mouldings around the west window echoed those of the elaborate west door. The west end of the aisles had four-light windows, surmounted by a raking cornice and parapet wall. On the north and south sides of the aisles the parapet walls were embattled, and each wall had four buttresses from which sprang flying buttresses to strengthen the clerestory walls above the nave.

A new chancel was also built, and consecrated on 17 July 1845 in the presence of a huge congregation and nearly 50 clergymen. A communion service followed, during which the sermon was preached by the Rev. R. Parkinson, Canon of Manchester; some hundreds took communion and the service finished at about four o'clock, six hours after it began. Afterwards the vicar gave a banquet in The Music Hall in Bath Street for nearly 400 people. The new chancel was designed by the Rev. Craig, assisted by Mr. Mitchell, a Leamington architect, and built by a local builder. Its great east window was based on one in Cologne cathedral.

The next project was the completion of the north transept and at its north-eastern corner a clock tower, first known as 'The Angel Tower'. The foundation stone of this tower was laid in June 1846, by when the Evangelist columns on the north side of the nave were almost completed, as was most of the ashlar work of the transept and the geometrical window at the end. The ceremonial on this occasion followed a similar pattern to the previous ones, with a procession and another banquet, the third given by the vicar.

At the Easter vestry meeting in 1847 the Rev. Craig, having spent about £4,000 of his own money on the parish church and about £3,000 provided by subscription, said '. . . that as soon as he received the sum of £2,500 he intended to complete the church, lantern tower, transepts and all'. This was interpreted as an appeal for funds to finish the work, and on 2 May 1847 a public meeting was held in the Scientific and Literary Institution to consider the completion of the church. An advertisement had already appeared in *The Courier* to launch a public appeal. A large number of local worthies signed this notice, in which they, although 'deeply sensible of the zeal and liberality with which the Vicar and friends have already erected the nave and chancel', said it was not desirable to levy a rate in order to finish the church, but they would 'cheerfully consent' to contribute at least what they would have to pay if a rate was made. At the meeting it was resolved that the completion of the church would be for the general good and that all classes of inhabitants should be asked to contribute voluntarily what they would pay in a rate. Contributions were to be paid into either of the Leamington banks in the names of six of the signatories. It should be noted that the money was not to be paid directly to the vicar.

The Rev. Craig thanked them, saying that he would gladly 'accept their offerings although the sum named would not cover the whole cost of the work'. Some of the town's foremost residents formed a committee to organise a house-to-house collection. Before starting work the members were invited by Dr. Hitchman to breakfast with the vicar at *The Regent Hotel* on 12 May 1847 to discuss their plans. A crowd of townspeople gathered to hear Dr. Hitchman announce after breakfast that Matthew Wise had donated £50 to add to the £168 collected at the breakfast. The canvass of the town started and £1,366 18s. 5d. was raised in two days, augmented by a legacy of £1,000 from Mrs. Burgess which was not paid until 1848 and was later the subject of much argument.

In 1847 the parishioners faced the same problems which had previously delayed work: lack of finance; the ambitious schemes of the vicar, who wished to see the church the largest and most impressive in the district; and, perhaps mainly, the fact that the plan was Craig's and the function of Mr. Mitchell, the architect, was really to draw out the vicar's ideas rather than implement his own. Difficulties resulted: the Evangelist columns would not take the weight of the lantern tower, the nave was disproportionately short for its height and the transepts were vast for a parish church. In spite of the generous donations made in 1847 and the vicar's promises of speedy results, the work dragged on and during the next two years the chancel was again enlarged.

The enlarged north transept was not ready to be opened until November 1849 although by that time the south transept was also half-built. Afterwards the Rev. Craig presided over the usual parochial feast, in the Music Hall, attended by 650 persons in the upper suite of rooms and 130 in the lower. This was the last such event, however, as soon afterwards a serious rift took place between the vicar and his parishioners.

Dudley, writing in 1896, comments about this saying:

> what was its nature has never been explained and probably never will. But it may have been the boundary wall question, about which there had been a long and fruitless correspondence between the Vicar and the Paving Commissioners. Finding his own views not approved he gave up the contest . . . and the Vicar retired sulkily to his tent, or to quote the words of the Memorial to the Bishop in 1854 'he became lukewarm and indifferent as to proceeding with the church'. The work stopped and the building remained for many years in an unfinished state.

The events which followed would not have been out of place in a novel by Trollope.

In September 1849 the commissioners bought some land opposite Victoria Terrace, in front of the church, to prevent any 'nuisance' being erected on it and to have that part of the town nearest the church under proper control. They started to have a wall built with gates leading into the churchyard, which made the front of the church more open to the view of people going between the Parade and Bath Street. The vicar and the commissioners differed over the exact boundary, however, and work soon stopped while a lengthy correspondence ensued. In September 1851 Craig wrote to *The Courier* about it. About this time too the vicar was accused by the vestry of delaying the provision of a new school to replace the 'workhouse school', demolished to make way for a railway, and of using the funds for other church purposes.

Although progress was slow the enlarged chancel was finished and opened in September 1851. The vicar, who was staying in Brighton, did not attend the ceremony. It was marked by another stained-glass window at the east end of the church, with glass by the Birmingham firm of Hunt and Ellis. Tablets bearing the Commandments, Lord's Prayer and Apostles' Creed were placed in the south transept. Collections were made at the services after the opening, but enthusiasm was waning; the offerings of £59 2s. 1d. fell far short of the vicar's expectations.

While the first disagreement between the vicar and the vestry did not affect directly the building of the church it has some bearing on the history of the parish and therefore needs to be mentioned to indicate the atmosphere at the time and the steady loss of goodwill towards Craig. At a vestry meeting in May 1852, without giving prior notice, the vicar laid claim to various pieces of the church plate, including the lectern, in the form of a large eagle, 'two antique silver-gilt chalices, two silver-gilt patens in oak case, antique paten, silver-gilt and flagon'. Craig stated that he had paid for this plate and so it was his. He intended it to be the parish plate after his death, but he would not let the churchwardens take it as 'theirs by right'.

Being unprepared, naturally the churchwardens were upset, but agreed that it be placed in custody of the vicar's representative, Mr. Roby. Craig did say the churchwardens could purchase it if they wanted to and he had no objection to going before the magistrates' court to settle the matter. He agreed to take no action until the vestry had time to consider it. Before this meeting took place in July 1852, however, his solicitors wrote requesting that the plate be delivered to him or legal action would be taken. The churchwardens replied that some of the parishioners thought the plate was theirs, and gave the name of their own solicitors. At the meeting, 'after a prolonged discussion, in which valour out-ran the discretion of many of the speakers', a motion was carried by 46 to 14 that the plate be kept and the churchwardens employ a solicitor on the rates to defend any action brought. A poll of the parish was demanded and carried out speedily; by 162 votes to 133 it approved the motion.

The vicar then commenced an action against the churchwardens. It should have been heard at Warwick assizes in March 1853, but at the last moment he withdrew it and the matter was left in abeyance until the following September. *The Courier* then published an open letter from the vicar proposing a possible amicable solution to the dispute, which now involved not only the church plate but also whether the unfinished church building belonged to the parish or not. The vicar suggested that the churchwardens should resign and substitutes be appointed by the bishop, and that the diocese be asked to grant a faculty to legalise the ownership of the church by the parish who would then be responsible for its completion. By the time of the vestry meeting on 15 September 1853 tempers had cooled and the argument about ownership of the plate gradually subsided, all action ceasing. The cost of the completion of the church still remained the vexed question it had been for several years, however, the vestry doubting that the money raised had been spent properly.

In 1850 the vicar had sent the Church Commissioners details of the costs and of those who had supplied materials, along with the names of the donors. After receiving a rebate on the tax paid on bricks and glass the Commissioners sent him a certified copy of the accounts. These, published by the vicar, showed that legacies amounted to £1,208 11s. 1d., collections at church services and other events to £4,058 9s. 2d. and parish subscriptions to £1,366 18s. 5d., which he said amounted to £6,631 18s. 8d. – there being some slight discrepancies in the figures – while the cost of the church up to then was £15,000. The difference had been paid by the vicar. In 1853 Craig wrote to *The Courier* that attempts to goad him on were likely to be counter-productive. He expected to receive over £3,000 over the next 12 months by free will offering, not a rate, which would allow the church to be completed. This money could be raised by collections at the proprietory chapels in the town, which could produce £50 a month and at the parish church which ought to produce £50 a week. This would prove that the townspeople would admit that the vicar was not responsible for finishing the church, as some people suggested. Mr. Cundall senior, one of the churchwardens, added a postscript supporting him and claiming that the church could be charged by the other churchwarden, Owen White, with diverting church funds. White went to see the bishop of Worcester personally about the matter. The bishop could not ignore such a charge and wrote to Craig stating that White had claimed that £1,500 had been raised by a voluntary rate and handed over to him, and that a bequest of £1,000 had been made, but it did not appear that any of this £2,500 had been applied to the completion of the church.

The vicar, indignant, published the bishop's letter and a refutation of the charge in *The Courier* and demanded an explanation from White. Craig pointed out that that the voluntary rate had amounted to only £1,366 18s. 5d. Dr. Hitchman wrote to the paper stating that the vicar was correct and a list of subscribers was printed. Craig also printed a list of all the subscribers and donations received by him from September 1842 to March 1844, which totalled £3,258 16s. 6d. He also published the cost of the building work except the price paid for the ornamental windows. This sum was £6,390 3s. 1d. He claimed that he had surrendered pews in the church to parishioners in lieu of those they had lost when the galleries were removed, and his own income had thereby been damaged.

A poll of the parish, however, approved of the decision to lay the case of the alleged diversion of church funds before the bishop, and a vestry meeting appointed a committee to draw up a 'memorial' of it. This committee included Matthew Wise, Dr. Jephson, the churchwardens and seven others. At the same meeting a report was heard from a Coventry architect, James Murray, on the state of the church and suggestions for its completion. Murray said that the work was well done as far as it went, but it could have been completed for far less than the vicar stated. He doubted that the Evangelist columns could bear the weight of a tower and spire, and in any case to build them over the crossing would be expensive. He proposed building them beside the north transept and lengthening the nave eastwards over the crossing. Galleries should be erected in the transepts which were 'quite out of proportion and character and therefore objectionable'. These plans were set aside.

On 7 March 1854 Mrs. Craig, 'a lady who had made herself popular in the parish by her goodness to the poor and her consistent piety', died. She was buried in the new cemetery in the Whitnash Road, and all expressed great sympathy to Mr. Craig. Nevertheless, at a vestry held on 29 March the memorial to be sent to the bishop was considered and sent soon afterwards.

It was a lengthy document. It began by describing how in 1842 when Craig wanted to extend the church the patron of the living (the Rev. Henry Wise) and the lay rector (Matthew Wise, Esq.) refused to sanction any alterations except on an understanding with him that he would indemnify the parish against all expenses resulting. At a vestry in 1843 Craig had again accepted full responsibility for the cost of alterations. A faculty was obtained to extend the church westwards at a cost estimated by J. G. Jackson, 'the then architect', at £3,500. Craig then carried on the work until 1847 with gifts from various parishioners totalling £3,300 – which were listed in detail. The vicar was also accused of receiving other gifts of which he did not notify the churchwardens, saying the donors wished to remain anonymous, and collections in the parish church and episcopal chapels in the town for the improvements of £887 2s. 6d.

By 1847 the alterations had been in progress for nearly five years, to the discomfort of those using the church, but then Craig had become indifferent about continuing. He said he would finish the church when he received £2,500, following which a local collection raised £1,533 14s. 2d. plus a legacy from Mrs. Burgess of £1,000, which was paid in 1848 following her death. Still no progress was made, however, and there were many complaints from those whose pews got wet when the roof leaked in rainy weather, forcing them to leave the church during Divine Service. A vestry meeting was held on 18 August 1853 to consider the condition of the church. It was unusually well attended. The vicar insisted on taking the chair and, according to contemporary accounts, 'he at first persisted in sitting at the extreme end of the Town Hall [to which the meeting had been adjourned] away from the chair usually accepted by the chairman and with his hat on'.

Murray's report was then discussed in the memorial. It showed that the work had not been done in accordance with the faculty, being shorter and wider, and allowing room for only 373 people instead of the 484 promised. The value of the work completed west of the transepts would not exceed £3,000. A lot of extra work had been done not sanctioned by the faculty. It would require about £5,000 to finish the south transept, entrance and bell-tower, whereas it could be finished differently for £3,000.

The memorial reminded the bishop that the original church contained 1,250 general sittings and 730 free sittings, a total of 1,980, while the present incomplete church contained 1,265 general sittings and 590 free sittings, 1,855 in all. There was a deficiency of 125 free sittings, for which no rent was payable to the vicar, and he should be asked how he was going to make it up.

The question of the church plate was also raised. It was pointed out that the vicar had presented it for use in the church on the opening of the new chancel in July 1845, and it had been in regular use for seven years until the vestry meeting of May 1852 when Craig had claimed it. He had also declared his right to remove the stained glass from the memorial windows in the apse, the £500 cost of which had been paid by the Misses Sutton-Manners, claiming that as it had been fixed without a faculty he was free to sell it if he wished.

The memorial also complained that Dr. Warneford had given £500 to the vicar to build a 'Poor Man's Church' in the High Street area of town and the money had gone astray. It was alleged that Warneford had required the first stone to be laid before payment and, although this was done on 15 September 1849 and the money paid on the 19th, no further work was carried out. The vicar eventually sold the site to the Primitive Methodists without accounting for the money to the donor.

The vestry asked the bishop for a number of things. First that he require the vicar to account for all money received by him in aid of the parish church, to complete it in accordance with the faculty or indemnify the parishioners against the cost of doing so, and that future work be placed in the hands of the churchwardens, to the exclusion of Craig. Second that the deficiency of free sittings for the poor be made up from the pews from which Craig received rents. Third that Mrs. Burgess's legacy and Warneford's £500 be refunded to the churchwardens. Fourth that Craig account for £27 19s. 9d. collected for the erection of a font in 1843 and £300 bequeathed by Sarah Campion in aid of a female school in the parish. Fifth that the vicar either discontinue his action for recovery of the plate or try it at the next Warwick assizes. Sixth that the vicar place a keeper in the lodge erected at the new cemetery in the Whitnash Road to preserve proper order there.

The bishop replied advising that legal action against the vicar in the ecclesiastical courts for misconduct would involve lengthy and expensive litigation. Instead he suggested proceeding in the diocesan court to compel him to get a faculty for alterations already made and to obtain a date for completion of the work. Redress over the bequests should be obtained through action in Chancery. The vicar had no authority to remove the stained glass. It was now against ecclesiastical law to let pews in a parish church without the sanction of a special Act of Parliament. In some other matters he advised arbitration. Meanwhile the churchwardens had sent the vicar a copy of the memorial, on the bishop's instructions. The principal points of the memorial were published in *The Courier* on 1 April 1854.

In December 1855, after a year, Craig wrote again to *The Courier*. His letter he regarded as an olive branch, but he freely criticised some of his detractors. It drew replies from Matthew Wise and Henry Young. In an exchange of letters which followed, all published in the paper rather than sent directly, the vicar alleged serious mistakes in the memorial, while Wise and the committee offered an apology if any errors had been made and to examine impartially all papers and deeds connected with the affair before Craig and his witnesses. The vicar then said that he considered the memorial to be libellous and began legal proceedings in February 1856. A writ was served personally on Wise.

The case began on 3 April at Gloucester assizes and a number of witnesses were summoned, including the bishop of Worcester. Wise pleaded not guilty to publishing several libels against the vicar in the memorial. The full document was then read, which took over two hours, and the opening remarks of Craig's lawyer took the rest of the day. On the second day the vicar, the first and only witness, gave in detail the facts relating to the building of the church since the first faculty was granted in September 1842. The judge intervened and suggested that it was desirable the parties reached a peaceful settlement without proceeding, as it was obviously bad for both parish and clergyman. They could not agree, however, so the examination of the vicar continued. After he had been in the witness-box for five hours the Rev. Craig became unwell, however, and after a second consultation it was agreed to withdraw the case and refer the suit to arbitration.

Mr. Whitmore, Q.C., was chosen as arbiter. He sat for three days from 19 May 1856 at *The Bath Hotel*, Leamington, and both sides were represented by legal counsel. Large numbers of local gentry attended, either as witnesses or spectators. The most important witness was perhaps Gilbert Scott, then one of the country's best-known architects. When first asked to inspect the church by the vestry in February 1855, he said that it was obvious that the church had been designed by an amateur. The nave was too short, the arches of the aisles too narrow and 'he considered the Evangelist piers to be fully capable of sustaining any weight it is necessary to place on them, but they are not, of course, intended to carry a central tower'. He suggested the work to be done should follow the style of that already finished, but his estimate of the cost of the work already done was not half of what the vicar had paid. Giving evidence he said that the work was well done, but the foundations were not large enough for the proposed lantern tower. The roof leaked because it was temporary. The arches over the crossing were not started. On 22 May the vicar's counsel announced that all litigation between Craig and Wise had ceased, and the vicar had decided to do what he had been thinking of, namely exchanging the parish of Leamington for another, and leaving the town.

After elections a committee was appointed to be responsible for finishing the church. The vicar had the church accounts audited and gave them to the churchwardens for public inspection. They showed that £10,695 12s. 7d. had been received in donations of various kinds, including the voluntary rate, while the work had cost £14,186 17s. 7d., including the £171 5s. 6d. spent on the plate. The vicar had also paid out just over £1,751 for the choir school and about £1,717 for running the Vicar's Grammar School. The arbiter had decided that each side in the libel action should pay their own costs, the church plate belonged to the church, no money belonging to the church remained in the vicar's hands, and he gave the committee full and exclusive power to direct the finishing of the church. It was also agreed that this committee should repay the vicar £1,200 for his outlay on the church on his resignation within the year. Since he never left the parish it is not clear if this was ever paid.

Only a week later Mr. Baker, a creditor for £500, affixed a sequestration notice to the door of the church in order to seize church funds. In August the bishop was forced to send a representative to the parish to investigate. He found a sad state of affairs:

> The church was in a disgraceful state, the cloths on the communion table were allowed to remain dirty and ragged, the walls blistered with untempered mortar, the galleries were propped up with dirty scaffold poles, the eagle lectern was tarnished, the font too dirty to be used and the pews covered with dust, the church being in a lamentable condition.

The vicar did not preach and the parish was in the care of his curate, the Rev. Thomas Bowen, who was trying unsuccessfully to cope. During this confusion the episcopal chapel, later known as Christchurch, reverted to its former proprietor, the Rev. Downes, saving Mr. Craig £730 a year rent, and Trinity Chapel, later Holy Trinity church, was sold to the Rev. Tilson Marsh. But the vicar recovered from his illness and resumed duties in the parish church on Sunday 21 September, preaching to a congregation of nearly 2,000.

The committee appointed by the arbiter to complete the church took three years, until late 1859, to decide what to do. It then offered a premium of 20 guineas for the best design for the completion of the church, but there was no work on the south transept until 1867 because the competition itself led to arguments among the members of the committee.

Though the vicar was among those who submitted designs, the premium was awarded to Mr. Murray of Coventry. He offered two designs, the one which gained the prize being to complete the south transept according to the original plan, but without the porch. Instead the porch was to be placed below the west window. A new Tower and spire was to be built over the top of the original clock or Angel Tower, with a vestry underneath. The Evangelist columns were to support a wooden roof. The committee could not agree over his ideas, so John Cundall was asked to prepare some designs. He suggested extending the nave for three or four bays, building a bell-tower at the west end and a lantern tower over the centre of the church to light the nave. Contemporary writers criticised it as novel and lacking in dignity, and again nothing was done.

By this time the original committee had been replaced by a new 'Church Completion Committee', formed in 1864. The new committee asked the well-known London architect, George Street, to prepare plans. He suggested entirely remodelling the church, putting a flèche over its centre and replacing the window tracery, the work to cost £20,000. This was dismissed as too costly. William Gascoyne, a Leamington builder, was also called in and his plans rejected. Instead the plans of the vicar revised in conjunction with Alexander Johnson, a Leamington architect, were adopted. This was just in time as in February 1866 the church had to be closed as the temporary roof had become so dangerous. Tenders were invited for the work and James Marriot of Coventry obtained the contract for £8,140.

Work began on the south transept in January 1867; by May all the walls had reached the height of 20 ft. and the 'foundation stone' was laid. The transept was opened in October 1869. It was in the Decorated style, and had a south porch. The old galleries were removed and many pews replaced by chairs.

The removal of the pews, which had a monetary value, brought complaints from their owners, who included the vicar. The churchwardens asked the bishop to appoint a commission to study the problem and propose a solution. The commission sat in April 1870 and empowered the churchwardens to appropriate pews at their discretion. The vicar appealed against this decision to the Court of Arches on the grounds that since the churchwardens had removed the galleries which provided 700 sittings, they were not entitled to allot pews in other parts of the church which belonged to him. Craig's appeal was dismissed later in 1870.

In 1871 the plan to build a tower over the centre of the church was finally abandoned. The previous year the committee asked London architects Slater and Carpenter to look at the church and also commissioned a structural report from Mr. Clarke, a civil engineer from London. Clarke's findings were discussed at a vestry meeting at the end of February, which *The Builder* reported. Both Clarke and the architects said that the Evangelist piers were incapable of supporting the tower and spire proposed; Clarke recommended that the weight on them should be reduced. The roof was therefore levelled off as it is today.

The following year another painful crisis took place with the Rev. Craig. In January it was alleged that he was unsober in the pulpit. Although many people thought it unwise because the vicar was known for his eccentric behaviour which might have been mistaken for tipsiness, the bishop was asked to investigate. He may have been reluctant to take the matter far, but the memorial was signed by Matthew Wise, patron of the living, so he had to act. A commission sat in Leamington shortly afterwards, chaired by the chancellor of the diocese, but the vicar was a sick man and, although it decided there were grounds for proceeding, no further action followed. He held the living until his death in 1877, after a long and painful illness. It was estimated that about 10,000 people paid their last respects to him; all the shops closed, the parish church was crowded for the funeral service and hundreds stood outside and lined the route to the cemetery in Brunswick Street.

John Craig was born in 1805 in Dublin. He was educated at Trinity College, Dublin, ordained as a priest in 1830 and in 1833 graduated M.A. from Cambridge. When appointed vicar of Leamington he was also pastor of the chapel in Eaton Square in London, but resigned at the request of the bishop of London. His father left him £20,000 plus an estate worth £1,300 a year. He married three times and his wives brought him nearly £63,000. Morley records that at one stage in his life he received about £100,000 in twelve months, and despite his eccentricities he was well-liked and benevolent towards his poorer parishioners.

Craig was a keen amateur astronomer. In 1852 he installed, at great expense, a five-ton telescope on Wandsworth Common. With a focal length of 85 ft. it was one of the largest then in the country, and by means of it, in October 1852, the existence of a third ring around Saturn was finally established with certainty. Craig seriously impaired his own fortune in the quest, however. Despite the telescope's many excellent qualities it was rather old-fashioned and was soon superseded.

To restore parochial harmony Mrs. Wise, now widowed and therefore patron of the living, quickly selected the new vicar, the Hon. and Rev. James Wentworth Leigh, then holding the living of Stoneleigh. He soon cleared the debt of £600 still owed to the builders who had completed the nave and south transept. During his ministry the church received many gifts, including a reredos representing The Last Supper from Mr. W. Willes, an altar cross from Mrs. Craddock, a pulpit from Mrs. Wise in memory of her husband, an altar cross for the Lady Chapel from Mr. James Mitchell, an oak lectern from the Misses Douglas and a font from the Rev. T. B. Beaumont, as well as several stained-glass windows from other donors. The new organ and organ chamber, and a new vestry, were added to the church in 1879, while in the same year a temporary mission chapel was built in Satchwell Street. The Rev. Leigh was a popular figure. He became chairman of the Warwick Board of Guardians, the first chairman of the Leamington School Board and supported many charities. He left Leamington in 1883 for St Mary's church, Bryanston Square, London, then in the gift of the Prime Minister, Mr. Gladstone.

He was succeeded by the Rev. Walter Copleston Furneaux. Furneaux was chaplain of the Pro-Cathedral in Lahore, India in 1883 and had previously been at Leeds parish church. Once settled as vicar of Leamington he took up the task of further improving All Saints' church and in February 1887 held a meeting to consider the removal of some buildings that were obstructing the view of the west end of the church and the erection of a bell-tower at the south-west corner of the building.

The first step was to acquire what was then a sizeable sum to buy the land at the west end of the church and to demolish the buildings on it, four shops and two cottages. A large open space was left with the Well House over the original spring in the centre. In 1888 the chancel was 'restored and beautified', a fine choir screen, the bottom section of the present screen, was given by Sidney Flavel, junior, and Gertrude, his wife, and a new choir vestry provided by Mrs. Beaumont in memory of her husband. The Lady Chapel was 'embellished' at the expense of Miss Hughes and a reredos for the chapel was given by the Rev. W. C. Furneaux and family in memory of his mother. Electric light was also installed.

54. The temporary wooden belfry which stood in front of the parish church until 1889. Eventually the bells were rehung in the tower built at the south-west corner of the church.

In 1889 the wooden bell-tower was declared unsafe and demolished, the bells being stored temporarily in the crypt. The Mission chapel in Satchwell Street was rebuilt as a church (demolished just before the last war). In 1894 the vicarage in Priory Terrace was sold, another being bought in Leam Terrace, which in turn was replaced by the present one. A major setback to the plan to build the bell-tower occurred when a local bank failed, in 1887, and much of the money was lost.

Mr. Furneaux was succeeded in 1896 by the Rev. Cecil Hook of Oswestry. Arthur Blomfield (later knighted) was consulted about the bell-tower and estimated that one 140 ft. high was needed and would cost at least £5,000. By then also the Warwickshire sandstone of which the church had been constructed had weathered badly and not a pinnacle remained, so it was decided to reface much of the church with Hollington stone and extend the nave two bays westwards as well as build the bell tower. The church could then be reseated to hold 1,500 people. An appeal for £20,000 was launched in March 1897.

The foundation stone of the two western bays was laid on 30 June 1898; these were built in a different style from the earlier ones. On 1 November 1900 the enlarged church was consecrated; three processions converged on the building: the Mayor and Corporation entered by the north door, the choir by the vestry, while the parish procession received the bishop of Worcester, the vicar and the patron of the living at the west door. In October 1902 the tower was dedicated. It had been finished thanks to the generosity of Mrs. Urquhart and a gift of £1,000 from Mr. Richard Badger. The bells were rehung thanks to Mr. John Hutchinson, in memory of his wife. The treble bell added to the peal was given in memory of William Milford Teulon by his three daughters. A baptistry was also built to commemorate the vicar's aunt, so the south porch was no longer needed for christenings. The interior of the church was further enriched using further donations, and the screen was surmounted by open ironwork designed by Blomfield.

55. All Saints' church. A view dating from 1881, before the present west front was constructed. On the left is the post office erected in 1870.

56. All Saints' church after the new west front and tower had been completed.

In 1921 it was extended across the side chapels at either side as the gift of Sidney Flavel, churchwarden since 1885 and six times Mayor, in memory of his wife Elizabeth.

The Rev. Hook was made an honorary canon of Worcester cathedral in 1903; two years later he was appointed the suffragan bishop of Kingston-on-Thames and left Leamington. He was succeeded by the Rev. W. Armstrong Buck. In 1909 all the seats except two rows on either side of the nave were made free for the first time since the early 19th century. As the vicar pointed out, 'all are equal within the church's gate'.

In 1916 the Rev. Buck exchanged livings with the Rev. B. Feist, rector of Thurlaston, near Rugby, whom the bishop installed on 9 July. The new vicar remained in the parish for nearly 30 years. After the war the raised section of the south transept was made the War Memorial Chapel, dedicated to All Souls in memory of the men of the parish who gave their lives for their country; their names were carved on the polished floor of the chapel and the inscription enclosed in a marble kerb. The parish church was then virtually complete in its present form. Only minor alterations were made until 1984-5 when a new gallery was added at the west end of the nave. A new parish room underneath it, the Urquhart Room, replaces the Urquhart Hall, the parish room built in Priory Terrace in 1904-5 with funds provided by Miss Urquhart, which had been sold.

There are many fine memorial windows in the church. Those in the chancel are to the Willes family, who settled in Newbold Comyn in 1539, one being to the memory of the Right Hon. Edward Willes, Chief Baron of the Court of the Exchequer and of the Privy Council of Ireland. The chancel also has the monuments of the Wise family, who came to the parish in 1714 and who were patrons of the living. The monuments in the north transept chiefly record those buried in the vault below the church, but there is one to the memory of the Rev. John Craig, inscribed '. . . to whose noble conception and munificence the parishioners are largely indebted for this church'.

Chapter Nineteen

Ways to Heaven: The Church Competitive

Those who came to take the waters found their spiritual well-being amply cared for, with a wide range of forms of christian worship to choose from. An inhabitant of another town described a similar situation to Robert Southey:

> Why Sir, there's the Old Church and the New Church, that's one religion; there's Parson Kiddell's at the Pitt Meeting, that's two; Parson Westcott's in Peter Street, that's three; and old Parson Terry's in Newport Street, is four, – Four ways of going to Heaven already!

The original parish of Leamington Priors, centred around the parish church of All Saints, was large though not populous. As the spa developed the parish church had to be enlarged to accommodate bigger congregations. But as the spa's visitors included many Nonconformists and Roman Catholics, all requiring their own places of worship, the 19th century saw the building of dissenters' chapels, a Catholic church and a number of Anglican proprietary chapels, as well as new parish churches.

Among the first to worship separately were the Congregationalists who in about 1812 began to meet at *The Blenheim Hotel* in Clemens Street, their services being conducted by the minister of the Brook Street chapel in Warwick. Holding their services in a hotel was rather inappropriate for a group which favoured the Temperance Movement, so from about 1814 the meetings were held at 6 Clemens Street, the home of Mrs Moody, widow of James Moody formerly minister at Brook Street. They opened their chapel, the **Union Chapel**, in 1816. A small classical-style building, it was the first purpose-built independent chapel in the town. It was in regular use until 1836 despite numerous setbacks. These troubles were partly because Clemens Street became less fashionable, but also because some ministers went over to the Church of England and there were arguments about the form of service to be used.

The first two ministers, the Rev. Arthur Bromiley, appointed in 1817 and the Rev. William Seaton, appointed in 1824, left to join the Anglicans. In 1828, during the incumbency of the Rev. Charles Bassano, proposals were made to drop the accepted Church of England liturgy in favour of a Nonconformist type of service. Bassano objected to this change and taking some members of the congregation withdrew to temporary premises further along Clemens Street. At the same time a number of Baptists, who had worshipped with the other Nonconformists in the Union Chapel, moved to their own premises. The Rev. Alfred Pope preached his first sermon in the Union Chapel in February 1828, replacing the person originally invited, stayed to preach on successive Sundays to increasing congregations and was formally appointed minister in April 1829. During his ministry the Union Chapel prospered so that in 1836 a new building was erected in Spencer Street to accommodate the bigger congregations. The original chapel was then sold and in 1844 was adapted as a theatre.

In 1866 it was reopened as a Congregational Free Church. The ceremony, on 24 April, took place in the presence of the 82-year-old Rev. J. Percy, the principal founder of the original chapel in 1816, and Mr. Jesse Johnson, aged 90, one of the first trustees. After a rather uneventful period, services were discontinued in July 1900, the church was for a second time disbanded and the premises were again sold. It became a corn store in 1902 and finally the first home of Automotive Products Ltd., who still own the building.

In 1819 the first group of Wesleyan Methodists moved from their small meeting room in

Satchwell Street to Brunswick Street near the first Union Chapel, and in May 1822 a group of Roman Catholics opened their first chapel in the Apollo Rooms in Clemens Street.

As the area north of the Leam became more fashionable, Clemens Street became less attractive, so the Nonconformists started to move into specially-built premises in the New Town. The first of these was the **Wesleyan Methodist chapel in Portland Street**, opened in 1825 by the Rev. J. Entwistle junior, and built by John Toone to the designs of William Thomas at a cost of £750, including the purchase of the site. In keeping with Methodist tradition all seats were free to a congregation largely drawn from the poorer classes. Despite great efforts to raise the necessary money the congregation could find only £150; to complete the building the trustees took out a mortgage for £600, becoming guarantors. Unfortunately the following year the members were unable to pay the interest and the mortgage was foreclosed. The trustees, a hairdresser, three carpenters, two yeomen, a baker, and the minister, were either arrested or went into hiding. Eventually the congregation raised the interest and the Superintendent of the Coventry circuit, to which the Leamington chapel then belonged, borrowed the money to pay off the mortgage.

In 1835 the rear of the chapel was enlarged, at a cost of £811. Much of the work was done for nothing by members of the congregation, while John Toone, builder of the original chapel, gave materials worth £80. Part of this extension formed a schoolroom. The original frontage was set back from Portland Street, and when the premises had to be enlarged again in 1845-7 the present front was erected. In 1870 the chapel itself was converted into schoolrooms.

By then the growth of the congregation necessitated the building of a new chapel. The last service in the Portland Street chapel was on 5 June 1870; thereafter it was used as a public hall and later for commercial purposes. As a public hall it won its place in national history when at a public meeting there on Good Friday 1872 the Agricultural Labourers' Union, the ancestor of the National Union of Agricultural Workers, was formed with Joseph Arch as its organising secretary.

In August 1823 a meeting of the parish vestry decided to build a chapel in the New Town, as there was no Anglican church north of the Leam. Mr. Willes generously offered to provide a site and build the chapel; Mr. Greatheed supplemented this gift by presenting the land necessary to extend the road from the top of Union Parade where it joined Warwick Street to the site fixed on for the chapel. This new road later became the Upper Parade. The new building was a proprietary chapel to be leased by a 'proprietor preacher', in this case a clergyman of the Church of England, who depended for his income on donations from the congregation or charging an entrance fee.

The opening service was held on 16 October 1825. Instead of adopting the Gothic-revival style then usual for churches, the architect, P. F. Robinson, chose a more controversial style based on the design of an abbey in Normandy. His chapel was one of the earliest Norman revival churches in the country. Known as **The Leamington Episcopal Chapel**, it became the private property of the Rev. Robert Downes, then vicar of Leamington, who conducted the services assisted by his curates. To meet the cost of maintaining and running the chapel admission was by ticket at 6d. each (five for 2s.), servants half-price. It was never owned by the parish of Leamington Priors but remained the property of Downes and his family, who leased it out for up to £700 p.a. When the Rev. John Craig became vicar in 1839 he leased the chapel from Downes and abolished the charge.

The building had galleries above the aisles and seated 1,000. Originally the tower had a pitched roof, but about 1870 this was removed and replaced by the parapet with corner turrets familiar to townspeople until its demolition. At the same time new dormer windows were inserted to light the galleries and other windows were changed. In 1829 the ground around the chapel was enclosed for use as a public garden, and about the same time a clock

57.   Christchurch, after the alterations of 1870.

was installed in the tower by the Rev. Downes. The vestry was responsible for maintaining the clock 'as this was a great convenience for the inhabitants of the upper town'. One of the more important features of the chapel was its excellent organ, used for many concerts.

Several clergymen leased the chapel. In 1840 the Rev. Craig unsuccessfully challenged the right of the Rev. Downes to the ownership of the chapel. After Craig's lease was terminated by Downes in 1856, the building was restored, renamed Christchurch and leased to the Rev. Dr. Bickmore of Berkswell Hall, a popular clergyman and preacher. His aim was to 'avoid every extreme both of doctrine and ritual', and during his 14 years there the congregation increased considerably. After his final sermon on his retirement on 18 December 1870 the congregation showed their appreciation by presenting him with £180. The lease was then acquired by Dr. Hall, from Halifax, but he died suddenly the following August. Then the chapel was vacant until 1872 when the Rev. Haden Cope of Wilmslow took it. After a short time he disagreed with Mrs. Downes over the rent, so gave up the tenancy early in 1873. A new arrangement apparently settled the dispute, but in September of that year he was given six months' notice to quit. The next leaseholder, the Rev. J. A. Nicholson, began his duties in 1874. He made extensive alterations to the interior of the chapel, 'including a reduction of the size of the columns by stripping them of an outer casing, the removal of the organ to a new position and the renovation of the chancel by the erection of choir stalls'. He introduced a high-church type of service attracting a large and fashionable congregation. Mrs. Downes refused to renew his lease in 1880 and 'Dr. Nicholson and his congregation were practically ejected from the building'. They moved first to the Public

Hall in Windsor Street, then to the church of St Michael's and All Angels, later renamed St Alban's.

Christchurch was sold to Mr. Dale, a prominent Warwick businessman, who conveyed the chapel to trustees 'for the purpose of being used for ever for Evangelical purposes'. The first incumbent appointed by the trustees was the Rev. Edward Wilkinson, who took services from September 1881 to 1896. The Rev. J. G. Gregory, from Emmanuel Church in Brighton, took over in July 1897 and the church was reopened after 'improvements' in January 1898. What befell the chapel during the early 20th century is uncertain, although it went through ups and downs and became less fashionable. There were centenary celebrations in May 1926, but so little notice was taken of them that *The Courier* appears to have ignored the event completely. After the last war the bishop would not license anyone to preach in it and demolition followed in 1959. When St Luke's church was closed in 1947 its congregation joined that of Christchurch and in 1951 the combined congregations moved to join St Mark's church in Rugby Road.

58. St Peter's church. The first Roman Catholic chapel, in George Street, about 1843.

When Christchurch disappeared its single bell was returned to All Saints' church, where it had originally hung. Cast by Hugh Watts of Leicester, it bore the inscription, in Latin, 'Jesus of Nazareth, King of the Jews, Son of God, Have mercy on me. 1628'. The Rev. Downes gave the bell to his new chapel in 1825. Now rehung in the clock tower of All Saints', it continues to ring as it has been doing for over 350 years.

The next new chapel to appear was Leamington's first Roman Catholic chapel. The building, in George Street, was designed by Mitchell and Russell, the architects of Wise Street. It cost £1,000 and was opened on 1 October 1828. This chapel, like the presbytery later built beside it, was paid for by Major and Mrs. Bisshopp, members of the congregation. They also bought a plot of ground adjoining for a burial ground and they were later both interred in it, their grave being marked by a large cross. The chapel, dedicated to St Peter, was in the classical style. Its façade had a pediment supported by four Ionic columns; a central niche over the entrance contained a statue of the patron saint. The building survives almost unaltered externally although the interior has been altered for other purposes. Canon Jefferies came to the chapel in 1851 and served Leamington's Catholic inhabitants for nearly thirty years; during his time the present Catholic church was built. In 1855 he was joined by Father Bittlestone, a convert from the established church who had been a curate at All Saints'.

Soon after the Catholic chapel opened, so did the nearby **Mill Street chapel** for the Nonconformists led by the Rev. Bassano who had separated from the Union Chapel. The new chapel was designed by Mr. Nicklin and stood on the corner of George Street and Priory Terrace. When first opened in August 1829 it was only partially completed. In 1831 the Rev. Rowland Hill, a national leader of those Nonconformists who wished to continue using the Anglican form of service, bought the chapel, completed it and built a minister's house at a cost of £2,000. He had a tablet placed inside the chapel, reading:

I, Rowland Hill, Clerk, having purchased this chapel for the express purpose of introducing the

Liturgical Service of the Church of England (after the said service was excluded from the Clemens Street Chapel) do hereby declare it to be my will that the said service shall be adopted and continue therein, without any material alteration, as long as it forms part of the service of that Church, as by law now established. Rowland Hill, Proprietor, November 2nd 1831, Witnesses. Edward Bates, Minister. John Hitchman, Surgeon. Charles Goring.

Bates was the first minister appointed by Hill.

The Mill Street chapel thus became the second proprietary chapel in the town. Upon the resignation of the Rev. Bates in 1841 it was presented to Lady Huntingdon's Connexion and later became known as Lady Huntingdon's Chapel. The next minister was the Rev. Alfred New who wrote an account of the life and work of the Countess of Huntingdon, and his successor in 1859, the Rev. W. H. Sisterson, remained for the next twenty years, helping to promote Sunday afternoon services for the poorer people at the Public Hall in Windsor Street. The chapel was sold by auction in March 1887 to the Presbyterians, who used it until 1897 when it was bought by the vicar of Leamington for a parish room and later the Parish Church Men's Club. The chapel was demolished in 1902 to allow the Urquhart Hall, a new church hall, to be built on the site. This hall still stands although not now used for church purposes.

The Baptists left Clemens Street in 1827, separating from the other Nonconformists in the Union Chapel, and becoming an independent society under their first minister in Leamington, the Rev. George Cole. They went first to a room in Grove Place, then to larger premises vacated by the Methodists in Brunswick Street, and finally to a small chapel in Guy Street, off Warwick Street in the New Town, built by John Toone. This they rented from him until 1833. The Baptist Church in Leamington was formally constituted on 28 November 1830. Two years later, on 14 October 1832, adult baptism by total immersion was carried out for the first time in the spa when six people were baptised at a service held at half-past seven in the morning.

A larger chapel seemed necessary so a site was acquired nearby, part of Squire Hooton's vegetable garden, on the corner of Satchwell Street. Some of the land was reserved for a burial-ground, and a chapel designed by the local architect William Thomas was built on the rest. According to contemporary accounts his new building was 'elegant and gothic', although in its original form it was a mere box with walls and a roof.

Cole was succeeded by the Rev. D. J. East. He resigned in 1839 when the chapel suffered severe financial difficulties after the failure of Ransford's Bank. During the time of his successor, the Rev. Octavius Winslow 'late of New York', extensive alterations were made, introducing side galleries to cope with larger congregations. Winslow was British, but took his M.A. at the University of New York after his widowed mother emigrated there. He came to Leamington in 1839, left for Bath in 1857 and in 1870 seceded from the Baptists and was ordained into the Church of England. According to contemporary accounts, 'as a writer and preacher he had few equals'.

In 1892 a new minister, the Rev. A. P. Phillips, arrived whose preaching drew congregations of a size that warranted further extensions to the old chapel. A pulpit was installed, the baptistry enlarged, the organ moved from the north gallery to behind the pulpit, the schoolroom became classrooms and a vestry, a new Sunday school and vestry occupied the site of the old burial ground and the seating was rearranged to make places for another 100 people. The bodies buried in the land at the side of the chapel were reinterred in the Leamington cemetery. Work began in April 1894 and the re-opening service was held on 30 August. Land behind the chapel became available after the closure of the Church of the Good Shepherd and was bought in 1938 by the chapel trustees. The Clarendon Street chapel, used as a Sunday school after the two churches amalgamated in 1921, was sold in

59.   The Spencer Street chapel opened in 1836, the first building to be erected in the street. A view
published about 1843.

1937 and the money allocated for building another Sunday school on this land, but the war
delayed construction. It was eventually opened in 1962, named the Clarendon Hall.

The Rev. Pope's congregation outgrew the original Union Chapel, and a site in Spencer
Street was chosen for a new building. Spencer Street was then a rough, unmetalled track.
The new Congregational chapel, designed by John Russell, opened on 21 July 1836.
Merridew's *Leamington Chronicle* said of it 'We must be permitted to congratulate the
inhabitants of Leamington on the acquisition of another public building, simple yet elegant
in design, and from its situation forming a great ornament to this town'. It had a portico of
four Ionic columns standing on a platform of two steps, on either side of which was a tall
circular-headed window. The ground floor had pews for 600, and a gallery running around
three sides of the building, supported by 'light enriched columns', could seat a further 470.
Above it on the south side 'a children's gallery is admirably contrived which will hold 200
children, all in full sight of the Minister'. The chapel was lit by six windows on each side,
separated by pilasters. Under it was 'a capacious school'. The school, for boys, which was
opened in 1840, shared the basement with the tombs of the dead. It was lit by two windows
only 18 ins. of which were above ground level and the only source of heating was a single
fire in one corner. Mr. Pope left the town in 1846 because of the ill health of his family.
They went to Torquay but found the climate unsuitable, so after twelve months he came

back to Leamington and resumed his ministry at the chapel. He continued until ill health forced him to resign in 1863.

The Rev. J. Sellicks came to the chapel in 1890. He managed to raise £13,000 for perhaps the last major changes to it. These were the building of a new lecture room, completed in 1891, and a renovation and redecoration of the interior of the chapel. This included resiting the organ. Nearly a century later, in 1982, almost the last trace of the original interior was removed when the choir stalls and pews gave way to new chairs and a modern style of decoration. The chapel is now the United Reformed Church.

Another important Church of England chapel of ease, or daughter church, was opened just beyond the parish boundary of Leamington Priors, in the parish of Milverton. Houses were built beyond Wellington Street and Portland Place and on the level ground above Milverton Hill and Church Hill from about 1827. Well-to-do families living in this area attended the parish church of Milverton, St James', some distance away. The inconvenience created a demand for a chapel near at hand, and after much discussion the vicars of Leamington and Milverton agreed to one although any new place of worship would reduce their income.

The new chapel was built on a site given by the Earl of Warwick at the top of Milverton Hill. It was an impressive stone-faced building in the Grecian style, but because it had a small round tower housing its single bell it soon became known locally as **'the pepper-box' chapel**. The site is now occupied by 22-6 Milverton Terrace, at the junction of Milverton Hill, Warwick New Road and Church Hill, which street was named after the chapel. These houses were built from its materials by G. F. Smith, the builder of St Mark's. The chapel, opened in August 1836, could seat 800 worshippers. Its gallery had a fine organ built by Hill of London, which had come from the Chapel Royal at St James' Palace, Westminster. The first minister was the Rev. J. H. Smith of Corpus Christi College, Cambridge. During his incumbency each service saw the chapel almost filled by a congregation of influential people drawn from a wide area, including the Earl, who had a private pew.

When he retired in 1871 Smith was succeeded by the Rev. Charles Carus-Wilson. By then the chapel could not accommodate the growing number of people living in this part of the town, so Carus-Wilson began to work towards building a new place of worship. In 1875 an Act of Parliament created a new independent parish by dividing the original Milverton parish into two: Old Milverton and New Milverton. The pepper-box chapel became the parish church for New Milverton, and was replaced by St Mark's church in 1879. It was demolished in 1882, so when he died in 1883 the Rev. Smith had seen not only the opening of the chapel but also its destruction.

The Rev. John Craig, the vicar of Leamington, was under continual pressure to allow his parish to be divided and another created to serve the growing population in the new part of the town south and east of the original village. This the vicar was loath to do since his income would be diminished, as would the importance of the parish. By 1839, however, he could no longer resist these requests, so the parish of St Mary was created although it did not become fully independent until his death in 1877. Though now surrounded by housing, the newly-built **St Mary's church** stood in the middle of open fields. It became a magnet for new building developments, as the original landowners had hoped.

Edward Willes, Esq. gave a site for the new church and the Church Building Commissioners and the bishop were asked to approve it. Construction started in October 1838 without any public ceremony. The work was paid for by the Rev. Dr. W. Marsh and his friends. Marsh had been rector of St Thomas', Birmingham, until ill health caused his resignation; the new church was to be somewhere 'where the work would be lighter and more proportioned to his strength'. The opening services and consecration took place on 27

July 1839 and Dr. Marsh settled in Lansdowne House, Leamington, although his poor health prevented his immediate assumption of duties at St Mary's; for a time they were carried out by his son, the Rev. W. Tilson Marsh. Despite the protests of the Rev. Craig the creation of the parish was approved by the diocesan consistory court and its boundaries fixed in June 1840. The new parish included most of the eastern part of the town.

The new church was a brick building, designed in 'the ecclesiastical style of the 15th century' by J. G. Jackson. It had a nave and aisles, separated by an arcade, and a gallery. There were seats for 1,136 including 415 in the gallery. It was lit by six windows on each side and a large stained-glass window, the gift of a member of the congregation, at the east end. At the west end was a tower, 75 ft. high, ornamented with battlements and pinnacles. Changes were made later in the 19th century: in 1870 the exposed brickwork was rendered, in 1882 the original 'three-decker' pulpit was removed and the font shifted, in 1885 the organ was resited and new choir stalls provided and in 1888 the whole interior was reseated.

The Rev. Marsh remained at St Mary's until he retired in 1851. In 1856 the trustees appointed the Rev. T. Bromley, whose achievements in the parish included paying off the heavy debt on the church school in Holly Walk, the establishment of a new infants' school in Queen Street and further schools in the Radford Road and New Street. His crowning success was the creation of the new parish of St Paul's and the building of St Paul's church. He died, aged 72, on 22 September 1886.

After St Mary's other church buildings came thick and fast. The Anglicans and Nonconformists alike built new chapels, often as a result of antipathy between small groups of people and the minister or congregation of their original chapel or church. Finding new sites in the town they had their own independent places of worship built.

Trinity Chapel, later Holy Trinity church, opened in 1847 as a proprietary chapel like Christchurch and only a stone's throw from it on the opposite side of Beauchamp Square. The chapel was designed by Mr. Mitchell, and opened on All Saints' Day 1847 by the Rev. Craig. Dr. Young, the first incumbent, stayed until 1850, but then for seven years there was no regularly licensed minister, so the services were conducted by Craig and his curates. The church was sold by auction on the vicar's behalf in 1856, and realised £2,680 plus an additional £200 for the fixtures including the communion table and organ.

The buyer was the Rev. W. Tilson Marsh, son of the builder of St Mary's. He became the incumbent on 13 August 1857, returning from Ryde in the Isle of Wight, where he had been rector of St James'. After he retired he leased Holy Trinity to succeeding incumbents. The church was enlarged a little in 1869 and extensively in 1881, when a new choir vestry was built and the north and south transepts extended. The Rev. W. Flory preached his first sermon in the church in January 1877 and remained minister there for 21 years. In 1898 he was offered the living of Snitterfield, but his congregation wanted to keep him in Leamington and tried to get a new parish created and assigned to the church. The bishop and the Rev. Hook, vicar of Leamington, whose parish included Holy Trinity, approved the idea, as did the Wise family, patrons of the living of All Saints' church, so when the necessary endowment fund of £1,000 was raised the application was granted. The parish of Holy Trinity was created and Flory appointed its first vicar. The consecration service was held on 16 November 1899 and the next year £5,000 was raised to cover the purchase of the church, to increase the endowment and to make necessary extensions and repairs. These included work to enlarge the chancel paid for by Mrs. and Miss Lee. The church was enlarged again in 1920, and still serves as one of Leamington's parish churches.

Two years after Holy Trinity opened, the foundation stone of a new **Congregational chapel in Holly Walk** was laid. This was another chapel created following disagreements among members of one of the Nonconformist chapels, in this case the Spencer Street chapel. During Mr. Pope's ministry at this chapel theological differences divided the congregation and some members left to worship separately. They first met in the Music Hall in Bath Street, eventually deciding to build their own chapel. D. G. Squirhill was employed to design the new building.

The chapel was built in the style of the reign of Henry VII. Its façade was of red brick, relieved by diagonal lines of blue, with Bath stone dressings for windows, doors, buttresses and walls. Inside were open seats and a gallery at the north end which provided room for about 600 people. It had also a classroom. Dudley thought that 'the structure itself was an agreeable contrast in its external appearance to the stereotyped plaster, or stucco work, so characteristic of every other sacred edifice in Leamington, excepting the Parish Church'. He commented that Squirhill must be awarded a special commendation for designing the most cheerful and comfortable building of the kind in Leamington at that period.

Several ministers served this chapel, including the Rev. Hamilton Davies, who stayed only a short time before being ordained into the Church of England in 1856. He then became curate at All Saints' where he stayed until 1874. The Rev. F. S. Attenborough was appointed in March 1869, who was very active in local educational matters. For some years he was a member of the Free Library Committee and introduced the idea of a childrens' department. In 1868 a two-storey Sunday-school building was erected at the back of the chapel, facing William Street. Attenborough felt that 'it was a great pity that two such excellent rooms as those lately built should only be used on Sunday', and persuaded his congregation to collect money to finance the establishment of a new British Day School. It opened in May 1870 and provided accommodation for 45 boys and 45 girls. Supervised by Mr. and Mrs. Stone, the master and mistress, the school ran for six years before being amalgamated with the Spencer Street school in 1876. The Rev. Attenborough was a regular contributor to the *Leamington Chronicle*, and after Mr. Vincent disposed of the paper he became its proprietor and editor. He also edited the *English Labourer's Chronicle*, the first paper of the National Agricultural Labourers' Union. He died in October 1879 at the early age of thirty-seven.

During his final illness it was proposed that the services be transferred to the Spencer Street chapel, but some of the congregation dissented and elected the Rev. Tuck to the vacant pastorate. Nevertheless after a short time the services were discontinued and in 1897 the chapel was sold to the congregation of St Luke's church, which had been forced to move from Augusta Place. This church in turn closed down after the last war and the Holly Walk premises were sold. The building survives, largely unaltered externally although almost nothing of the original interior remains intact.

St Luke's church, or, rather, 'proprietary chapel', was built in Augusta Place in 1850 on land formerly used for commercial purposes. About August 1832 Stephen Peasnall, a plumber, had workshops there but after his bankruptcy Mr. Healdey, a coachbuilder, acquired them as a coachbuilding works. He sold the land in 1850 to the Rev. Edmund Clay, who demolished the buildings and erected the new chapel at his own expense. St Luke's was built with the sanction of John Craig, the vicar of Leamington, who preached at its inaugural service, a licence was granted by the bishop to use the chapel for preaching and it was opened on St Luke's day, 18 October.

Like the Congregational chapel in Holly Walk, St Luke's was designed by Mr. Squirhill, this time using the Early-English style. It seated 400 in the body of the building and a further 150 in the gallery on the north and west sides; many of these seats were let at low rents for the benefit of the 'less opulent classes'. The main front facing Augusta Place had eight lancet windows and a cornice and battlements. It was rendered. Both the communion table and the pulpit were on the south side because the site was too small to allow the usual orientation. The roof timbers were of deal, stained and decorated with tracery.

Mr. Clay was a 'low-church' clergyman who achieved some local notoriety for his great interest in Spiritualism, giving lectures on the subject to the town's many sceptics. Despite conflicting evidence, he displayed a too credulous acceptance of the alleged manifestations at seances of 'spirit-rappings', a subject of much interest during the 1850s. In a more practical vein he was in advance of his time in advocating early closing for shops in the town. He remained at his proprietary chapel until 1856, during which period it was enlarged and improved three times.

The evangelical Rev. Henry Fisher succeeded him at St Luke's and for the next 38 years denounced all ceremonies, ornaments and 'high-church' practices, which he regarded as alien to the Church of England. He continued the day and Sunday schools established by Mr. Clay and stayed on in Leamington until he died aged 79, in 1894.

60. St Luke's church, Holly Walk, in 1929. The church was formerly a Congregational chapel.

Fisher was succeeded by the Rev. J. W. Dance. During his proprietorship there was a dispute over the ownership of the chapel in Augusta Place and the minister and congregation were expelled from the building. Dance purchased the Holly Walk Congregational chapel for £2,000, and on 18 February 1896 he and his congregation held their first service in their new home. Their right to establish a church in the existing parish of St Paul's was challenged by its vicar, since he feared his income might be reduced, and a bitter quarrel ensued. The bishop at first refused to grant a licence for the chapel, but public sympathy was with Dance and his congregation and the bishop allowed them to stay. The Augusta Place chapel was eventually sold at auction in 1899 and its use as a place of worship ended.

After the Rev. W. A. Salter resigned from the Warwick Street Baptist church in 1860 he and his supporters held services in Beck's Rooms in the Upper Parade. In August of that year he announced his intention of remaining in Leamington and plans were made to build a new meeting place for the 'Baptist Union' in Clarendon Street, to the designs of Mr. Bradshaw, a local builder. The chapel, erected on the site of the former *Clarendon Inn*, was in the Early-English style, and excluding the classroom cost £2,098 2s. 11d. Built to hold 400, it was of red brick with Bath-stone dressings, lit by three brass 'sunlights' suspended from the ceiling. At the west end was a gallery for a choir and a small organ built by Mr. Wyatt of Milverton. Fronting the street were three stained-glass lancet windows manufactured at the St Helen's glassworks in Lancashire, owned by the Pilkington family; these windows were given by Miss M. Pilkington in memory of her sister Ann, who died in 1862. The local press reported that 'the arrangements evince a rare combination of beauty and commodiousness'.

When the new chapel was opened the day school for girls and infants which the congregation had started in the public hall in Windsor Street was moved to the classroom behind the chapel and renamed The Clarendon Street British Girls' and Infants' School. The children were transferred in 1881 to the Board School which had been built in Leicester Street. The chapel also maintained a Sunday school, with girls' and boys' departments, as well as a senior young women's bible class. In 1861 Mrs. Salter started a Mothers' Meeting, the pioneer of all such meetings in the town, while a night school for boys was also held in the Tachbrook Street Mission Room, south of the river.

The inaugural service took place on 22 June 1863. At that time £1,500 had been raised and not long afterwards the whole debt was discharged. After 20 years in Leamington Mr. Salter died in 1879, aged sixty-seven. The chapel closed in 1921 and the congregation transferred to the Warwick Street chapel. The Clarendon Street premises were used for some time as a Sunday school, then sold.

In the early 1860s the Roman Catholics, finding their original chapel too small for their increasing congregation, started to plan a new church. This was designed by Mr. H. Clutton of London and built by Mr. G. Gascoyne of Leamington on a site in Dormer Place. The foundation stone was laid on 1 May 1862 by Bishop Ullathorne, the Roman Catholic bishop of Birmingham. The new **St Peter's church** opened on 18 August 1864, and the bishop took the service, attended by many prominent catholic clergy and laity. The occasion was marked by a public dinner held at The Royal Assembly Rooms.

The new church had a fine organ made by Messrs. Bevington & Sons of London and played by Signor Aspa, the director of music, who lived in Priory Terrace. It cost £425, paid for by Miss France, who also paid for the decoration of the sanctuary. The church fittings were donated by many local people. The altar was brought from the old chapel; it had been given by Sir Edward Mostyn, and was made of stone from his quarries to the design of E. W. Pugin, the celebrated architect. The new church was given a tower in 1878, with a small copper spire which was removed after the last war. The first peal of bells, cast by Messrs. Blews & Sons of Birmingham at a cost of £562, were hung in 1878.

The original chapel remained in use for some years, but eventually it was sold and altered internally. It still survives, tucked away among the houses and commercial premises of George Street. Its outside looks very much as it did when it first opened.

On 19 December 1883 a calamitous fire broke out in the organ gallery. The church was almost destroyed, for the roof was completely wrecked, the altar ruined and the rest of the structure damaged. After the fire the fire brigade was criticised because Leamington had only manual pumps while Warwick had bought a steam fire-engine. Mr. Duke, the Town Council's chief fire officer who was in charge of the appliances, defended the brigade in a letter to *The Courier*, ten days later. Only ten minutes after the alarm was raised 80 yards of hose were connected to the hydrant in Bedford Street as there was no hydrant or water main in Dormer Place. Jets of water were pumped through the north windows of the church at a pressure of over 50 lbs. a square inch. He denied that the hose was out of order when it arrived: red-hot tiles had fallen on it and burnt it.

At the suggestion of two Anglican ladies of the town an appeal was launched immediately, and within a week £1,000 was raised so that restoration work could start. Catholics and Protestants contributed so generously that when the reconstruction, costing £6,690, was completed in 1884 only £200 was needed to pay off the entire debt. The grand reopening took place on 11 November 1884 and a pontifical high mass was celebrated by the bishop of Birmingham in the presence of a large gathering of Catholic clergy and laity. Lunch followed at *The Regent Hotel* and 200 guests applauded the speech by Lord Braye which emphasised the rare and noble example set by the non-catholics in the town in giving so generously towards the restoration.

In 1894 a new reredos was consecrated, designed by A. J. Pilkington, the carvings being by Mr. Boulton of Cheltenham. An altar designed by A. E. Purdie was given by C. J. Shaw in memory of his wife, Nora, who died in 1891. Since then the church has remained very much as originally designed, surviving one of the greatest floods ever known in Leamington, on 31 December 1900, when the Leam rose to reach the church door and halfway up Augusta Place. Fortunately it subsided enough to allow the celebration of the midnight mass marking the turn of the century.

The early years of the new century were marked by the decoration of the sanctuary, in 1902, with paintings of the popes who had most influenced the history of the Catholic Church in England. In 1903 the wooden framework of the belfry tower was declared unsafe, the bells and framework were dismantled and a new peal of eight bells was cast by Messrs. Taylor & Son of Loughborough, hung in the reconstructed belfry and dedicated on 16 November 1905. Because of further structural problems these bells were lowered within the tower and are now used as part of a carillon.

In 1852 there were problems among the Wesleyan Methodists in the town and some members broke away from the chapel in Portland Street to form their own congregation. They established the **Wesleyan Reform Chapel** which opened on 7 September of that year. Little is known about this group except that the chapel was built in Clarendon Street, on the Lillington Road corner of Moreton Street. Beck's *Guide* for 1852 describes this chapel as

> of simple construction, built more for inward accommodation than for outward appearance. It is capable of holding 400 persons. A Sunday School is established in connection with this place of worship.

The chapel did not last long as by 1887 it had been sold and converted into a private residence, Chesford House. Enough of its main elevation still survives intact to recall its original use as a chapel. At present it houses retired people.

Also in 1852 the **Ebenezer Primitive Methodist Chapel** was built on the corner of Wise Street and High Street, on the western side of the road junction. Again, little is known about the building except for a single illustration published at the time, although the chapel served a congregation until 1921 when the small group joined the Wesleyan Methodists at the chapel in Dale Street. The Ebenezer Chapel was eventually closed and part of the site redeveloped.

Other small groups using temporary accommodation in 1852 included those who met in the Temperance Hall in Clemens Street for services and Band of Hope meetings, and those who formed the United Free Methodist Church. This latter group first met in Colley's Temperance Hall in Oxford Street, and held a Sunday school nearby at 11 Kenilworth Street. The congregation increased and a chapel became essential. With Mr. Colley's help a site was acquired in 1864, now known as 120 Warwick Street; two houses between Gibbs the butcher's and Harris the baker's were bought, demolished and work began in April. The architect was Mr. Timms and the chapel was built by Messrs. Hunt & Co. Morley, in his *History* describes it as 'a most unpretending place of worship in the plain Grecian style of architecture'. It held 500 and was furnished with an organ by Wyatt & Son of

Binswood, Leamington Spa. At the inaugural service on 1 September 1864 Mr. Colley officiated as organist. In 1966 the small congregation departed to join the town's other Methodist chapel in Dale Street, leaving the site to be redeveloped as a modern office block.

By 1866 the old Methodist chapel in Portland Street was too small, so a new chapel on another site was planned. When the Rev. B. Waddy arrived in the town in that year, however, he found a debt of £1,260 outstanding on the Portland Street property. He determined that it should be paid off and by December the congregation had raised £1,275 to do so.

Several possible sites were considered for the new building, but it was decided to buy one in Dale Street. By January 1868 the congregation had secured promises of subscriptions amounting to £2,123, so in July Cavendish Cottage was bought for £1,500 and the site was cleared to build the chapel and a new schoolroom. This schoolroom escaped the demolition of the chapel in 1971.

In October 1868 the committee instructed the architect, G. Woodhouse of Bolton-le-Moors, that the new building was 'to be as much like a chapel as possible', but it was to cost no more than £4,500. On 15 April 1869 Mr. Green's tender of £4,548 was accepted. At the ceremony on 19 May at which the foundation stone was laid were 120 ministers and friends who were attending the annual meeting of the Birmingham and Shrewsbury District of the Methodist Church, held in Leamington for the first time. By means of 'Collecting books for the New Chapel and School Alterations' £4,820 was collected, which allowed for the building of a new manse to be completed while tenders for new schoolrooms in the original Portland Street chapel were also accepted. On 9 June 1870 the new chapel was dedicated. It could hold 1,300 people, while the congregation was then only 400; as a result there were problems paying for the work for some years, but eventually the debt was met without the difficulties which had beset the trustees of the first chapel.

The centenary of the Leamington Circuit was celebrated on 21 October 1937, but membership reached 1,000 for the first time only in 1961. In 1968 it was decided to dispense with the large **Dale Street chapel** and it was demolished. The present modern chapel, to accommodate 250, was erected on the site in 1971.

As the Methodist movement continued to flourish in the 19th century, however, a new chapel, which became known as the **Trinity Methodist Chapel**, was erected in the Radford Road. The foundation stone was laid in 1876 and the chapel, built by John Fell, opened in September 1877. The architect, John Cundall, used the 'Geometrical Gothic Style' The building is still a place of worship and although the interior has been drastically altered the exterior is much as built. The cost of the chapel and adjacent minister's house, £4,568 with furniture, was borne entirely by Mrs. Holy.

When St Mary's parish was formed in 1838 much of its area was undeveloped land. By 1871, however, its population had grown to over 7,000, 3,000 or so of whom lived north of the Leam, a mile from their parish church. The Upper District School in Holly walk, on the site of the present St Paul's Infants' School, was used also as a church on Sundays, but this was unsatisfactory. In July 1872 the vicar of St Mary's, the Rev. Thomas Bromley, called a parish meeting to discuss building a new church in the northern part of the parish, and the response to the proposal was enthusiastic.

A plot of land in Leicester Street offered by Mr. Samuel Bird, a member of the original building committee, was purchased for £533 15s. When **St Paul's church** was built Leicester Street was no more than a country lane serving a few buildings, but Bird, who was a local builder, foreseeing the future growth of the area had acquired land along it for house-building. The houses between the site of the church and the junction of Leicester Street with Clarendon Street are the fruit of his policy.

It was thought that £5,000 would be necessary to build and endow the new church, and by 1872 a fund-raising appeal had produced £3,312. The committee told the architect, John Cundall, to make the church 'plain and inexpensive with very little carving or ornament'. In December 1872 he reported that the church, excluding the chancel, could be erected for £4,000 and the whole for £5,000 if the tower and spire were left for a later date. It would accommodate 780 persons. The committee wanted the church to open unburdened by debt, so with some misgivings the tender of Thomas Kibler of Wellesbourne for £6,240 was accepted and work started in February 1873.

Mr. William Willes, then owner of Newbold Comyn, laid the foundation stone on Ascension Day, 15 May 1873. The first phase of building, the nave, aisles and transepts, proceeded until there was insufficient money to build the chancel and vestries. The Rev. Bromley agreed to foot the bill for these himself so that the building could be finished without delay and be ready for opening in May 1874. The construction of the tower and spire began in February 1874, after £1,196 was raised quickly to allow it to take place. They were completed in 1875 in accordance with Cundall's designs although in slightly different materials.

The church, cruciform in plan, is 130 ft. long and 86 ft. wide, the spire being 150 ft. high, the whole being in the Gothic style of the 13th century. Its nave has a clerestory lit by 16 two-light windows and aisles separated from it by arcades of four arches. The clerestory walls were of white and red brick in geometrical patterns, but the lower walls were plastered and colour-washed to save money rather than constructed in exposed brickwork as the architect wanted. The short chancel also has aisles, one housing the organ and the other leading to the vestries. The dressings of the windows, doors, tops of piers, etc., are of Bath stone or Aberdeen marble, the roof is of exposed timbers, strengthened with iron rods across the church. There were galleries in the transepts, set back so as not to project into the nave. Of the 1,123 seats, 146 were in these galleries; 500 were free sittings. Below the east window was arcading with recessed panels on which the decalogue, Lord's Prayer and creed could be inscribed – to save money this was not done at the time.

The tower and spire were not included in the original building plans and to compensate for their omission a turret was built at the corner of the north transept, with space for one bell and capped by a stone spirelet. The first storey of the tower was intended to form the north porch and principal entrance to the church, through an outer door set in a richly moulded arch, perhaps the most decorated part of the building. Until the tower was built the church was entered by doors in the north transept and at the west end through a porch removed when the school and other rooms were added in 1887-8.

The church was not consecrated at first, being only dedicated for services, so it could not have an independent parish but only a minister under the jurisdiction of the vicar of St Mary's. The dedication took place on Ascension Day 1874 at a service conducted by the bishop of Worcester. It was followed by a public luncheon in St Mary's School in Holly Walk at which the Rev. Bromley and his committee received congratulations and expressions of great satisfaction that the organisers never had to resort to 'collecting cards, boxes or bazaars'. When the accounts came to be settled in April 1875 there was a balance in hand of £2 16s. 11d. after an outlay of nearly £9,000.

About the time the church was opened the Rev. Bromley tried to obtain more land at the west end of the church from Mr. Willes to provide extra space for ancillary buildings, including a church hall. Although eventually land was acquired, Bromley died before the work was completed. In 1878 the church was allotted a separate parish and granted an endowment of £200 a year. When the bishop consecrated the church on 2 July the curate-in-charge, the Rev. J. Bradley, became the vicar; he remained in the parish until 1893. During his incumbency the church had to be reroofed as in 1881 the original slates proved faulty and the ancillary buildings were completed in 1888 to the designs of W. H. Lloyd of Birmingham and Leamington. The chancel was re-ordered and some interior alterations were made in 1974, but the exterior remained largely as first designed until some additions and alterations were made at both ends of the building in 1985-6.

When in 1861 the Rev. John Craig wished to provide more church accommodation for the poorer people of the parish he put up a corrugated-iron building in Priory Terrace on the opposite side of the road and to the east of All Saints' church. This building held 1,000 people and became known as 'The New Opposition Church', some people even calling it 'The Vicar's New Shop'. Services were taken by one of Mr. Craig's curates until 1864 when it was bought by the Rev. T. S. Millington. He had it moved to a new site at the junction of Warwick Street and Portland Street, where it was reassembled on part of the garden then belonging to Orleans House, now used by the Conservative Club. The 'Iron Church' was licensed for use as a proprietary chapel and a chancel was added which was designed to be part of a permanent church.

Shortly afterwards the Rev. Craig bought the property back again and held services there until 1871. It was then sold to the Rev. Wilkinson who appealed for funds to build a permanent church on the site. Miss G. Unett laid the foundation stone of the new church, named **St Michael's and All Angels**, on 7 June 1877. It was designed by John Cundall and built by John Fell for less than £2,000. In 1881 the chapel again changed hands when Dr. Nicholson, having left Christchurch with his congregation in 1880, purchased it for £5,600. Soon afterwards he changed its name to St Alban's, and began improving the interior. In 1887 the tower was erected to commemorate Queen Victoria's Jubilee. Nicholson died in July 1902 and on 1 January 1903, no longer a proprietary chapel, St Alban's passed into the care of the vicar of Leamington. A district was allotted to it although it never became a fully independent parish church. A church room was added, there were extensions to the chancel in 1913-14 and the interior was decorated with wall-paintings of various religious subjects and texts – the congregation was high-church. It served a dwindling number of worshippers until it was closed and demolished in 1968; the chapel was replaced by a block of offices known as St Alban's House.

The next church to become a mark on the skyline of the town was **St John the Baptist's**, opened to serve rapidly-developing south Leamington. Among those who readily supported the project were the Rev. Canon Young of Whitnash, Mrs. Matthew Wise and Dr. Jephson. At a preliminary meeting held at *The Crown Hotel* in 1875 eight sites were considered, one being offered by Mrs. Hitchman who not only gave a large sum to the building fund but also agreed to give a site free of all charges. Her offer was accepted and the site in Tachbrook Street was transferred to the trustees, but the church was slow to be built. Near the chosen site Dr. Hitchman had established a large hydropathic treatment centre, The Arboretum. It had a two-storey private chapel which his widow offered for the use of local people, and in 1875 the Rev. Franklin came to take services there until St John's was opened. He also opened a school in temporary premises in 1876, which had nearly 300 pupils.

The new church was designed by Cundall in the Early-English style. It held 873 worshippers. The foundation stone was laid in April 1877 but funds were short and the church had to be free of debt when consecrated, so building went on in stages between 1877 and 1888. The final cost was £7,700, the contractors being successively: John Fell of Leamington, who built the nave; Thomas Mills, also of Leamington, for the chancel and choir vestry; William Dawkes of Leamington for the south transept and the clergy vestry; and G. F. Smith of Milverton for the tower and spire added in 1887-8. Among the stained-glass windows by Hardman & Co. of Birmingham and Holt of Warwick there is a memorial window to Dr. John Hitchman, given by his widow in 1882 and one in memory of John Cundall, the architect, given in 1889. Cundall also designed the original vicarage standing beside the church; it was sold in 1984 and converted into flats.

The church was opened in 1878 although unfinished. There were no objections when the Rev. Franklin became the first incumbent and vicar of the new parish as the Rev. Craig had died the previous year and his successor as vicar of Leamington welcomed the creation of a new parish from the poorer part of the medieval one. In 1882 Franklin was succeeded by the Rev. W. G. Wise, from Leeds parish church, the son of Mrs. Matthew Wise who had given some of the money for building St John's.

The religious revival of the mid-19th century brought many other groups to settle in the town; The Brethren, The Believers, the Christadelphians and The Church of Christ all held meetings in various public halls and assembly rooms, some eventually occupying their own buildings. Some took root and flourished, others were short-lived. Among the most fashionable was the fast-growing Catholic Apostolic Church, a group started in London in the 1850s by the followers of Edward Irvine, and despite its name a Nonconformist movement. Members opened meeting-houses in all the larger towns. Their form of service was derived from high-church worship, using a vast number of ornaments, symbols, and copes and encouraging the use of exotic ritualism. Their ministers were 'ordained' by the 'Twelve Original Apostles' and after the last one died in 1902 there could be no more ordinations, so the sect gradually disappeared. In 1867 the Leamington group used the former Roman Catholic chapel in George Street, then moved to other premises, meeting in Chapel Street in 1890 and in a private house, 14 Leam Terrace, in 1900. A few years later they ceased to exist in the town.

The town also had its share of missions, for example The Railway Mission, which used a building in Church Street for some years in the 1880s. The most important mission was started by the parish church in Satchwell Street, one of the humbler areas of the town. It first occupied a temporary corrugated-iron building, erected by public subscription and seating about 300 people. Later a more substantial structure was put up and the mission became **The Church of the Good Shepherd**. The building was enriched by numerous gifts, including the oak screen and choir stalls originally in St Alban's church, Oxford. In the alterations of 1903 the chancel was lengthened, vestries enlarged and a new altar installed. The church continued its work, helping those living in the squalid conditions prevalent in the neighbourhood, for some years, but despite more renovations in 1923 the building was shortly afterwards demolished.

Perhaps the most recent of the pre-war religious buildings in the Regency town was the chapel in Charlotte Street used by a group of Anglican nuns. Opened in 1926 by the bishop of Coventry, it was attached to the St Michael's Home next door. This church was a Gothic structure in the style of the 15th century, built in brick. It is now used as a Pentecostal church.

The medieval parish of Leamington Priors was surrounded by the parishes of Cubbington, Whitnash, Lillington and Milverton, all then quite separate from the village of Leamington. As the spa grew and spread out the boundaries became less distinct and in 1890 parts of Lillington and Milverton were absorbed into Leamington. By 1902 the whole of Lillington, Whitnash, Cubbington and New Milverton had become part of the Borough of Royal Leamington Spa and their medieval parish churches now serve the built-up area of modern Leamington.

The church of **St Mary, Cubbington**, originally Norman and 13th-century, was heavily restored in 1855 and has remained largely unaltered since then. **Whitnash church**, dedicated to St Margaret, was also originally medieval with a Perpendicular-style tower. It was thoroughly rebuilt to the designs of Sir George Gilbert Scott between 1855 and (after his death) 1880. **St Mary Magdalene** at Lillington suffered a similar fate and apart from its Perpendicular-style tower the church was rebuilt at various times 1847-84.

Architecturally the most important church is **St Mark's**, built in 1879 to serve as the parish church of the newly created parish of New Milverton. This fine Gothic-Revival church was designed by George Gilbert Scott, junior. Until 1979 the church was the only church by this architect surviving intact – unfortunately this is no longer the case, its unique interior being altered forever. Scott was also responsible for the design of the first vicarage, next to the church; this has recently been converted into flats and new houses built in the adjacent garden.

St Mark's was built at the expense of the Carus-Wilson family. Charles Carus-Wilson, the moving spirit behind its construction, was to have been the first vicar but died before the church was complete; his widow survived him by 45 years, dying in 1921. The Rev. Frederick Carus-Wilson, son of Charles, held the living from 1890 until 1898.

Paving the 'way to heaven' was a thriving business in 19th-century Leamington. Although the story of the town reveals much sincere religious devotion, perhaps there were also a few clergymen such as the one described by Robert Southey in *Letters from England*, published in 1807:

> . . . the height of the popular preacher's ambition is to obtain a chapel of his own, in which he rents out pews and single seats by the year; and here he does not trust wholly to his own oratorical accomplishments; he will have a finer-tuned organ than his neighbours, singers better trained, double doors, and stoves of the newest construction, to keep it comfortably warm. I met one of these chapel-proprietors in company; self-complacency, good humour, and habitual assentation to every body he met with, had wrinkled his face into a perpetual smile. He said he had lately been expending all his ready money in religious purposes; this he afterwards explained as meaning that he had been fitting up his chapel; 'I shall think myself very badly off' he added 'if it does not bring me fifty per cent.'

Chapter Twenty

A Postscript

The Parade had its new Town Hall in 1884 as a symbol of the town's importance as a Borough, but the Pump Rooms lacked the crowds of visitors who had once come to take the waters, marking a decline in the town's economic well-being after the peak years of the 1850s. The new century soon brought the end of Victoria's long reign. The Queen died in 1901 and her statue by Albert Toft, costing £1,400, was unveiled on 11 October 1902 in front of the Town Hall. Later the same month All Saints' bell-tower was consecrated marking the completion of the parish church after 60 years of effort. These events really marked the end of the Victorian era in the town. Victoria still observes the traffic in the Parade, but from a slightly different angle having been dislodged although not overturned by Second World War bombs.

At the start of the new century the somnolent spa was home to the retired well-to-do: ex-colonial civil servants and their families, retired Army and Navy officers. They had settled there in considerable numbers as Leamington was rather less fashionable than its rivals Bath and Cheltenham, and therefore cheaper to live in. All three places faced competition from popular south-coast resorts, from Brighton to Weymouth and beyond. This period of comparative quiet ended with the Great War. The town's losses are recorded on the War Memorial in Euston Place.

Post-war Leamington continued to decline in importance as a spa, as did other spa towns; its Pump Rooms and mineral spring remained, but its visitors rarely came again in large numbers to take the waters. The town's future prosperity seemed to lie in local industries, which had varying degrees of success in the competitive world of the 1920s and 1930s. Its economy revived for a period with the establishment of new engineering firms, including the Lockheed Hydraulic Brake Co., supplying parts for the expanding car industry in Birmingham, Coventry and Oxford, a reliance on one industry which the town has had some cause to regret in recent years. Horse-drawn vehicles disappeared and the old-established local iron foundries and coachbuilders survived by adapting to the needs of the motor car, or went out of business. Many old firms which had seen the town expand and prosper in the 19th century disappeared for good. Several of the more adventurous produced a few cars of their own before succumbing to more successful competitors. In the early years of the century one of them, C. T. Crowden, made cars and commercial vehicles, but eventually left the town and continued in business elsewhere; one of his Leamington-made cars survives for visitors to admire in Coventry City Motor Museum.

Industrial expansion brought large numbers of people from Scotland, Wales and the north of England to Coventry and Leamington in search of work. The newcomers found a town living largely on its reputation and, to quote from the town's Development Plan of 1947, too little attention had been given 'to the future of the Borough as a living and healthy community. At present it represents a business which is under-capitalised.'

The population stagnation of the late 19th and early 20th centuries was reversed by 1921, and the number of people in the town grew significantly and remained fairly stable up to the last war. Thus in 1901 the population of Leamington was 26,888, in 1911 it was about 27,000, but by 1939 it had grown to about 31,000. The change came with the rapid expansion of Coventry's motor industry and the accompanying growth of that city's population, which resulted in a shortage of housing there. Leamington, with a railway link to its larger neighbour, benefited from the 'overspill', although in 1931 there were still 246 unoccupied houses in the Borough. Against the national trend, deaths in Leamington exceeded the number of births, however, and in 1947 nearly 30 per cent of the townspeople were over 50 years old, a proportion maintained for some years. Leamington remained popular with retired people. The town had 42,953 inhabitants in 1981.

Even in 1947 housing conditions in the town were still unsatisfactory. According to the Development Plan much of Leamington's attractiveness was 'in the nature of a surface veneer hiding a lack of recreational facilities and not a few black spots, within a stone's throw of the Parade are slums as bad as those in our industrial cities, where back-to-back houses with no sanitation are still inhabited'. Many of these had been declared unfit for human habitation as long ago as 1850. Nevertheless, during the inter-war period the first of the private and local authority housing estates were built on the fringes of old Leamington, including those at Shrubland, Rushmore, on part of the Stud Farm and Manor Farm estates, as well as at Cubbington, Lillington and Whitnash, while the infilling of the open land between Leamington and Warwick began in earnest. After 50 years or so the gap between the two towns has finally been closed and the only open space between their boundaries is a thin wedge of floodland close to the confluence of the Rivers Avon and Leam, near Emscote.

In 1926 a local charity, called Leamington Slum Clearance Ltd., set about the problem of bad housing in the Borough, and with local authority help had cleared 104 slum properties by the late 1930s. The Corporation demolished the home of the Wise family, Shrubland Hall, and began to build upon the site in 1934. This land has been used for both houses and factories. By then the slum-clearance charity had finished building the Windmill estate, near the old windmill which stood in the Tachbrook Road until its demolition after the last war. The last 'official' slums in the town were not pulled down until the 1960s, however, so difficult was the problem.

Housing schemes were halted during the last war when the town again became drastically overcrowded, accommodating many troops. These included members of the Polish and Czech armies in exile. The Czechoslovak Government-in-exile occupied part of the Compton Verney Estate and its fine house, not far from Leamington, while the officers were billeted in the town iself. A fountain in the Jephson Gardens, erected in 1968, now commemorates their stay in the town; it is a tribute

> . . . to all Czechoslovak soldiers, airmen and patriots who fell in World War II. From Leamington Spa in 1941 volunteers from the Free Czechoslovak Forces stationed in the town were parachuted into their homeland to rid it of the tyrant Protector S.S. General Heydrich. Two of them – Jan Kubis and Josef Gabcik – accomplished their mission in May 1942. They and their companions laid down their lives for freedom.

Other Allied forces also found a temporary home in the town, and the British Camouflage Corps took over many buildings for the duration of the war, including the Art Gallery, Pump Rooms and *The Regent Hotel*. The clubhouse of the Leamington Golf Club became a reception centre for troops after the evacuation of the army at Dunkirk, and these were followed by another wave of evacuees, this time children from London and the south-east. Some firms whose output was vital to the war effort moved their factories into the centre of England, marked in this case by the Centre of England Oak standing alongside the Cubbington Road. The tree finally succumbed to old age and was felled in 1960, to be replaced by a sapling.

The arrival of these firms during the war caused an expansion of Leamington's industrial estates, a process which is being repeated in recent years. The Ford Motor Co. took over the Imperial Foundry on the Warwick Old Road from Flavels in 1940 and has stayed on. It has modernised the foundry, making it one of the most efficient in the country. Smaller businesses found a place in premises in the crowded side streets and some are still operating in the same buildings they took over in the 1940s, but which are not suited to modern industrial use. Moreover many are in the town's residential areas.

Fortunately Leamington escaped the serious air raids suffered by Coventry, and damage in the town happened only when a target was mistaken or bombs were jettisoned by a plane returning to enemy territory. Shops and properties on the Parade and a building in Dormer Place were destroyed on 14 November 1940. After the raids on Coventry on that night and those following, people who had lost everything streamed into the spa for shelter. The people of Leamington rose to the occasion and provided accommodation on a scale never known before for those less fortunate than themselves.

Following the V.E. and V.J. celebrations, homes were also found for displaced persons from all parts of Europe, including Estonia, Latvia, Lithuania and Poland, and many of them stayed to become permanent residents. Unrest in Egypt·and Uganda brought others in need of help; families from India, Pakistan and the Far East have also settled in the town and become members of the community. An Indian businessman, elected a member of the Warwick District Council and one of the spa's Charter Trustees, became Town Mayor in 1987.

In the post-war years many Regency buildings have been demolished to be replaced by modern ones. As the original buildings suffered in the process the townspeople have begun to notice changes in the town centre; some of the more important historic buildings have been repaired, some adapted to new uses and, particularly in the centre of the town, others demolished and replica façades grafted on to 20th-century offices and supermarkets. No building seems safe, even the future of the proud Town Hall being questioned by the present local authority in the search for new office accommodation.

The town has retained its importance as a prosperous shopping centre for the whole of mid-Warwickshire, however, and as a centre for light industries based on modern technology, although heavy industries have declined and are under threat of closure. The offical end of the Borough of Royal Leamington Spa came in 1974 when the town ceased to be a self-governing body and became part of the Warwick District Council area. The spa is the administrative headquarters of the new council, but has no power of its own.

Those who helped to establish the Royal Spa as a prosperous 19th-century town might have regretted the conclusion of their efforts. With the Pump Rooms passing out of local authority control into private hands the town's future may lie elsewhere than in medical treatment, but its surviving historic streets and buildings can still remind townspeople and visitors alike of the town's past. Leamington may now be best appreciated, strange as it may seem, by an increasing number of people who know it well yet have never seen it. These are the blind who come to the town for a new start in life, as Leamington is now a renowned centre for the training of guide dogs for the blind, and it is perhaps to them that this book should be dedicated.

Bibliography

Manuscript Sources

A wide range of manuscript sources have been consulted; only the most important documents or collections are listed here but details of others can be found in The Warwickshire County Record Office, Warwick. All the documents mentioned below are in the W.C.R.O.

Official documents include:

Warwickshire Quarter Sessions Records, Classes 1-119, Class 78, Leamington
Warwick Poor Law Union and Board of Guardians Records, CR. 51
Leamington Priors Inclosure Act, 1769, CR. 222/5
Leamington Priors Improvement Act, 1825, CR. 784/5
Leamington Priors Poor Rate Books, CR. 1538-253-8
Leamington Priors Improvement Commissioners Minute Books, 1825-52, CR. 1563/160-70 (also known as the Paving Commissioners)
Leamington Board of Health Minute Books and other records, 1852-76, CR. 1563/171-90
Leamington School Board Records, 1881-1903, CR. 298
Royal Leamington Spa Borough Council Records, 1888-1947, CR. 1538

The Leamington Borough Library Collection, deposited in the W.C.R.O. at the time of Local Government reorganisation in 1974, CR. 1563, includes a large amount of Ms material. Bertie Bertie Greatheed's Journal, 1805-26 is among the Heber-Percy Papers, CR. 1707. The Packington Accounts and papers relating to the lord of the manor are in the Finch-Knightly and Aylesford Papers, CR. 47 and 669. Other collections which contain large numbers of manuscripts relating to Leamington, especially property deeds and plans, are those deposited by solicitors (only the reference number of the largest group of documents is given):

Campbell, Brown & Ledbrook	CR. 556
Field & Son	CR. 1103 & 1247
Heath and Blenkinsop	CR. 611 & 919
Moore & Tibbits	CR. 1097
Slatter, Son & More	CR. 619 & 1596
Wright, Hassall & Co.	CR. 734

Leamington Spa Ms materials can also be found under CR. 1218, 1233, 1354, 1733, 1736, 1745, 1825, 1852 and 1877. The Aylesford Estate Maps are catalogued under CR. 2317 and the Willes Estate Maps under CR. 1247/1-40.

Printed Sources

Newspapers The dates given are the first year of publication to the last year available in the W.C.R.O. and the Leamington Spa Library collections. There are no indexes to any of these newspapers.

Leamington Chronicle	1835-59
Leamington Press	1834-5
Leamington Spa Courier	1828 to the present day
Warwick Advertiser	1808 to the present day

The County Record Office, the Leamington Library and the Coventry and Warwickshire Collection in the City of Coventry Library have many local guidebooks and other works relating to Leamington Spa; only the more important are listed below.

Guides
Beck, J., *Beck's Leamington Guide*, 8th edn., 1848, to 14th edn., 1871.
Bisset, J., *A Descriptive Guide of the Celebrated and Fashionable Spa of Leamington Priors*, 1814 and later edns.

Black, A. C., *Black's Guide to Leamington and its Environs*, 1868 and later edns.
Corporation of Royal Leamington Spa, Official Town Guide, various edns.
Fairfax, J., *Fairfax's New Guide to Leamington Spa*, 1833 and later edns.
Heywood, A., *A Guide to Royal Leamington Spa*, Abel Heywood's Penny Guide, 1869 and later edns.
Knibb, T., *A Guide to Leamington Spa and its Vicinity*, 1844.
Leamington: The Tourist's Picturesque Guide to Leamington, Warwick and Stratford-upon-Avon, 14th edn., 1872.
Leamington: A New Guide: An Historical and Descriptive Account of Leamington and Warwick, 1817, 2nd edn., 1825.
Medley, S., *A Visitor's Descriptive Guide to Leamington and Warwick*, 1826.
Merridew's Improved Edition of Moncrieff's Original Guide to Leamington and its Vicinity, 7th edn., 1837.
Moncrieff, W. T., *The Visitor's New Guide to the Spa of Leamington Priors*, 1815, 2nd edn., 1822, and later edns.
Reeve, W., *The Vicinity of Leamington: A Guide to the Neighbouring Towns of Warwick, Coventry, Stratford-upon-Avon and Kenilworth*, 1844 and later edns.
Roth, D., *A Pocket Guide to Royal Leamington Spa*, 1978.
Smith, F., *An Historical and Descriptive Guide to Leamington Spa*, 6th edn., 1826.
Ward, Lock & Co., *Illustrated Guide to Leamington*, 1866 and later edns.
William's Guide and Directory of Royal Leamington Spa, Warwick and Kenilworth, 1846.

Directories
Beck's Leamington Annual Directory, Diary and Almanack, 1870 and later edns.
Dewhirst, T. S., *Directory of Royal Leamington Spa*, 1849.
Kelly's Directory of Birmingham, Staffordshire, Warwickshire and Worcestershire, 1876 and later edns.
Kelly's Directory of Warwick, Leamington Spa, Stratford-upon-Avon, Kenilworth, etc., 1927 and later edns.
Kelly's Directory of Warwickshire, 1890 and later edns.
Percy, Butcher & Co., *Stratford-upon-Avon, Leamington and Warwick Directory*, 1873-4.
Pigot & Co., *Warwickshire Directory*, 1821-2 and 1829.
Pigot & Co., *National Commercial Directory*, 1835.
Pigot & Co., *Royal National Commercial Directory*, 1841.
Slater's (late Pigot & Co.) Royal National Commercial Directory, 1850.
Slater & Co., *Warwickshire Directory*, 1850.
Spennell's Directory of South Warwickshire, numerous editions, 1880-1927.
Stevens, Geo., & Co., *Directory of Coventry, Leamington, Kenilworth, etc.*, 1880.
West, W., *History, Topography and Directory of Warwickshire*, 1830.
White, Francis, & Co., *History, Gazetteer and Directory of Warwickshire*, 1850 and 1874.

Secondary Works
Arnison, C., The Speculative Development of Leamington Spa, 1800-1830, unpublished M.Phil. thesis, University of Leicester, 1986. ·
Baxter, E. G., *Dr. Jephson of Leamington Spa*, 1980.
Chaplin, R., 'New Light on the Origins of Royal Leamington Spa', *Transactions of the Birmingham and Warwickshire Archaeological Society*, vol. 86, 1974, pp. 148-66.
The Character of Leamington as a Village, the Celebrity of Leamington as a Town, 1847.
Clarke, H. G., *Royal Leamington Spa: A Century's Growth and Development, 1800-1900*, 1947.
Clarke, G. T., *Report to the General Board of Health on the town of Leamington Priors*, 1850.
Drew, J. H., *The Book of Royal Leamington Spa*, 1978.
Dudley, T. B., *A Complete History of Royal Leamington Spa, from the earliest times to the Charter of Incorporation*, 1896, revised edn., 1901.
Dudley, T. B., ed., *Memoir of James Bisset*, 1904.
Dugdale, Sir William, *Antiquities of Warwickshire*, 2nd edn., 1730.
Einarson, N., William Thomas (1799-1860) of Birmingham, Leamington Spa and Toronto, unpublished M.Phil. thesis, University of Essex, 1980.
Field, W., *The Town and Castle of Warwick*, 1815, reprinted 1969.
Gardiner, R., and Currie, B. J., *Royal Leamington Spa*, 1954.
Gibbons, W. G., *Royal Leamington Spa*, Pamphlets: 1. *Social Life*, 1985; 2. *Town Growth*, 1985; 3. *Signs of the Past*, 1986; 4. *On the Move*, 1986; 5. *On the Rails*, 1986; 6. *Law and Order*, 1987.

Gibbs, J., *Notes on the Past, Present and Future of Leamington Spa*, 1873.

Granville, Dr. A. B., *The Spas of England, and Provincial Sea Bathing Places, 2, The Midland Spas*, 1841, reprinted 1971.

Hanks, K., ed., *The Leamington We used to Know*, 1977.

Hanks, K., ed., *More Looking Back*, 1980.

Hanks, K., ed., *A Last Look Back*, 1983.

Hopper, R., *The History of Leamington Priors: from the earliest records to the year 1842*, 1842.

James, C. H., and Rowland Pierce, S., *Royal Leamington Spa. A Plan for Development*, 1947.

Leamington College – Jubilee, 1902-1952, 1952.

Leamington College, 1902-1977, 1977.

Leamington Library, *Village into Town: Royal Leamington Spa*, 2nd edn., 1980.

Lee, E., *The Mineral Springs of England*, 1847.

Luckett, F., Flint, K., and Lee, P., *A History of Brewing in Warwickshire*, 1982.

Mannings, J. C., *Glimpses of our Local Past*, 1895.

Morley, G., *History of Leamington Spa* – photostat copies of articles from *The Leamington Spa Courier*, 1887-9, in Leamington Library.

O'Shaughnessy, F., *A Spa and its Children*, privately printed, 1979.

Parry, A. B., *The Kingsley School: A Dream Realised, 1884-1984*, 1987.

Pratt, J. S., *Local and Literary Account of Leamington, Warwick, Birmingham, Stratford, Coventry and Kenilworth*, 1814.

Roth, D., *Early Nineteenth Century Decorative Ironwork: A Study based on Leamington Spa*, privately printed, 1976.

Roth, D., ed., *Random Papers from the Leamington Society's Collection*, 1985.

Scudamore, C., *A Chemical and Medical Report on the Properties of the Mineral Waters of Buxton, Matlock, Tunbridge Wells, Harrogate, Bath, Cheltenham, Leamington and Malvern*, 1820.

Simpson, M. A., and Lloyd, T. H., *Middle Class Housing in Britain*, 1977.

The Victoria History of the County of Warwick, vol. 6, 1951.

Willington, J. R., *Catholicism in Leamington: Past and Present*, 1906.

Winterburn, J. M., *A Brief History of Municipal Elections in Leamington*, privately printed, 1960.

Winterburn, J. M., *The Development of Local Government in Leamington Spa*, privately printed, 1962. Duplicated copies of these two studies are in the Leamington Library.

Winterburn, J. M., *A History of Arnold Lodge School, Royal Leamington Spa, 1864-1984*, 1984.

Index of Persons

General Index

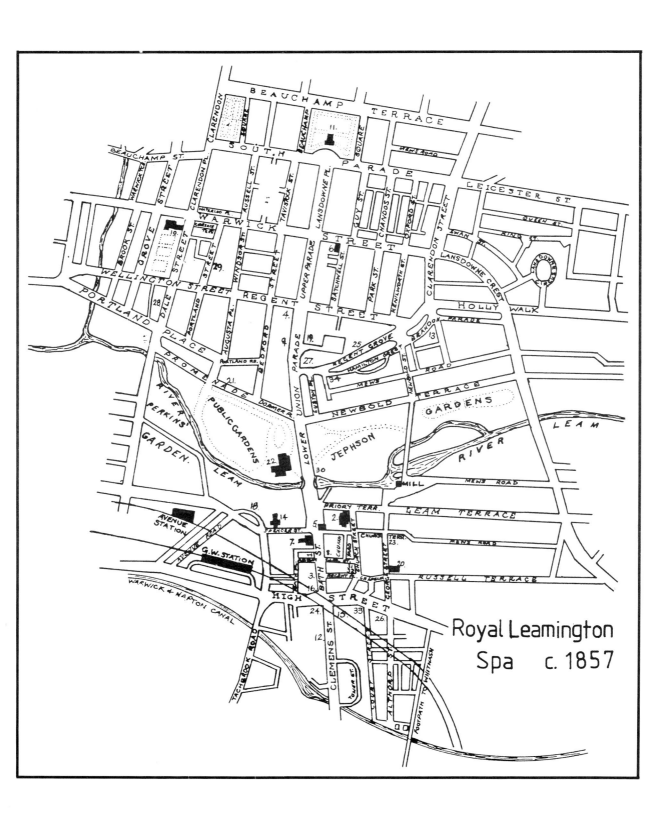